CRISIS UNAWARES

CRISIS
UNAWARES

A doctor examines the Korean church

Dr Peter R. M. Pattisson

OMF BOOKS

© Overseas Missionary Fellowship

First published 1981

ISBN 0 85363 135 2

Published by Overseas Missionary Fellowship,
Belmont, The Vine, SEVENOAKS, Kent, TN13 3TZ, UK,
and 404 South Church Street, ROBESONIA, Pa 19551, USA.

Produced in Hong Kong by OMF Communications

OMFC/CTC/TH 2/81 5K

Contents

Chronology

1866	Robert Thomas landed with Bibles at Pyong Yang and was killed
1884	First resident missionaries in Korea
1907	Pyong Yang revival
1910	Annexation by Japan
1945	End of second world war. Liberation from Japan. Division of the country
1950-53	The Korean War
1966	Pattissons first arrival in Korea
1969	First OMF team arrives in Korea
1972	Korea Scripture Union founded
1975	Adult in-patients first admitted at Masan Hospital
1977	Planning committee for OMF Home Council first formed
1980	OMF Home Council constituted

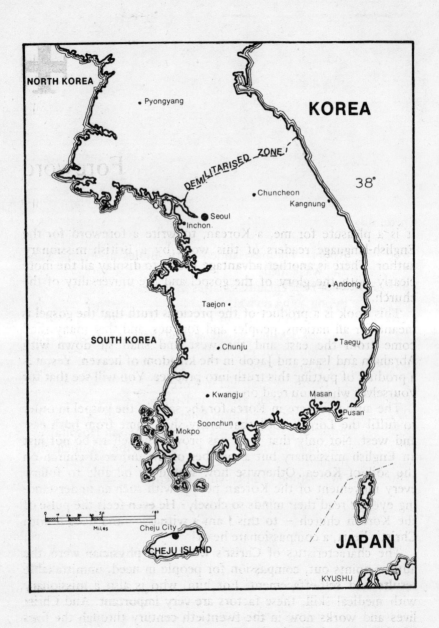

Foreword

It is a pleasure for me, a Korean, to write a foreword for the English-language readers of this work by a British missionary author. There is another advantage too – to display all the more clearly both the glory of the gospel and the universality of the church.

This book is a product of the precious truth that the gospel is meant for all nations, peoples and tongues, and that many shall come from the east and the west and shall sit down with Abraham and Isaac and Jacob in the kingdom of heaven. Yes, it is a product of putting this truth into practice. You will see that for yourselves when you read on.

The author is here in Korea for the sake of the gospel in order to fulfil the Lord's word that many shall come from both east and west. Not only that – he has proved himself to be not just an English missionary but a member of the universal church on the soil of Korea. Otherwise how would he be able to follow every movement of the Korean people with such an understanding eye, or read their minds so closely? He even feels the pulse of the Korean church – to this I am a witness – and does it with Christ's heart, a compassionate heart!

The characteristics of Christ's work as a physician were, the author points out, compassion for people in need, unmistakable results and self-effacement. For him, who is also a missionary with medical skill, these factors are very important. And Christ lives and works now in the twentieth century through the lives of His servants in the land of Korea.

What is the answer to all the challenges and problems of the church of God in Korea? With the experience of more than a decade in Korea behind him, the writer prescribes: emphasis on

Scripture; and particularly on reading it regularly and putting it into practice. Having read the manuscript of this book I, a Korean, not only concur with what he has diagnosed and prescribed but, from his actions also, I feel that he is first of all one of us, one member of our church, and only secondly an English missionary. So here you readers will see the struggle of a servant of Christ to build up and reform the church of God in Korea.

The format of the book also, you will find, reflects this emphasis. Each chapter is a study of one chapter of Matthew's gospel and its application to Korean church life or to mission.

May this book be used in God's hand to strengthen and purify His church in other parts of the world as well as in Korea.

Choe Nack Jae
Pastor, Kang Byun Church, Seoul.
Formerly professor in New Testament Studies, Presbyterian General Assembly Seminary, Seoul.
Korea.
March 1980

Introduction

The aim of this book is to bring before the reader aspects of life in Korea today as seen in the invigorating light of Scripture. It seeks to provide glimpses of a country that has been in the Christian and secular news in recent years. At the same time it offers some modern illustration of the portion of Scripture handled.

The book is structured around Matthew's gospel with a chapter for each of Matthew's chapters. Each chapter seeks to draw a seed thought or incident from the corresponding chapter of the gospel, and to illustrate it from modern Korea. There is a deliberate attempt to allow our thinking to be guided by the balance of the gospel narrative. Matthew's gospel was the first portion of Scripture that we studied with Koreans. Its impact was enormous. The reader may like to read the appropriate chapter of the gospel story before the corresponding chapter of the book. In this way the book could be used to augment a month's readings of God's word.

It is never easy to write about people with whom one is closely associated and for whom one has a warm affection. This is all the more so when what is written is necessarily critical in parts. If it is to be true to the balance of Scripture this is unavoidable. Critique of certain trends will be resented by some but, knowing the havoc that similar trends have wrought in our own churches, we would long for our brethren in the churches of Asia to understand and avoid the pitfalls. Thank God that, as in the gospel narrative, there is also much that illustrates and magnifies the grace of God.

The reader will find little direct account of the past history of the Korean church. This is deliberate. This glorious history of revival and growth, of suffering and faith, has been well-documented in other books (reference to which will be found in the text). It is with present-day Korea that we are concerned. Many imagine that the church in Korea today is the same as in former years, only larger. This is far from true. Profound changes have come over the church, as over the nation, in the last thirty years and we shall be looking at some of these.

The contents is not strictly chronological, though there is a general drift from earlier events to more recent ones as the book proceeds. Material is dealt with according to subject matter as suggested by the context of the gospel narrative. The brief chronology and dramatis personae and the map may help the reader to keep himself oriented.

In some instances names have been changed in deference to personal privacy, but the incidents recorded are factual.

My thanks are especially due to my good friend Rev. Choe Nack Jae for consenting to write a foreword, and to Miss Thelma Brown of Glasgow who kindly typed the first draft. My thanks are due too to all those who have read and commented on the manuscript, particularly Rev. John Wallis with whom we shared those first years of joy and sorrow in Korea. The views expressed however are my own, and the responsibility for the defects of the book must be mine.

Peter Pattisson

Dramatis Personae

Masan Hospital staff

Mr Choo Young Moo	clerk
Mr Jee Hyun Duck	driver
Mr Lee Chong Sup	physiotherapist
Mr Kim Dong Suk	clerk
Mr Park Seong Won	field worker

Korean friends and associates

Mr Kim Chin Kyung	our first Korean friend, when he was a student in Bristol
Mr Lee Jung Soo	early convert, later SU Council member
Mr Yune Zong Ha	general secretary of Scripture Union
Rev. Yune Bong Ki	father of the above. Presbyterian pastor
Dr John Kim	sometime OMF member, who opened the way for OMF to enter Korea
Dr Chun Chaeok	former missionary to Pakistan. OMF Home Council member

Fellow missionaries

John and Kathleen Wallis	OMFers from Britain who with us made up the first OMF team to Korea in 1969
Margaret Robertson	
Cecily Moar	Australian OMFer who first came in 1974

11

The book of the genealogy of Jesus Christ, the son of David, the son of Abraham. (Matthew 1.1)

1

Genealogy

My heart sank as I turned to the opening words of Matthew's gospel. A genealogy! Would they lose interest before we had started? Would they ever understand? It seemed an impossible task to communicate the riches of Christ to these who knew so little of Him; who had so many other presuppositions to life which I only dimly understood.

It was April 1970. We had just returned to our home in Masan — the long, low, ramshackle, Japanese-built house with kitchen at one end and bathroom at the other. In between, like a railway carriage, lay a line of rooms with a corridor running along the back. Provided for us, this spot had been home for two years while we had worked in secular employment in the Government Tuberculosis Sanatorium in Masan. Our first two children, born in Pusan 2½ hours away, had been welcomed to this home. Here we had made our first steps in language learning; here we had made our first cultural blunders such as when the hospital superintendent's seven-year-old boy had come on New Year's day and made his traditional courteous deep Confucian bow before us as a neighbouring 'uncle' and 'aunt'. How indignantly he had exploded in his parents' home when we had sent him away without the traditional courteous 100 won[1] in his pocket. Here we had welcomed a variety of neighbours, hospital staff, church leaders and friends, Korean and foreign, over those two years.

Now we were back after further language study, and asking ourselves what should be the first steps of our missionary outreach, as we picked up the threads. Bible study with our closest associates seemed the most natural initial move. Formerly we had been responsible for a children's tuberculosis unit attached to the Government Tuberculosis Sanatorium. This had had 70-80 beds, out-patient clinics four days a week, and forty to fifty staff. Now the wards had been placed under the umbrella of the Government Sanatorium, and we were responsible for out-patient work only, with just four staff. Besides this we had some medical, but not administrative, oversight of the wards. We welcomed the change. National initiative and leadership is always preferable to foreign control. More time was available for development of missionary outreach beyond the immediate medical context. Our whole approach to tuberculosis care centred on out-patient work, anyway, with the wards available only for selected difficult cases: we were still able to make the main part of our medical contribution. The changes definitely indicated progress.

But how could we make the gospel real to this first group of four staff? There was Mr Cho, in his late twenties, the only Christian among them and the most widely read. I had given a brief congratulatory speech at his wedding a year before — my first public attempt at spoken Korean. Yes, he would come along, but 'It was an impossible task'. Even if they started to come — those others on the team — they were just not the sort of people who could become Christians. Such was his assessment of the prospects.

Mr Jee was the hospital driver, in his mid thirties with a family of three boys. He was hard-working and friendly, but had limited education. From an intensely traditional local family steeped in Buddhist assumptions about life and death, he was held too in the rigid Confucian hierarchical structure, and deeply conscious of the influence the spirits of his ancestors could bring to bear. Even if he gave mental assent, what chance would there be for such as he to break free of the social web that binds men in a framework of security, yes, but binds them too from release into life in Christ? When we had discussed, the previous year, his continued employment in the clinic, I had said that God would bless him if he gave himself to this work — but I wondered if I believed my own words. On one of the few occasions that we had discussed spiritual matters (eight weeks of formal language study and daily tutoring with Mr Cho when it could be squeezed in with other work, up to a level about equivalent to one year's full-time study, made communication at that level a hazardous

14

adventure) he had said that when he set out in the hospital Land Rover northwards he prayed for safety to his ancestor who was buried there, and when he travelled westwards, he prayed to another who was buried in that direction. 'Were these the most powerful spirit beings?' we asked him. 'No, but the closest to me,' was his reply. We loved him and longed to introduce him to the Friend of sinners who would be closer than any. He agreed to join Bible study with us, but could we expect results? We were sceptical.

Mr Lee was in his mid-twenties. Working now as hospital physiotherapist, he had first come as a patient some years before from a country home 1½ hours away, having had tuberculosis in his spine for many months without treatment. He spent nine months in the hospital: treatment was successful but left him with a severely-curved spine. In spite of his short stature, he was strong and possessed a good mind and indomitable will to succeed. Having finished schooling at twelve years of age due to his disease, he had skipped the next three years, taught himself high-school subjects by correspondence and passed the exams. After his recovery he had stayed on at the hospital, first to look after pigs for a hospital feeding project, graduating to cleaner, and subsequently to physiotherapist. He taught himself the basics of anatomy, physiology, and physical therapy, rounding it off with three months at the National Rehabilitation Centre in Pusan. Almost certainly capable of passing his exams to qualify in physiotherapy, he had been bitterly disappointed to find himself debarred from sitting the exam by a rule that excluded those with a physical deformity. This rule was subsequently rescinded, but once again he was disappointed to learn that with general upgrading of facilities, new laws required a man to have attended the full three-year training course, before he could sit the exam. This was out of the question financially, and he found himself relegated to continuing work in this small provincial clinic, skilled but unlicensed.

Two years previously he had married a simple country girl by mutual arrangement of the two families — a pretty girl in spite of her pock-marked face. She had had the unusual advantage of three qualified nurses in attendance at the birth of their first son in their little one-roomed house next to the hospital (and the pigsties). An occasional attender at church, now he would join

15

with us in Bible Study — but could that strong independence of spirit and determined self-interest born of years of hardship and disappointments be brought to submission to Christ? Time would tell.

Fourth of that small hospital team was Miss Chang Young Ja, nurse-aide who owed almost all her training to the years she had spend working in the hospital. She was now in her early twenties. Her father had died while she was still at school. As the eldest of four, her family circumstances demanded that she leave school and find work so she had found a place in the hospital. A good worker and conscientious, yet she was almost obsessionally worried about a small mole on her lip. Repeated surgery had failed to remove it completely, but it was not startlingly obvious. However, in a society where marriages are still frequently arranged by the family, a society which hardly knows a place for the single woman, and a society where physical defect — especially visible defect — plays a large part in marriage chances, the problem understandably loomed large. Yes, she agreed to come to the Bible Studies, but only, we were to learn later, grudgingly, because everyone else was doing so.

So it was agreed. We were to meet each working day for twenty minutes before work in our house. The hospital being a government institution it was easier to meet in the house, and provided a more homely atmosphere.

Audrey hurriedly cleared the crumbs off the breakfast table, and wiped the marmalade off the faces of our two toddlers, while I pushed the carpet sweeper up and down the threadbare mock-persian rung and hung the little blackboard on the wall.

Hours of preparation had gone into this first meeting; we had agreed that the most natural place to start was the life of Christ, and Matthew's gospel coming first in the New Testament we would start with that — but a genealogy!! I remembered John Stott dealing with the same passage at Cambridge, quoting 'All scripture . . . is profitable'! and proceeding in a masterly way to reveal its import and nourish our minds and hearts. But that was the Cambridge Union Debating Chamber — this was Masan. That was the Cambridge Inter-Collegiate Christian Union — this was a small group of unbelievers with almost no background, in provincial Korea. That was in native English — this was in a fog of Korean. Why *did* we start with Matthew?

That day the first lesson was mine. We had set out with the approach, 'Who is this Jesus Christ? Is He really the Son of God as Christians claim?' and the passage provided the perfect introduction. Only in Europe and North America — and that only in recent years — are people relatively uninterested in family trees. The rest of the world is intensely interested in its origins. It is essential to understanding your place in society that you know your family tree. This is a very large part of the answer to the question of every young person, 'Who am I?' (And also magnifies the plight of orphans who know nothing of their origins.) Nowhere is this more true than in a Confucian society. If Jesus Christ was someone important, then of course He had a long and traceable family tree. It was the natural place to start. The Word of God immediately struck a chord of relevance that we had never even glimpsed. We were to find this happening again and again.

The setting was laid into which could be placed the immediate claims inherent in the Name of the Lord.

Jesus — He shall save His people from their sins (1.21)
Immanuel — God with us (1.23)

1 £1 = 1242 won; $1 = 570 won

2

Now when Jesus was born in Bethlehem of Judea in the days of Herod the king, behold, wise men from the East came to Jerusalem, saying, 'Where is he who has been born king of the Jews? For we have seen his star in the East, and have come to worship him.' (Matthew 2.1, 2)

2

Nativity

Myung Ja was well-suited for the part of Mary. Seventeen years old, a little shy and of gentle nature, she had been in the hospital four months already. She always wore a thin silk neck-scarf tucked into the top of her blouse or jumper. This served to conceal the dressings covering her suppurating tuberculous neck glands. It hurt her to move her neck more than a little. The dignity of movement that this necessitated served only to accentuate her qualities of patience. Her deep brown eyes — unusually big for one of Mongoloid race and therefore unusually pretty to Korean thinking — would look at you with that deep expressiveness of patience under suffering and the questioning glance that conveys more than words of a heart that is ever asking, 'How long will it be? Will I *ever* get better?' Behind those questions, too, lay the very practical ones of, 'When will I be able to go back to work? Will I be so disfigured that my marriage prospects will be dashed?' and a host of other less well-formulated but equally vital questions along with them.

Yes, Myung Ja came from a working home in Pusan. Her mother had died some years ago and, as the eldest, she carried a lot of responsibility for the home besides her job in a sweater factory, one among many in Pusan producing clothing for export to many parts of the Western world. Some such factories, like the major one in Masan employing over 15,000 staff, are large and modern — clean and airy with a shift system, adequate salary and generally good working conditions. Others are small and poky, old-fashioned sweat-shops straight out of Dickens, demanding 14-16 hours a day from their employees. These operate outside the law and happily are diminishing in number, but even a pittance of income under such conditions may be preferable to idleness and dependence at home — 'playing' as the Korean expression is, a term applied widely to anything that is not work, encompassing everything from unemployment to a day off. Myung Ja's place of work was somewhere between the two extremes — employing a few hundred girls on mechanized looms and requiring twelve hours a day with one day off a fortnight.

When first the glands in her neck had begun to swell she tried to ignore them. Time was precious; so was money. It was embarrassing to ask for time off, would cost money to go to hospital and might involve loss of her job. As the weeks went by the increasing swelling on both sides of her neck could no longer be ignored, and when one began to discharge her father recommended a local herb practitioner whom she could visit in the evening and who wouldn't charge too much. He applied a thick brown paste to both sides of her neck and in front over the sternum, bound it up with a layer of polythene and a coarse dressing, asked a few hundred won and recommended cat meat as an adjunct to treatment. That evening she donned the silk neck scarf and it was to be many months before it would be shed again in public.

These pastes are made of a variety of leaves, roots and herbs. Many of them are corrosive on the skin, especially when bound down in an airless space below a layer of plastic. This one proved to be such and it was only a few days before Myung Ja's neck was covered with ulcerating sores on both sides. Work was out of the question, though the kindly supervisor told her she would be welcome back when she was better. She visited a local doctor's clinic where the paste was removed, the sores redressed and the whole bound up in white cotton bandages around her neck. An injection given, some pills to eat, and three thousand won to pay; she was told to come back tomorrow and every day for dressings and an injection. It was hopeless! Out of work and three thousand won a day. Where could she find that? From being the mainstay of the family, she was reduced to helplessness and that sense of burdening others that drove Oates in Antarctica to selfless suicide and countless others in more humdrum circumstances to the same.

Father still had his labouring job so the family was not destitute, but there were a younger sister and two brothers to feed, school fees to find and, with winter approaching, briquette coal to be bought to warm the single living room floor and make life bearable in the cold months from November to March.

Then one day father had come in with news of a hospital in Masan that would take patients like Myung Ja, and that without treatment charge — just twelve thousand won a month for food and the rest would be provided. Could it be true? Rumours abounded and when it came to the treatment of sickness everyone had their word of advice. All too often such advice proved fallacious, as Myung Ja had found out to her bitter cost, or so expensive that it became like looking up at luscious orange persimmons against a high blue Korean sky in autumn, and no ladder to reach them.

Could it really be that when no one in the great urban sprawl of two million people that makes up Pusan seemed interested in the likes of Myung Ja at a scale within her resources, a hospital in provincial Masan two hours away could provide the answer? Perhaps it was worth a try — just this once. By bus the fares for father and daughter would come to 2,000 won, but train, though slower, was cheaper. Perhaps they could make the whole trip for 1,000 won.

Fortunately the informant had also passed on the news that Tuesday was the day when the hospital saw new patients. So next Tuesday morning the rising sun found Myung Ja and her father at Pusan railway station headed for Masan for the first time in their lives. It was not hard to find the National Masan Tuberculosis Hospital. Everyone seemed to know its whereabouts. 'Get the bus to Kapo Dong — two kilometres beyond the far end of town. No, not this one: wait for one that says "Kapo Dong". Then you won't have to change. 35 won each — only five won more than in town.'

Myung Ja pulled the silk scarf a little closer round her neck as she settled in the bus and furtively glanced around, hoping no one had noticed why. Amongst the crowd of market women and working men that glance revealed, she was surprised to note several who seemed to be going the same way as herself — that thin, gaunt man with a crutch; that girl about her own age, but nine inches shorter, with an obviously hunched back; that mother with a crying three-year-old, its right arm swathed in bandages hanging free from the cloth that bound her tightly to her mother's back. It was good not to be alone, but 'I hope there won't be too many: I hope I don't have to wait too long,' she thought as she climbed out of the bus with the others, father bringing up the rear. The bus stop was right in front of an imposing gateway with white three-storey hospital buildings behind. Beyond that and behind her too, the wooded slopes climbed to the skyline with some of the largest fir trees she had ever seen standing amidst an undergrowth of scrub fir and dry mountain-grass. Away to the right a glimpse of the sea down the valley, and to the left mountain slopes again. It seemed a forgotten backwater: could someone here provide the answers to her problems?

Some of those who alighted from the bus with her had headed straight up the hill the way the bus had come, but the mother and child followed her to the gatehouse of the entrance that proudly declared in shining brass plate that it led to the National Masan Tuberculosis Hospital. Her heart pounded as father asked at the gate. It was said that so many forms and documents were needed before you could be admitted to a government hospital, especially if you hoped for free treatment. They had come empty-handed, but for a few thousand won. Would their journey be fruitless?

'No, you've come to the wrong place' — her heart sank. 'You should go just up the road: follow that man with the crutches.' Hope sprang again. A shy smile of thanks and they were on their way. It was still barely ten o'clock as, three hundred yards up the hill and round the corner, they came upon the low single-storey white building standing fifty yards back from the road. It had no gateway or gatekeeper, only a single white board hanging from the doorway indicating in black lettering that this was the 'Spinal Tuberculosis Clinic'! She was surprised to find as she approached that the building was much larger than she had at first imagined, stretching away from the road in a single, long expanded L-form. The crowd was daunting: would they really all be seen today? A little man, hardly taller than her own shoulder height and dressed in white trousers and jacket, was calling out for all newcomers to come round to a side door, where he would see them one by one and hear their troubles. The conversation flowed between patients while they waited. 'No, this wasn't the doctor. He helped the doctor, by finding out first what was wrong with each patient. He might just give you some pills if it was a minor thing, or he might advise you to go elsewhere. If you were poor and really sick he'd ask you to see the doctor.'

'Oh! I *do* hope I get to see the doctor,' thought Myung Ja. He seemed kindly, this man, and spoke gently to those in front of her, though he gave the appearance of knowing what he was talking about and stood no nonsense from those who wanted to jump the queue. She didn't see anyone passing money over. Perhaps he would have mercy on her. Then in the conversation she heard that the doctor was a foreigner — he came from England, and this was a 'Jesus' hospital. She had seen some booklets lying on a table in the hallway; perhaps they were Jesus booklets. But all she knew of Jesus hospitals in Pusan was imposing buildings where you needed lots of money. This didn't seem like that at all.

Now it was her turn — father told the story. Mr Lee (for that is who it was) gently removed the silk neck-scarf and lifted the dressings on her neck. He didn't move them much, but even that hurt.

'You must see the doctor: I think you'll have to come into the hospital for these, but first an X-ray!'

Her heart leapt. Hope! But would the doctor understand her if he was a foreigner? How much *would* it cost? She didn't dare ask Mr Lee. He was already turning to the next patient.

As she waited, conversation flowed among the crowd. Father did the asking.

'Yes, it is quite true. Twelve thousand won a month for food — and no extras.'

'The staff won't accept gifts either,' said another.

'But will she get better?' asked father.

'Well, *I'm* a lot better and I was worse than her when I came in,' answered a voice. The speaker was a man in his late 20's who had obviously drifted down from the wards to pass the time of day with some of those awaiting their turn in out-patients.

'But how will she manage?' pursued father.

'Well, you'll have to bring her bedding and her rice bowl and *suje* (spoon and chopsticks), but they'll look after her here. She'll have to do her bit, of course. She can get around more than some of us, so they'll probably ask her to help in the laundry, or with the little ones. They don't like you lying around here, you know, if you can do something useful.'

Myung Ja's interest rose. It would be more fun to do something than just to sit around, and glancing down the veranda in front of the line of wards she could see among the groups of patients a few girls of her own age. I do hope they'll have me, she thought.

But that was all four months ago now. Myung Ja was a lot better, but not yet ready for home. Now it was Christmas, and time for a nativity play among the festivities for staff and patients.

- - - - - - - - - - - - - - - - - - -

When you've been used to nativity plays from infancy — when even the littlest angel in the pageant has himself seen two or three before and heard the story even from before that — it is hard to imagine the impact that dramatic presentation of the Christmas story can have on children, teenagers and grown men and women who are seeing it for the first time. For most of our patients and their relatives Christmas has but shadowy connections with the birth of Christ. Both for the participants themselves and for the seventy to eighty who gathered to watch, that nativity play had a deep impact: the plight of Mary, the young woman; the bitter fury of Herod; the flight into Egypt; the angels and the star — all would strike chords within their experience

- the struggle of childbirth in dirty surroundings
- the fear of war and bloodshed
- refugee existence
- the impact of the supernatural upon everyday life. Not a person present, but they or their immediate family would have had some deep experience of these things.

And in the midst of all these commonplaces of human life — the Incarnation of God.

Emmanuel — God with us.

Jesus — He will save His people from their sins.

Mary still wore her neck-scarf. Two of the wise men used crutches, and Herod himself had to sit propped up straight on his throne, for he couldn't bend his back more than a fraction; but out of that service and the teaching that led up to it, seventeen patients indicated their desire to follow the Lord.

'First of all I give thanks to God,' wrote Jung Hi, eighteen-year-old high-school boy just recovering from paralysis. 'From the time I was admitted to this hospital, I have prayed to God, confessing that I must put my trust in Christ. Up until the time that I was admitted to hospital I lived without knowledge of Christ. But now, most of all I give thanks that through your words and those of all the staff and through the words of Scripture you have sowed the words of faith in my heart.'

'In the Name of Christ I give thanks for the gift of new life to this dying soul and body,' wrote Kim Kwon, a 24-year-old young man recovering from months of a painful skin condition and arthritis. Although from a Christian home, like many his age he had been in a spiritual wilderness for some years. 'In the past eight months,' he went on, 'I have learned again to follow the Lord. I give thanks for the grace that, forgetting the countless sinful acts of past days, welcomes me again to the warm embrace of my Lord. From henceforth, even when I return to society, I intend not to walk in the paths of sin!'

You shall call His name Jesus, for He will save His people from their sins.

From another, more simply, 'I will believe,' or again from a relative newcomer with less certainty — 'I'll have a go at believing.'

A missionary's life and work is in some senses a projection of the incarnation. 'He shall see of the travail of His soul and be satisfied.'

In those days came John the Baptist, preaching in the wilderness of Judea, 'Repent, for the kindom of heaven is at hand.' ... Bear fruit that befits repentance. (Matthew 3.1-2, 8)

3

Repent!

Repent! The word rings through the history of the Korean church. It was the hallmark of the revival that broke out in Pyong Yang (now capital of North Korea) in 1907. Dr William Blair, one of the early American Presbyterian missionaries, writes as an eye-witness of the event:

'The whole audience began to pray out loud, all together. The effect was indescribable — not confusion, but a vast harmony of sound and spirit, a mingling together of souls moved by an irresistible impulse of prayer! . . . Man after man would rise, confess his sins, break down and weep, and then throw himself to the floor and beat the floor with his fists in perfect agony of conviction . . . Some threw themselves full length upon the floor, hundreds stood with arms outstretched toward heaven. Every man forgot every other. Each was face to face with God. I can hear yet that fearful sound of hundreds of men pleading with God for life, for mercy. The cry went out over the city till the heathen were in consternation . . . A meeting the like of which I had never seen before, nor wish to see again unless in God's sight it is absolutely necessary . . . We may have our theories of the desirability or undesirability of public confession of sin. I have had mine but I know now that when the Spirit of God falls upon guilty souls, there will be confession and no power on earth can stop it!'[1]

That revival transformed the church of the day, added numbers to the body of Christ, and set the tone for the ensuing decades of mounting pressures under Japanese colonial domination (1910-1945).

Repent! Again the call rang out through the Korean church in 1945. 15th August 1945: liberation had come at last from the hated Japanese. Scenes of wild exultation were sobered by the rapid realization that the northern half of the country had been 'liberated' by Russian forces and these had no intention of uniting the country except on their own terms, still less of restoring to the church the basic freedoms that had been steadily suppressed by the Japanese during the tense days of the second world war.

Repent! Japan had progressively foisted its own national religion of Shinto upon Korea. Japan argued that attendance and bowing at shinto shrines was essentially a secular activity — demonstration of fealty to the Emperor, the nation and the empire. Inextricably bound up as it was with emperor-worship and bowing at the shrines of the ancestors and to the spirits that these shrines housed, most Christians saw such observances as 'bowing to other gods than Jehovah' and sought to resist. However, over 35 years of persuasive arguments by Japanese authorities linked with police questioning, closure of Christian schools, imprisonments, tortures, and sometimes (though rarely deliberately) death, many Korean Christians were persuaded to go along with the outward form of such ceremonies. The situation had been very closely akin to that of the Christians in ancient Rome faced with the demands of emperor-worship, but the Japanese had sought to portray the ceremonies as no more than exercises of national solidarity akin to saluting the flag or standing for the national anthem. While many Korean Christians had concurred with this, there were numbers, too, who had firmly resisted the pressures. For some of the leaders this had meant extended and often repeated periods of imprisonment under severe conditions. In a few cases it had meant death in prison. For many others, less prominent, it had meant social ostracism and loss of opportunity.

Now all this was past (in South Korea at least) and the call went out — Repent! Repent of compromise with shrine worship.

The repentance movement gathered momentum — not without acrimony, mutual accusations, struggles for power, and ultimately fragmentation of the hitherto united Korean church. However, in the aftermath of war, the movement for truth and purity was a vigorous and largely creative force. Student groups sprang up (especially in the city of Pusan), many of them predominantly high-school age; with the vision and vigour of youth they demanded uncompromising purity; the older men who had suffered in prison were their heroes; they sought to gather in their fellow-students with intense fervour. With the initiative of such and under the benign influence of the American occupying forces, the church grew by leaps and bounds. In 1945 Pusan had seven churches (two of them Roman Catholic). Twenty years later there were two hundred Protestant churches in the city, and by 1975 there were five hundred. Such figures could be repeated for almost every part of the country south of the 38th Parallel (border with communist-dominated North) and especially for Seoul, the capital, which in 1977 topped seven million people — 20% of the 35 million people in South Korea.

Dawn (or more strictly pre-dawn) prayer meetings had long been a feature of the Korean Church. They had sprung up in the revival of 1907, but their roots lay further back. It had long been the custom in the Buddhist temples (in Korea mostly beautifully situated in high, secluded, tree-decked valleys among the remote mountains) to rise at two or three in the morning for prayer. In the Korean church it became the custom to rise for corporate the prayer at the church. Traditionally this hour of prayer should finish before the sun rose. With its origins in what was already a local pattern for the expression of religious fervour, it had much to commend it in the early days. A lone Christian in an unbelieving family could not find peace for communion with God in the narrow confines of his home. In a farming community where work started at sunrise, the pre-dawn hour was the only time for quiet.

The repentance movement provided the momentum for the revival of the pre-dawn meeting and it became normal for every church to hold such. It was expected of every keen church member to attend as often as possible, and especially on Sunday. Like so many emphases in church history, its roots were healthy, but projected into a changed (and now largely urban) community and used as the seal of orthodoxy rather than the channel of spontaneous seeking after God, its status as an institution is more problematical.

August 1970

Repent! The strident, rather high-pitched voice rang out from the platform over the sea of four hundred high school boys and girls crowded into the provincial church where we were gathered. Repent! Repent! The tone rose to its highest pitch and all bowed, many with faces to the floor at the close of the 45-minute sermon. A crescendo of noise rose from the body of the church, some calling out, some shouting, some beating the floor with their fists. Repentance was being offered at the shrine of the speaker whose voice, like some officiating high priest — or perhaps 20th-Century cheer-leader — could be heard from time to time above the tumult calling out 'Oh Lord — Oh Lord — O-o-o-h — L-o-o-o-rd' — urging to greater intensity of responses.

Ping-ping — the little finger bell on the speaker's desk sounded twice. The tumult subsided, and as the speaker's voice alone rose in prayer, handkerchiefs were drawn out, brows mopped, eyes wiped, and normality once again restored. Was that normality now pervaded with the peace of God that passes all understanding — that peace which comes from assurance of sins forgiven? I wondered.

I had been a missionary in Korea only a year and was attending 24 hours of the four-day area conference of students, held each year in the summer holidays. These students were the successors of those who had been deeply involved in the repentance movement in Pusan 25 years before. The majority were of high-school age, and another large section in the 'middle-school' bracket (12-15 years old) — some of these only just out of primary school. A smattering of college students were leading and organizing.

The speaker at this evening meeting was a much-respected local minister. Now in his mid-sixties, he had taken a courageous stand against Japanese Shinto shrine worship thirty years ago. Along with others of his friends he had suffered beatings and imprisonment. I was later to know him personally as a kindly man with a real personal love for God's word. With only limited language at this stage, I could only catch trends in his sermon — not enough to understand its main thrust — but I was disturbed. This scene that I was surveying almost as a spectator with little emotion other than perplexity — was this biblical Christianity? Was I so cold-blooded and analytical that I could not catch the breath of the Spirit of God? Was I so hide-bound in Western thought that I could not make allowances for different expression in a different setting? The speaker — a man of esteem; the student movement — one of the vaunted bright-spots of the Korean church scene. Yet I couldn't get away from the sense that the great majority present had got no more from the address than I had — Repent! Repent! — and had produced a mechanical response as indicated. We were to see the pattern repeated on countless occasions, and generally to look in vain for a heart that had been taught to rest upon the finished work of Christ and find there the fears of a guilty conscience assuaged and peace with God restored.

- - - - - - - - - - - - - - - - - -

October 1970

'Do you know where the old paraffin stove that used to be in the garage has got to?' It was two months later and I was talking to Mr Jee, our hospital driver.

'No, I don't know,' was the reply, and I thought no more of it.

A few days later he caught me in a quiet corner behind the house. A slight pause — 'I've got something to say that's not much fun to say,' he started. I waited.

'You know that stove — ?'

'Yes.'

'Well — it's in my house.'

'Oh?'

'I didn't think it was wanted, so I took it and patched it up to use at home. When you asked me the other day, you caught me unawares. Then I thought, "Oh! Here I am, coming morning by morning to study the Bible, saying I am looking for the truth — and here I've told a downright lie!" I'm sorry!'

My heart sang. Here was a man not yet a Christian, but the Word of God with its standards of truth was having its impact on his heart. The fate of the stove was, by comparison, utterly trivial. Here was a conscience awakened, and we rejoiced to reassure him of forgiveness and acceptance on our human level — though he had as yet not made peace with God. It is hard to 'own up'. In Asia this is doubly so. Discussing the story later with some Korean Christian friends of some standing, they were amazed. Face-saving is common to us all.

'We hardly ever see this in our churches,' they said. 'This is real

discipleship.'
Repent! Repent!

- - - - - - - - - - - - - - - - - -

'I want to repent.'

It was early December in that same year of 1970. Mr Lee, our hospital physiotherapist, stood before me entirely on his own initiative. Starting with that genealogy which had been more problematical for me than for them, we had been working through Matthew's gospel over the intervening eight months. Now we were nearing the end.

'I want to repent.' I wondered what he meant. Had he collected some phrase of religious jargon that he thought would please me? My cautious nature and little faith hesitated.

'Yes — good — what do you mean by that?' I asked. I had not urged repentance or decision on any of them except in so far as the actual passage of Scripture we were reading at the time did so itself.

'I want to repent of this,' went on Mr Lee, pulling out a piece of paper from his pocket and showing me, on it, a list of the specific matters that lay on his conscience.

The first dated back fifteen years to a time when as a school boy he had hitched a ride on a railway train without buying a ticket. 'I've just sent the station-master the money for that ticket,' he said.

The remainder were all items he had stolen from the hospital. None of them was large or very serious; some could even have been regarded as rightful 'perks'; none of them was ever suspected by me. Mr Lee had always been a hard-working and exemplary member of staff. I was dumbfounded, not at the revelation of crime — there was nothing very major in human eyes anyway — but at the impact that God's Word had had even amidst our struggling, fumbling Korean, and at the tenderness of an awakened conscience.

'I want to repay the cost of these items to the hospital over a few months out of my salary,' Mr Lee went on, 'and I would like to tell to the whole group what I have told you today!' Restitution and utter honesty without thought to the cost of 'face'!

'Well, this is wonderful,' I said. Then, knowing the hard streak in his nature among the many other fine qualities, I asked further,

'What brought you to this?'

Mr Lee paused.

'It was when we were reading the story of the cross that I found my heart was changed,' he replied.

A heart taught to rest upon the finished work of Christ and to find there the fears of a guilty conscience assuaged and peace with God. A child of God was born that day and through all the ensuing ups and downs he has never forgotten it. Repent! Repent! Oh Korea!

Bear fruit that befits repentance, and do not presume to say to yourselves, 'We have Abraham as our father.'

1   Dr William Blair, *The Korean Pentecost* (Banner of Truth), pages 71-74

He went about all Galilee, teaching in their synagogues and preaching the gospel of the kingdom and healing every disease and every infirmity among the people . . . and great crowds followed Him. (Matthew 4.23, 25.)

4

Temptation

Every missionary, like every servant of Christ, faces at the outset of his ministry a barrage of temptation — some of it conscious, much of it below the threshold of conscious analysis. He is young and impressionable. He has been taught to listen before he speaks, to learn from his elders and to recognize from the start that just because things are done differently in a different culture it does not necessarily mean they are wrong. The guidelines for his own ministry are being laid down and he is easily swayed by those with whom he first comes into contact. It is only by careful sifting of impressions over a considerable length of time and in the light of Scripture that he will be able to separate the true and the false and have the courage to hold to the one and discard the other. Something of this process must have lain behind our Lord's preparation for ministry. It reached its climax in the temptations in the wilderness, but years of close observation of the religious climate of His youth in the light of Old Testament Scripture must have preceded this. We found ourselves subjected to the same cross-currents, often perplexed, not infrequently swept off course, and again and again driven back to the Word of God for light on fresh experiences.

- - - - - - - - - - - - - - - - - -

Saturday, December 17th 1966. The Cathay Pacific flight from Hong Kong circled Kimpo Airport, Seoul, for its landing early in the afternoon. Audrey and I pressed our faces close to the window for our first glimpses of Korea. Brown, empty fields . . . clusters of thatched roofed houses, many of them in the traditional stumpy L-shaped design . . . the wide flat basin of the Han

35

river west of Seoul . . . and, in the distance, mountains on every side except westwards where, thirty miles on, the river empties itself into the sea.

Through customs and immigration formalities and out to the welcoming handshakes of a small group of Koreans who had come to greet us. There was the inevitable photograph, with Audrey clutching the bunch of presentation chrysanthemums (an accommodation to western practice — more commonly they would be given to the man). Foremost among the welcomers was our friend, Kim Chin Kyung, whom we had known during his two years at Clifton Theological College, Bristol (now Trinity College), and through whom our first knowledge of Korea and our call to the land had come.

'This is my friend, Yune Zong Ha' — yes, I had seen his photograph and we had corresponded a few times while he had spend a year at the Red Cross Tuberculosis Sanatorium at Inchon, port-city an hour west of Seoul. This was to be the first of very many happy and profitable hours spent together.

'And this is his sister, Zong Ae' — yes, she, too, had written before, and with some knowledge of English proved herself an early and warm friend to Audrey.

'And this is their father, Pastor Yune Bong Ki' — we turned to greet an unassuming little man in his early 60's with greying hair, warm, twinkling eyes, and a face whose lines seemed well-practised in the art of creasing into smiles.

And so into cars for the centre of town. On the way Pastor Yune excused himself to visit one of his church members who was in hospital, a custom we were to find over the next ten years was one of his characteristics. He seemed to be for ever calling on the sick, visiting the bereaved, comforting the distressed, shepherding the flock — mostly by bus and on foot, rarely by taxi in spite of the fact that, in a society where private cars are relatively few, taxi would be the commonly accepted normal means of transport within the city for professional classes.

Many were the times subsequently when, on a visit to Seoul, I would be asked to go with Pastor Yune to visit a child in hospital and reassure his parents, to see an X-ray and advise, to explore the possibilities of a cheaper form of treatment than that which had been recommended, and so on. These reflections of the Master's pattern of compassionate ministry were precious and reassuring.

Next morning we awoke at early dawn to the sound of multiple church bells sounding out over the city. It was immensely comforting in a strange land to huddle under the quilt on the hot floor and to listen to this familiar token of Christian worship. The house where we stayed was set on the slopes of Nan San (South Mountain) in the centre of Seoul, and when we rose and pushed back the shutters, a number of spires and church towers could be seen from the windows.

In the intervening years these church bells have been multiplied, many adapted to produce transistorized hymn tunes, vying with neighbouring churches for earliest start and air-space. At times such is the volume that housing adjacent to church property is commonly said to be less valuable — it is too noisy.

By 11 o'clock that morning we were at Paster Yune's church, the Central Presbyterian Church, which, in spite of its imposing name in a city that even then had many hundred churches (and now thousands), was a low-roofed building with Japanese-style *tatami* floor on which the congregation sat. It was in fact several Korean houses run together, the partitions removed but the wooden uprights remaining as pillars dotted around the floor space. Of course, we understood not a word of the service in Korean, but we have abiding memories of that day and similar ones spent there during the ensuing two months while we were taking our first steps in language study in Seoul — the warm singing of the choir, the recurring use of the name *Yesu* (Jesus) in Pastor Yune's preaching, and the warmth of the Yune family's hospitality over lunch prepared by the pastor's wife for the choir, various other church members, and ourselves.

As we stood after lunch on the raised cement platform, used for storing earthenware *kimchi* (winter pickle) jars through the winter, Zong Ae told us of her forthcoming marriage and impending departure with her husband for study in the States. It was to be five years before we would see them again, and Audrey lost a good friend almost before friendship had started. However her brother, Zong Ha, being currently self-employed preparing a church Sunday School syllabus for publication and therefore master of his own time, undertook to be our first language tutor, and came morning by morning to the house where we stayed in Seoul, patiently working at grammar and vocabulary with us.

Those sessions would always end hurriedly as we dashed out down the hill in the breath-taking cold of January and February in Seoul, grabbed a hurried doughnut and milk at a bakery for lunch, and made our way across Seoul to the language school for four hours' class beginning at one pm. In the goodness of God our paths were to become even more closely entwined with that of Mr Yune.

New Year's Day saw us on our first visit to a smaller provincial town where we were to have our first brush with a pattern of ministry very different from Pastor Yune's: a pattern caught up in the temptations which the Lord resisted, but which have enmeshed many men since. We had spent Christmas with our friend Kim Chin Kyung and his family and he was taking us to his home church where his mother still worshipped. I was to speak at the morning service. Entering the gateway of the church we were surprised to be directed not to the stone-built church in front of us where many were entering for morning worship, but to the less pretentious wooden building at the side which appeared to do service as a church-hall. Here the elderly minister welcomed us warmly and ushered us to the front. Pastor Kang was in his early seventies, with piercing eyes and hair showing grey at the roots where the black dye, which many older Koreans of both sexes apply to their hair to preserve the appearance of youth, had begun to grow out. The congregation, mostly elderly ladies in their traditional *hanbok* or long Korean dress with a high bodice, with a smattering of students in their black smocks, was seated on square cushions on the wooden floor with a higher concentration of cushions around the two stoves that warmed the building — like ants around a jam pot.

This church was the first in that town, with a history of over fifty years — a mother-church to many others in the city and the area. We were later to learn that the church had split in the wake of the repentance movement following liberation from the Japanese. For fifteen years the two factions had used the same front gate but worshipped separately, one in the church and one in the former church hall, while protracted legal suits were pursued in the secular courts over right to ownership of the property. Finally judgement was given that ownership of property was vested in the local congregation and that in case of division assets should be divided. Pastor Kang's section then received a substantial sum of compensation from the other section of the church and were able to build themselves a separate church building 300 yards up the road. The protracted nature of this visible quarrel in the central church in town, and all the bitterness associated with it, meant that very few educated people there were drawn to the churches, and today it remains one of the hardest parts of the country for the gospel.

I was to learn more of Pastor Kang in the ensuing years. He had been a policeman before entering the ministry, and had a considerable legal knowledge and a flair for ruthlessly applying the full scope of legal powers to achieve his aims. It was well known that one could not cross him and expect to remain at peace in any position of leadership in the churches of that presbytery – nor even beyond. Many a young man in the ministry had found himself compelled to toe the line and to support Pastor Kang in Presbytery and Assembly – or to get his fingers burned. Many was the time when younger men knew they needed to support his candidacy for chairman of key committees or boards, or they would find life exceedingly uncomfortable.

Some years later I was visiting him to seek his help in promotion of Scripture Union Bible Reading aids in his church. I found him seated crosslegged on the floor of his inner room at his house attached to the new church they had constructed. Beside him on the floor lay a carefully stacked pile of 500-won notes – probably several thousand of them. He listened to what I had to say and, lifting two notes from the top of the pile, passed them to me in payment for ten copies of the Scripture Union notes. *All these I will give you, if you will fall down and worship me.* I shuddered and extricated myself as quickly as possible. I knew instinctively that to win his influence would be the death-knell of all we were seeking to do.

I think of him again five years later, now in his late 70's but still with fresh jet-black hair. He is seated in 'general assembly', but it is not a large gathering. The previous year, following years of tension, his party was defeated in all the major posts at general assembly, and he took with him a sizeable group of churches in his area to form a new 'general assembly'. It is this assembly that is meeting – many of them younger men who have found themselves step by step enmeshed in his power structure and unable to extricate themselves. But this time it is not the pastors who are dominating the assembly; it is the lay elders. And it is not the cultured city elders with new suits and newly-dyed hair for assembly; it is the country elders — farming men with baggy creaseless trousers that have seen ten assemblies or more; men with gnarled hands and good country earth so ingrained down the sides of the fingernails that even the extra scrubbing that general assembly calls for has not entirely removed it. It is these men who are on their feet one after another:

'You have led us astray.'

'You pastors have been concerned only with your power, not our progress.'

'You are engaged only in politics and have no concern for the spiritual life of the church.'

'We have been deceived: you have brought us on a pathway to death.'

'We trusted you and you have betrayed that trust.'

One after another the accusations of peace-loving men stirred to indignation fall upon the ears of the leadership.

Pastor Kang rises slowly to his feet. All are hushed. What will he answer? Many has been the time when, under attack, the legal skill of his tongue has turned his opponents' criticisms upon their own heads.

'Mr Chairman, I am an old man and it is getting late. Please will you have me excused.'

Gathering his hat he turns and makes his way slowly out into the night. *You shall worship the Lord your God and Him only shall you serve.*

This cameo is exceptional only in that it is more dramatic than most. Temptation besets the path of every young servant of Christ. It is hard to preach the gospel of the kingdom and to practise a ministry of compassion. The practice of the pre-eminence of God is at a premium.

Blessed are the poor in spirit, for theirs is the kingdom of heaven.
(Matthew 5.3.)

5

Happiness

It is significant that Jesus begins His teaching in the Sermon on the Mount on the theme of happiness. Where does it lie? Upon what conditions may it be obtained? It immediately relates Him to the real position of His hearers, for everyone wants happiness.

Part of the task of the preacher and especially of the missionary in a foreign culture is to understand the aspirations of the people and through the teaching of Scripture to bring them into line with the purposes of God. Nowhere is this more needed than in the context of the younger churches growing up in a culture totally alien to the principles of the gospel. Where the church is vigorously expanding, as in Korea, it is yet more necessary, for unless the principles of Scripture are brought carefully to bear on the assumptions of those entering Christ and those entering His church, the traditional value-system remains unchanged with merely a veneer of Christian terminology. People remain Buddhist, Confucian, materialist in their thinking and Christian values and even vocabulary are interpreted within this framework. This may be true whether people truly come to Christ or are merely incorporated into the fold of Christianity in a mass-movement, though of course in the latter case, where there is no true conversion to Christ, the problems are compounded. Very often it is impossible, and anyway probably wrong, to distinguish the two. The only sure path is for the teaching of Scripture (what Paul calls 'that mould of teaching to which you were committed' Romans 6.17) to be so persistently brought to bear upon people's lives that its form and value-system progressively transforms people in their thinking, and therefore in their living, into the pattern of Christ. This can be illustrated by reference to Christ's teaching on this basic human aspiration for happiness.

Confucian teaching has five beatitudes:
Blessed are the rich
Blessed are the popular
Blessed are the healthy
Blessed are the long-lived
Blessed are they who have many sons.

A moment's thought will show that these aspirations concur very closely with the values of the Buddhism that lies yet further back in Korean history than does Confucian social structure, and with perennial materialism that is in its full flower today. The Buddhist seeks release from desire: this is a somewhat easier proposition for one who already has what he wants. The materialist seeks fulness of joy in this life: these beatitudes are, on the surface at least, a good prescription for this. The blessing of many sons, furthermore, not only ensures material comfort in old age, but bridges Confucian social structure and ancient animistic roots in the continuing family rites of ancestor worship. The gospel cuts into all of this. It is indeed fire upon the earth.

- - - - - - - - - - - - - - - - - -

I was asked to speak at morning service in a church the other end of town. The minister, a man now around forty, had over the years progressively become a disciple of the man we saw in the last chapter. When we had first known him, five or six years before, he and several other of the younger ministers in town had invited us to a meeting where they had discussed their strategy for advance. Within five years, they said, the reins of power would pass from the hands of the old guard into their own, and they had begun to outline their plans for control in the churches and influence in the town. In my naivety at that time I had been excited at the prospect of release for the churches from the strait-jacket of authoritarian control by the old guard, but the emphasis on 'power', 'influence', 'control' should have alerted me.

In the interval I had seen his church grow from around 150 to over three hundred members — largely with the influx of young people from the country areas into work in the industrial zones in the city. But I had seen him, too, grow in girth, aloofness from the people, and demands upon his flock. I knew that there was currently strife between him and his church over pastor's pay and that growing demands from the pulpit for increased giving to meet this and the projected building fund goals were creating friction and making heavy demands on the conscience of some church deacons, already heavily committed in personal house mortgages and children's education. I knew that a sizeable group of deacons and their families had recently defected to a new church that had opened half a mile away, where the pastor was a somewhat older man with a warmer pastoral care over his people.

Where could I as an outsider bring Scripture to bear upon this situation for the good of pastor and people? The beatitudes seemed the answer.

True happiness lies in right relationship with God — not merely in status in human society.

True happiness is found in the context of here and eternity held together, not just in the here and now.

True happiness is found in giving, not getting.

Above all, true happiness is found in the meekness of faith — faith that God means what He says, and if I am right with Him I do not need to politic for influence to protect and extend my own rights.

Whether the message penetrated I don't know: certainly some of the congregation found their intuitive sense of values in Christ nourished. Not long after this the pastor left to begin a new church in Seoul. Prospects for advancement (and temptation) are always greater in the capital.

Do we condemn such a man? Let him who is without sin cast the first stone. The enormous weight of an anti-Christian cultural heritage lies at his back. The pattern of life of his seniors has provided the precedent. What of those seniors? — the missionaries were their prototype. Too often in the eyes of the church and the world in Korea today Christianity is seen to be preoccupied with power and riches. This, of course, was the predominant emphasis of organized religion in our Lord's day and makes His words the more piercingly relevant. The early missionaries preached a wonderful biblical gospel and planted a vigorous and self-sufficient church amidst much hardship. However, a discerning observer of the early years of the century said that the Korean church had a wonderful future if it could deal with the question of power and money. In the ensuing decades the missionaries' pattern of life all too often served to enhance the already strong belief that if you were good you would be rich.

Extensive mission compounds on quiet wooded slopes at the edge of many major cities — compounds where all too often house servants were the only Koreans gaining regular access — served to reinforce the image. Following the second world war and again following the Korean war (1950-53) many new missions entered Korea. The economic situation was such that relatively small amounts of capital could secure very desirable land and properties. This meant that the public image of Wealth = Blessing of God was yet further strengthened. The atmosphere has become such that it is now very hard for the young Christian, be he worker or layman, foreign or local, to exercise faith in setting his goals on the sources of true happiness as taught by our Lord.

- - - - - - - - - - - - - - - - - -

'It is very hard to exercise faith ...' but it can be done. *Blessed are the meek for they shall inherit the earth.* (5.5.) Among the refugees who poured into Pusan in the latter part of 1950, swelling the population from 200,000 to over a million, was a surgeon of considerable renown and strong Christian character. Just turned forty, Dr Chang had become famous in the city of Pyong Yang (capital of North Korea) when he had carried out an appendicectomy on the North Korean leader, Kim Il Sung. Now in the tides of war he had taken the opportunity, like countless others, to escape from the Communist purge of Christians and had made his way to the far south east, where at that time the Pusan perimeter taking in Taegu and Masan was all that was left of the peninsula not in Communist hands. Again like countless others in the chaos of flight he had lost touch with his family and to this day does not know whether they are dead or alive in North Korea.

Touched with the tremendous need among the refugees living in shacks, tents, lean-tos and any conglomeration of wood, stone, tin and cardboard that would provide some shelter, he, along with two non-medical friends, had started a Christian hospital in tents borrowed from the American army.

Following the war, such was his standing among rich and poor alike that the hospital qualified for Armed Forces relief in the construction of permanent buildings, which we were to see ten years later standing on a hillside at the southern end of Pusan with a magnificent outlook to the open sea looking towards Japan. I shall always remember the night I spend with him in his little semi-westernized house below the hospital not long after our arrival. His insistence that I sleep in the bed while he lay on the floor beside me spoke volumes about his humble disposition to me almost thirty years his junior. Dr Chang was the sort of doctor who is the despair of a hospital business manager trying to balance the books. His ear was always open to the patients' needs and many was the time that he ordered charity care or substantial cuts in charges to meet a patient's straitened circumstances. I have long been of the opinion that in Christian medical work in the developing world, while it is important that the doctor be a man of faith, it is even more important that the business manager exercise the meekness of faith. If not, the poor are inevitably and progressively excluded.

About the time we arrived the hospital received recognition as a surgical post-graduate training institution, and from that time has had between six and twelve surgeons in training — by no means all of them Christian. Some five years later a nursing school was added and substantial funds received from overseas for nursing school buildings and hospital expansion. As the institution grew it became progressively harder for one man to imprint his ethos on the whole against the prevailing preoccupation with bigness and profits. Trusteeship fell into the hands of those more interested in profit than patients. Their protégés were to find their way on to the staff and the dreary trend towards medicine for the benefit of administation rather than patients was to become all too apparent.

But not all was loss. Wherever a man of faith can reproduce one in his own image there is hope. For many years Dr Chang trained up as his right-hand man Dr Park, a young surgeon. Dr Park had been converted as a high school boy in the student movement mentioned in chapter 3. He had become one of its leaders in the early days of spiritual zeal and had been much torn between medicine and the ministry. Choosing the former, he had in course of time found his way to Dr Chang's tutelage — not only in surgical skill, but in the fight of faith. Today he is one of the leading surgeons in Pusan. Yet I vividly remember his unprecedented eagerness to come with us on trips to country villages, bringing with him a team of hospital staff for a day's treatment centred on the village church or other local building. On one such occasion, in the relaxation time, a group of us were singing together:

I'd rather have Jesus than silver or gold,
I'd rather be His than have riches untold.
I'd rather have Jesus than houses and lands,
I'd rather be led by His nail-pierced hands.

It was new to Dr Park, but so expressed the true aspirations of his heart that he never forgot it.

Blessed are the peace-makers.

Dr Chang and Dr Park manifested this quality in marked degree, but *blessed, too, are those who hunger and thirst for righteousness. They shall be satisfied,* but it often takes courage and leads to persecution for righteousness' sake.

In one stormy board meeting the generally taciturn and peace-loving Dr Park rose to his feet and declared roundly:

'The most important person in the hospital is not the chairman of trustees, not the medical superintendent, but THE PATIENT,' and stormed out. The point was made, but Dr Park lost his post at the hospital for three years. Now he is back, and on Dr Chang's retirement in 1975 he took up the reins as medical superintendent. In his speech at the hand-over ceremony, dressed in his work-a-day white coat amongst the dapper-suited celebrities, he declared firmly, 'This hospital was founded by Dr Chang as a Christian hospital to care for the poor. Today there is a change in superintendent, but no change in that basic policy,' and everyone, current staff, guests and patients, knew that the call had gone out, 'Let's get back to the principles with which we started.'

The path is a long and hard one strongly against the tide – it is very hard to exercise faith that Jesus' prescription of true happiness is the correct one . . . but it can be done.

Blessed are those who are persecuted for righteousness' sake, for theirs is the kingdom of heaven.

In praying do not heap up empty phrases as the Gentiles do; . . . pray then like this: 'Our Father who art in heaven . . .' (Matthew 6.7, 9.)

6

Prayer

I was sitting in the staff common-room of a large seminary with an international missions leader who was visiting Korea, and some of the staff.

'This is a revival church; we have our dawn prayer meetings,' declared one of the staff members.

'There is very, very much fasting and prayer in Korea. Most of the Christians, about sixty percent of our congregation, fast for at least five or six days a year. They go up to the Prayer Mountain,' states one leader, pastor of a congregation of many thousands in Seoul, in an interview with a Christian magazine in the West.

'Sorry, he's not available,' says his wife as I call to visit a minister friend in Masan, 'he's gone to the prayer-place in the mountains to fast and pray. He'll be away all week.'

'My elders and I don't agree,' said another young minister friend, discussing his plans for study overseas, 'but we are praying. God will hear the minister's prayers more than the elders', won't He?' he added, half-jokingly, but with sufficient proximity to commonly-held belief to cause a question mark to be raised over the nature of such prayer.

'Father, thank you *very* much. Amen,' prayed the hospital cleaner in his first verbalized prayer when we had completed the study of Mark's gospel together over a period of some weeks.

'I need sometimes to go up on the mountains and shout at Satan,' said the former evangelist of the local church a few hundred yards from our house. A man of little education but strong faith mellowed by much suffering, he had escaped from North Korea in the war and tells of weeks on the mountains existing on tree bark and such; of lying hidden in the long grass with the boots of Communist soldiers tramping past his nose. A visit to his shack constructed with his own hands on the hillside is always a spiritual tonic. His wife had almost died in childbirth shortly before our last return from furlough, but visiting her I was the greater recipient of blessing. 'I pray for you,' she said, 'that you will be a motor-car and God will be the Driver.'

The rostrum shook as the elder thumped it with his fist and his voice rose in a crescendo. The occasion was the annual conference of a Presbyterian Men's Association. Some three hundred men between 25 and forty years old, from all over the country, assembled in a Pusan church for three days in the midst of a steaming summer. To lead such an assembly in prayer was a rare opportunity not to be missed, and the leader was using his opportunity to the full — opportunity for what?

Nic Deane and I had survived three hours on the corner of the platform in a chilly wind from a nearby open window in the depths of bitterly-cold early January. The occasion was an annual students' conference. Over a thousand students (mostly of high school age) gathered for five days of meetings beginning daily with dawn prayer meeting and continuing at high pitch through most of the day to its culmination in this lengthy evening session.

The preacher, a gifted man well-liked by the students, had concluded his hour-and-a-half sermon on Daniel — much good content, but beyond the great majority of the young people after the first thirty minutes. The points which stuck in the memory were that every student should spend at least two hours a day in prayer and Bible study, and that the corollary of the fourth commandment ('Remember the sabbath day . . .') was 'six days shalt thou work . . .' If they would work properly the other days, they would be free to keep Sunday for the Lord without doing homework.

Korean school children are worked extremely hard. High school students will be in school from eight to six with homework assignments after that and, if the family can afford it, often private tutoring as well late into the night. In the house where we stayed in Seoul during those early days of language study, we were woken on many occasions at midnight, one am, even three am, by the murmur of voices. It was the family tutor (a university student living in and earning his keep) coaching the boys for their high school exams.

Yes, the preacher's emphasis on prayer and Bible study and the Lord's day was attractive, but added up and looked at in the light of the realities of a high school student's life, it was a formula for despair. Few high-schoolers find two hours a day to do anything other than their studies and the bare necessities of living.

The preacher had finished, the subsidiary speakers had had their say — an amusing army chaplain telling of life with the paratroopers. 'Left-Right-Left-Right I — AM — WITH — YOU. (In crisp marching time) 1 — 2 — 3 — JUMP. 1 — 2 — 3 — Oh Lord'. Here was practical Christianity — vigorous and relevant.

The students — many of them to be in like circumstances within a few years — woke up and enjoyed it.

Then the meeting closed in prayer — all heads bowed and the crescendo of noise rose from a thousand tongues — to sing my great redeemer's praise? — or to cry out in the unrelieved gloom of a guilty conscience whose burdens had been multiplied not lifted.

As I looked out over the sea of black smock uniforms, my attention was focussed on one lad of about sixteen near the front — on his knees with his head to the floor and thumping the boards in front of him while he cried out in ever-increasing intensity. The sweat poured from his brow and his motion increased until his whole body was shaking up and down — only to be subdued into silence and stillness by the ping-ping of the rostrum finger-bell. Was this Christian prayer? The scene would be repeated night after night and year after year at similar meetings up and down the country in churches of all denominations and with groups young and old. But, 'Burdens are lifted at Calvary.' Where was the peace and joy of sins forgiven? The quietness of a conscience at peace with God?

The spectrum of activity included in the term 'prayer' is very wide. How are we to distinguish that which rightly comes within the term of 'Christian prayer?' Like every other aspect of Christian living, it is only in the light of Scripture that we can discern the genuine and that which, although it may carry Christian terminology, in fact manifests activities other than those of the gospel.

The strength of Korean dawn prayer meetings is much vaunted abroad. 'The Korean church is a praying church,' it is said, but prayer divorced from the teaching of Scripture as to the nature of Christian prayer reverts to type — the background culture:

Buddhist —
— prayer means merit
— more prayer — more merit
— much prayer — much merit
They think that they will be heard for their many words (6.7.)

Shamanist — 'Lord, you are more powerful than I. Therefore I invoke you that *my* will may be done.'
The Kingdom come.   Thy will be done.

Materialist — 'If I am a good boy I will get rich quick.'
You cannot serve God and mammon.

There is much in both church and society in 20th-century

Korea that is analogous to Victorian Britain. The impact of the headlong rush into industrial revolution and its aftermath has been enormous, and Dickens and his critique of society is amazingly relevant. It is not surprising that, just as in 19th-century Britain the YMCA and YWCA attracted the interest of much of the best in Christian service, by virtue of their deep involvement in the social needs of young people, so today, in Korea, many thinking and involved Christians have found outlets for service within these movements which have a long history in Korea. This is especially true of the YWCA which has had a succession of outstanding leaders. In Masan over the last five years the local YWCA chapter has acquired premises, and opened a night school for factory girls who have not been able to acquire more than primary schooling. YWCA also runs a series of evening clubs in arts and crafts for older girls living in lodgings and dormitories while working in the industrial zones. Senior support has come from a wide body of Christian women, mostly the wives of professional men and active members of their churches.

Three of the Masan leaders, a school-teacher's wife and two doctors' wives, have also for the last three years been members of the Masan Scripture Union Committee — formed to promote Bible reading in the churches. At the instigation of these three the local YWCA invited Mr Yune Zong Ha, mentioned in chapter 4 and now general secretary of Korea SU, to address three special meetings arranged for the local 'Y' leadership. They stipulated that they did not want the usual type of 'revivalist' meeting — flogging without feeding. They wanted Bible teaching. Mr Yune came in the autumn of 1977 and the first meeting coincided with a meeting of the local Christian doctors' group. This somewhat fragile group, revived two years before at the initiative of Dr Chang of Pusan, met monthly for a meal, a formal homily by a local minister and a collection of membership fees. The husbands of these two YW leaders were members but less active in Christian things than their wives. They say that in Asia the man rules the household, but there is plenty of scope for the skilful wife to exert her influence. These two did just that, with the effect that the doctors' meeting was curtailed and the doctors' group combined with the YW ladies for the first of Mr Yune's addresses. He chose Matthew 6 and the subject of prayer. It is always revealing to see how a national, seeking to bring a biblical critique to bear upon his own culture and traditions, deals with Scripture. What follows is sermon notes from Matthew 6.7-15 as they came over that evening:

(1) *Prayer is conversation with God* (v 7.)

It is a two-way process: sharing life with a friend.

This contrasts with the prophets of Baal on Carmel.

Communication *both* ways is important, but it is more important to *listen* to God than to speak to God.

'Please do as I have planned . . .' is not Christian prayer.

God speaks not by a voice of revelation, but through the Bible. Thus the Bible is essential to an understanding of prayer, and prayer is essential to an understanding of the Bible.

(2) *I must know to Whom I am praying*

I must concentrate my thoughts on Him.

Our Father Who art in heaven (6.9)

I need to remember His greatness.

If I concentrate only on keeping up an unceasing flow of words I forget Him (v. 7). Shamanism (which is a form of animism) teaches that the world is full of evil spirits. If I invoke the power of a greater spirit I may overcome them. The centre of activity is *me,* not God.

(3) *Many Christians think that God is sitting by idly until they ask His help.*

On the contrary, God is working out His plans and wants to draw us into them. (v 10.)

(4) Many think that if we have committed big sins, when we repent God will forgive, but we shall have to pay for them (v 12.)

This is to ignore the death of Christ.

If when trouble comes we think it is punishment for past sins of which we have already repented, we are subjects of Satan's deceit.

(5) *God is not tied by cause-and-effect determinism.*

Job grappled with this problem and eventually ends silent and worshipful. God can do as He wants and Job gets no explanation of his circumstances. We must ask if this circumstance is a warning about something I had not noticed, but in many cases we shall not know *why* events turned out this way or that.

God is not a tour-guide!

(6) *Content of Prayer*

Hallowed be Thy Name — through me!
Thy kingdom come
Thy will be done — I will do as You tell me
We have totally forgotten to pray this way.

Always we make our decisions and ask His blessing — house, job, school, marriage, etc. etc.

The answers are not in the Bible, but God will guide us as we read and obey His Word.

Eg Jesus in Gethsemane — not an endless flow of words, but seeking the Father's will.

Give us this day our daily bread — Daily — don't rely on your bank balance or rice store.

Forgive ... as we forgive others — we need to develop the habit of forgiving.

Lead us not into temptation — not only just 'not into sin.'

Greed is the greatest temptation today — hence the relevance of the latter parts of the chapter —

Do not lay up for yourselves treasures on earth ... lay up for yourselves treasures in heaven. (19-20.)

- - - - - - - - - - - - - - - - - -

The response was enthusiastic. It had the ring of truth about it it. The message corresponded with reality and they wanted more. Here were sophisticated professional men and highly-educated, cultured housewives in middle life. They had been active members of their churches for many years and were able members of society by any standard, but this sort of exposition of Christian prayer was almost entirely new to them. The doctors especially, though able men, were children in the faith — not so much by deliberate default as by starvation. It was a situation we found repeated on every hand: able men who were loyal to their churches remained subservient and dissatisfied, and repeatedly the more able thinkers rebelled and absented themselves. As another senior physician in town — a man from a strong Christian family with one brother a minister and two others church elders, and who had trained in the Christian medical school in Seoul — said to me, 'I don't go to church. There is too much shamanism in the church and the doorstep is too high — but I think my name will be written in the book of life.' That we are not to know, but it is tragic when able well-disposed men are kept out by that which goes by the name of Christian zeal, and is falsely so-called.

In praying do not heap up empty phrases as the Gentiles do.

Do not be anxious ... seek first his kingdom and his righteousness, and all these things shall be yours as well. Every line of the Lord's words in Matthew chapter 6 is piercingly relevant to the needs of today's church in Korea and beyond.

In the next chapter we shall explore some of the causes of this wandering from Christian truth, and an approach to dealing with the problem.

Not everyone who says to me, 'Lord, Lord' shall enter the kingdom of heaven, but he who does the will of my Father who is in heaven . . . everyone then who hears these words of mine and does them will be like a wise man who built his house upon the rock. (Matthew 7.21, 24.)

7

His Word

'May I help you?'

Audrey, my wife, was startled by a voice in English at her shoulder. It was pouring with rain, nearly lunch-time and, cluttered with purchases, she was looking for the bus home from a shopping expedition in the centre of Seoul escorted by our two small children.

It was October 1969. We had returned to Seoul for further language study six weeks before in company with John and Kathleen Wallis and Margaret Robertson, the first team of OMF missionaries to Korea. Korea had been surveyed along with the other countries of East Asia in the early 1950's when the China Inland Mission had withdrawn from China and redeployed throughout the rest of the area. At that time, with a relatively strong national church and a large input of missionary contribution from American denominational missions in the aftermath of the Korean War, an OMF contribution had been deemed unnecessary.

Fifteen years later the situation had been reviewed. In 1965 Dr John and Susan Kim, Korean nationals completing post-graduate theological studies in the States, had applied to OMF in America for service in Japan. They were the first Asian members of the mission following the decisions reached in the 1965 centenary year, that membership of the mission should be actively sought among all races for service in East Asia in countries outside their own native land. Although they were accepted in America, it had been deemed wise that John and Susan should return to Korea first and strengthen their links with their Korean home base before moving on to Japan. Following their return with their family to Korea in 1966, through their initiative the question of

OMF involvement in Korea was again raised. It was said that the churches were eager for cooperating missionaries and, in line with the new policy, Korea seemed an excellent potential recruiting ground for missionaries to the rest of Asia.

Accordingly, in September 1966 Arnold Lea as Overseas Director, and Michael Griffiths who was then Superintendent in Japan, visited Korea for three weeks, spoke at the general assemblies of two Presbyterian denominations, visited many areas and spoke to a wide range of Korean Christians and missionaries. Strong invitations were received from these two denominations to send cooperating missionaries, and literature and youth work were particularly cited as areas where help was needed. In their report Mr Lea and Mr Griffiths recommended that these invitations be accepted subject to suitable candidates coming forward.

We ourselves had already had two years in the country in secular employment, but our return in the late summer of 1969 as part of a team of five OMF missionaries was the direct fruit of these early deliberations. John Wallis had been at Clifton Theological College at the same time as our friend Kim Chin Kyung and his interest in Korea had been born at that time. Margaret, quite independently, had had a deep interest in Korea and sense of call to that land from twelve years previously. God drew us together through these various unconnected events to form a team and to confirm to us all that it was His will at that time for a new contribution from OMF in Korea. And now we were all in Seoul in two adjacent houses rented from another mission. Extracts from a prayer letter written at that time give some glimpses of the setting in which we were placed:

'Even in the seven months we have been away the changes in Seoul have been tremendous — everywhere new roads, new buildings, new businesses — the universal trend towards the common denominators of city life. We notice the change too from provincial Masan — bread and milk delivered, newspapers, mail through the letter-box, bacon and butter available on a limited scale — and of course we notice the rising prices — an average of some fifteen to twenty percent per annum.

'Looking out of our study window here in Seoul I can see across the valley which was largely paddy fields when we came 2½ years ago. Now tall apartment blocks crown the opposite hillside, and everywhere new houses are filling in the remaining gaps in the landscape below us. The other day as I was looking over at this I was reading Genesis 11. "Go to, let us build us a city and a tower . . . lest we be scattered . . . ," they said. "Go to, let us go down and there confound their language," God said, and "the Lord scattered them abroad." The tower was begun in a frenzy of self-effort born of deep-rooted insecurity, and the very thing they feared came to pass. One sees this as a spiritual danger for Seoul and perhaps for Asia. Change, development, progress are exciting things under the direction and blessing of God, but brash self-sufficiency is ugly and destructive. As Christians we easily and unconsciously absorb the spirit of the society in which we live and this is a warning for the development of our own work. "He who believes shall not make haste." '

The story of Babel, of course, had other relevance for us too, immersed as we were at that time in the complexities of Korean language. Korean is a distinct language in its own right, although a great many of its words come from Chinese in the same way that many English words come from Greek and Latin, and its grammar is closely related to Japanese. Its complex honorifics reflect the Confucian stratification of society and its own phonetic 24-letter alphabet (invented under the aegis of King Sejong the Great in the 16th century in order that his people could read) make reading a relatively easy matter. However, there 'easiness' ends. Reading with understanding and, still more, understanding and reproducing the spoken word are taxing and intensely difficult exercises. Two-thirds of the seven hundred Protestant missionaries in Korea have never acquired enough language to preach acceptably or carry on a conversation on spiritual matters in Korean. That same prayer letter added, 'It is hard to understand at home that, even if we do really well in the next year's study, even ten years from now language will still be a major limitation.' Nearly ten years later we would endorse this prediction.

Of course, language study has its amusing aspects. Audrey, one day at the market, asked a stall-holder, 'Where are the mush-rooms?' 'Where do you want to go?' was the reply. Non sequitur! Try again. 'Where are the mushrooms?' 'Yes, but where do you want to go?' No good! Forget it! — thought but not said amidst a somewhat shamefaced withdrawal from an embarrassing situation. Only later we found that the Korean word for 'mushroom' and the word for 'bus' are very similar.

'Where are the buses?'

'Where do you want to get to?' Ah! I see — but too late.

Eggs are plentiful in Korea, but battery hens are not infrequently fed on fish-meal as part of their diet — result: fishy eggs! On one occasion, John, shopping for Kathleen in the nearby market, wanted to avoid fishy eggs on the breakfast table.

'Ah-em ... excuse me ... ' ... picking up an egg ... 'the mother of this egg' — (thinks: no, start again.) 'Did the mother of this egg ... ' (no: that's not it. Try once more.) 'Was the honourable mother of this egg a fish-eating chicken?' Blank amazement on the stall-holder's face. End result: buy some eggs and hope for the best!

If it's that hard to buy a dozen eggs (ten in a decimal society) no wonder it takes time to feel the pulse of the church and the spiritual life of the society in which we found ourselves. Over the next three years we were repeatedly to groan, 'Lord, why have you brought us here? What is the specific contribution you have for us to make?' Only gradually did the pattern emerge. 'He who believes shall not make haste.'

That same prayer-letter ended with the words, 'Perhaps in our next letter we can say something of the links we have begun to form. Isaiah 43.5 says "Fear not for I am with thee. I will bring thy seed from the East." This is the central purpose of our being here and must remain dominant in our thinking.'

And now that voice at Audrey's shoulder, 'May I help you? May I carry your bags for you?'

Turning, Audrey found a young man in his mid-twenties, not tall even by Korean standards, with high cheekbones made the more prominent by his sallow, slightly indrawn cheeks and lack of spare flesh anywhere. The offer was genuine; surprising, too, from a man to a woman in a society where the woman is the beast of burden. The English was unusually good and the shy, hesitant smile engaging. She accepted thankfully. He accompanied her to the bus, helped the children on and joined the family aboard. On the way she elicited that he was a university student in his final year. When it was time to alight, he stayed with the family, carried the bags right to the door of the house — 'No, he wouldn't come in just now, but yes, he'd be happy to come back on Saturday evening when we had some friends in.'

On Saturday evenings, we had begun having open house for various folks we had met. Singing and Bible study mostly in English was the main diet, with odd words of Korean thrown in where we could. Several of those who came were seminary students introduced to us by John Kim. John and Susan, unable to obtain a missionary visa for Japan, had been obliged to remain in Korea; he was teaching Church History at a Seoul seminary, and pastoring a pioneer church in the first floor of an office block in Central Seoul. He had welcomed us at Seoul station with some of his students (flowers for John this time!), had introduced John to a weekly class in English at the seminary, and welcomed John and Kathleen (and their two long-suffering children) to his church. (Missionaries without language — and their children — understand the meaning of the word 'long-suffering' after 1½ to two hours in a church service without understanding a word of it.)

We found some real friends among these seminary students. They had great warmth and enthusiasm, considerable theological knowledge and, like students everywhere (especially theological ones), an intense concern for orthodoxy; but all-in-all a surprising lack of personal devotional life centred around the Word of God. It was a clue to a situation we were to find repeated far and wide.

Stephen Lee, who had helped Audrey with the shopping, joined with these and others on Saturday evenings. He confessed that his original purpose in coming had been curiosity (home life had been far from easy. He had a deep longing for 'sweet-home.' Could these foreigners have something to give?) and a desire to practise his English. He had been to church a few times as a student, but was critical of what he had seen there. Gradually spiritual interest was awakened as we shared the Scriptures together.

One Saturday morning early in the New Year we sat together at the dining room table with the Bible open before us.

'He came to His own home, and His own people received Him not. But to all who received Him, who believed in His Name, He gave power to become chidren of God.' We read John 1.11, 12 together. The time seemed right. Yes, he would like to receive the Lord Jesus and become a child of God. Yes, he would like to pray together now, and with heads bowed we each prayed, he to welcome the Lord, I that God would confirm His child in the faith. He confesses that he doesn't remember the incident at all (so much for decision evangelism!) but, be that as it may, about that time he undoubtedly passed from death to life and into the family of God.

From the start he developed a great love for God's Word, read it avidly, discussed it at great length with John over the next two years after we had returned to Masan, and in consequence grew by leaps and bounds.

Everyone who hears these words of mine and does them will be like a wise man who built his house upon the rock.

Our paths were to become intricately intertwined in the ensuing years.

- - - - - - - - - - - - - - - - - -

All through this period while we grappled with the question of what was to be the central thrust of our ministry, the matter of Bible study kept recurring. What we had found among the theological students we were to find general throughout the church. Dawn prayer meetings had been the predominant pattern of daily devotions. They still were for a number of older folk, but the great majority of younger church members rarely attended them, and nothing had taken their place. Bible reading was often stressed from the pulpit, but more as a religious duty than as a channel of fellowship with the living God. Emphasis was on quantity, not on method.

'If you read three chapters a day and five on Sundays you'll read the whole Bible in a year — and if you read six a day and ten on Sundays you'll read it twice in the year — and if you manage nine chapters a day and fifteen on Sundays you'll cover the whole Bible three times in a year,' declared the invited speaker at a Bible reading rally we held in Masan.

Many churches held competitions for a tally of aggregate total of chapters read per month by the members of the different Friday night home worship groups — with individual and group prizes for the winners. Students' meetings held Bible memory competitions — perhaps the whole Sermon on the Mount for middle school level (13-15 year old), with Romans 8 in King James Version English for the high-schoolers. The powers of absorption were tremendous. I heard one lady in a Taegu church recite the whole of Philippians without hesitating like an express train to thunderous applause in an afternoon service. As with other aspects of church life, we found tremendous zeal, but searched hard to find that careful hearing and doing that Jesus declared is the mark of the truly wise man.

Gradually the impression formed that there was what we termed 'a Scripture-Union-shaped gap in Korean church life.' The more we probed the more we found this opinion validated. We had all, in different ways, been influenced by Scripture Union. We were familiar, to some extent, with the two interrelated arms of SU work — Bible reading promotion at all ages, and evangelism among young people. We knew that the SU approach to Bible reading, including the production of daily reading notes and associated Bible study literature, emphasized the bringing of God's Word and the reader together in such a way that his knowledge of God and fellowship with Him was enhanced and his behaviour conformed more nearly to the will of God. We knew that SU work with young people involved understanding them and relating the gospel to them where they really stood, and that camps, schools work, rallies, and some SU literature were all related to this aim.

Yes, the more we saw of Korea the more we were confirmed in the view that all of this was the area of need to which out of our background and heritage we were potentially most qualified to minister. And, incidentally, this concurred very closely with the needs cited by the church leaders who had invited OMF to send cooperating missionaries in the first place — literature and youth work.

- - - - - - - - - - - - - - - - - -

At this time the development of Scripture Union work in Korea was in the hands of a university students' movement. Back in 1965 SU in Australia had seconded John and Judy Price to Korea to pioneer SU work, but they had had to return to Australia the following summer while still in language study, due to their child's health. John Price had returned for a month in December 1967 with a view to placing the production and distribution of *Daily Bread* Bible reading notes in the hands of someone local as an initial step. In the predominantly Amecan-in-fluenced culture SU was little known and few had a vision for the sort of approach to Bible reading that Scripture Union stood for. However, in this students' movement, an indigenous work of some six years standing, and in an American missionary associated with them, John found kindred spirits, and the group undertook the production of Daily Bread notes. These were written by their general secretary, and produced primarily for their student and graduate readership, with distribution into the churches only peripherally through graduate readers. Their leader himself benefited greatly from the discipline of Bible study necessary for note writing, and the whole movement grew in the use of SU approach for its Bible study. At the time we were in Seoul in 1969/70 we enjoyed close fellowship with them, attended and spoke at some of their meetings, and were thrilled to find large groups of students, mostly from the elite universities and mostly converted out of totally non-church backgrounds, eagerly Bible centred and Christ-centred in their approach. I remember speaking at their summer conference in 1971. The theme was 'Jesus — the rural missionary.' The whole morning was given up to it — firstly group study on Matthew 8 and 9, then report sessions, and finally the whole drawn together in an exposition of the two chapters on the basis of the previous personal study. Nowhere else had we found this sort of careful attention to Scripture and practical application of it. Our hearts were warmed and we were glad to use the Bible reading notes in our initial outreach among the churches.

Everyone then who hears these words of mine and does them will be like a wise man who built his house upon the rock.

A strategy was beginning to take shape and a group of people with whom to share it was at hand, but there were undercurrents at work of which we were not yet aware. It would be several years yet before these surfaced. Meanwhile there was much to occupy our time and energies.

That evening they brought to Him many who were possessed with demons, and He cast out the spirits with a word, and healed all who were sick. This was to fulfil what was spoken by the prophet Isaiah, 'He took our infirmities and bore our diseases.' (Matthew 8.16, 17.)

8

Healed!

I suppose every missionary doctor has asked himself at some stage in what respects his medical ministry is a perpetuation of Christ's healing ministry on earth, whether it is part of what Jesus predicted in John 14.12 ('He who believes in Me will also do the works that I do; and greater works than these will he do, because I go to the Father'), and what relation it bears to the varied claims of 'spiritual healing' in all its forms. We have tussled with this issue over the years and the present chapter seeks to illustrate some aspects of this.

In March 1975 a young man came to us from the small country town of Chilwon an hour north of Masan on the Taegu road. Choi Oo Yong was in his mid-twenties. His thick-set features tended towards a habitual scowl, but on occasion could wrinkle into a warm smile. He came alone at the end of a long line of patients on Tuesday afternoon, and obviously with only half an expectation of success. He had had tuberculosis of the hip for fifteen years with virtually no treatment. Fourteen years before, in the early stages of the disease, he had come to the hospital (before we were there) at a time when, because of pressure of work, it was only taking patients from Masan city itself. Living outside the area, he had been turned away. There was no alternative means of treatment so for fourteen years he had endured progressive destruction of his hip from the disease, and deformity had progressed so that now the hip could not be straightened beyond a right-angle. Pus had developed and had been discharging for many years. Only rudimentary and inter-mittent home treatment had been applied. As the pus-laden wrappings of old cloth were removed from the deformed hip, the picture, all-too-familiar among our patients, of chronic neglected tuberculosis of the joint with long-standing secondary septic infection, revealed itself.

Why hadn't he come before? we asked. The story of his earlier visit emerged. He had only recently heard that we now took adults as well as children, and patients from anywhere in the country. Whom did he live with? we pursued. He had no father; he had been married, but his wife had left him. He had one eight-year-old daughter, and lived with her and his mother.

What did he do for a living? He was a village barber. There were two barbers' shops in the small market town so he did not have a monopoly and business was poor.

At that time we did not have facilities for the in-patient care of adults so his pus-draining sinuses were dressed, he was instructed in drug-taking and home dressing and despatched home with an appointment a month later. It was arranged that the staff would visit his home to reinforce the teaching about drug-taking and dressings as well as to encourage him. We will take up his story again a little later.

When we first took up responsibilities at the children's wing of the Korea National Tuberculosis Sanatorium, Masan, in March of 1967, the unit was supported by Save the Children Fund. We were under contract with them for two years. My predecessor had done an excellent job in the control and treatment of children's tuberculosis in Masan City. In addition a project for the treatment of spinal tuberculosis in children from a wider area, sponsored by the Medical Research Council, had been running for two years. Since careful follow-up of treatment was essential to the gathering of clinical data for research purposes, home visits by members of the hospital team were already playing an important part in the overall programme. These served not only to check on regular drug-taking and to chase up defaulters who failed to return on the appointed day, but were also an important means of health education. The whole plan of treatment over eighteen months would be explained to a circle of relatives and neighbours; hitherto undetected possible contact cases would be sought out, and general advice on tuberculosis prevention and health care would be passed on. Public health and preventive medicine, which is rightly emphasized in many medical mission circles today, is much more effective in the context of a continuing treatment programme than as an isolated project.

Grateful patients and their relatives are far more receptive to new ideas than the general populace anywhere in the world.

When we arrived the control programme for children's tuberculosis locally in Masan had been so effective that we were poised for further outreach. Government immunization and case-finding programmes were developing. This meant that although we saw the importance of prevention our contribution was less and less needed in this area. The wider spread of cases of spinal tuberculosis provided the natural starting point for a more widespread service for the *treatment* of children's tuberculosis of all forms. While prevention programmes were available, treatment programmes for children's and bone and joint tuberculosis were almost non-existent. While continuing with local clinics and the care of around seventy children in the wards, we selected four surrounding counties and, borrowing facilities from their government county health centres, ran a monthly clinic in each. We selected Monday, the first working day of the week, as the day for these out-clinics, thus seeking to indicate to ourselves and others that we regarded this as the most important work in which we were engaged.

These centres varied between one and two hours' distance from Masan, all of them along bumpy unmade roads. Many was the bumpy ride in the back of the hospital Toyota jeep returning from the clinic at Chung Moo, a small port city down on the coast, centre for ferries from all the surrounding islands. However, these were minor hardships. We did not yet know Choi Oo Yong whose story began this chapter, but we were aware of many scattered up mountain valleys and on south-coast islands for whom a journey to Masan was a daunting prospect, and for whom there was no other means of treatment than what we could provide. As yet, because of language limitations, there was little or no opportunity for direct gospel outreach, but we had other good news to share. These long-standing and often unsightly tuberculosis conditions could be treated and we were prepared to do it, the only charge to the patient being the bus or boat fares to and from the clinic. Sankey's famous old hymn often ran through my mind:

> There were ninety and nine that safely lay
> In the shelter of the fold,
> But one was out on the hills away,

Far off from the gates of gold.

While there were patients we could treat in the area we could reach we could not be content to leave them. It seemed as important to go out and find the needy ones as to treat those who came to us of their own accord.

These who were already registered were referred to the clinic nearest their home for monthly follow-up visits. Word spread, and before long we had sixty patients registered for regular treatment at the Chung Moo Centre alone. When clinic was over, a late lunch of noodles and *kim-pab* (a core of spicy vegetable in a ball of rice rolled in a covering of thin dried seaweed and dipped in hot beancurd sauce for added flavour), prepared us for the rest of the day given to home visits. On occasion a small ferry boat was hired for a visit to an island home. On many others long diversions up narrow dusty roads, winding up through mountain passes, negotiating the occasional bus or heavy lorry on a sharp corner, and the last mile or two along cart tracks between the paddy fields, added charm and interest to the work. Fascinating scenes occurred along the way — a secluded Buddhist temple in a wooded valley high in the mountains; hand-loom weaving of hemp cloth in a dry paddy field in autumn, a custom unchanged in centuries; the occasional live hen trussed up and deposited in the back of the car by a grateful patient — but in and through it all —

> *. . . although the road be rough and steep,*
> *I go to the desert to find My sheep.*

August 25-29th SAN HO PRIMARY SCHOOL PLAYGROUND
THE GREAT CITY CRUSADE

The posters and banners stretching across streets at various points in town proclaimed the coming event. Several months of planning had preceded it and nearly all the churches in town had pledged their support. Large evangelistic meetings have been held in many towns in Korea in recent years, but never before in this town. The initiative had come from a Californian evangelistic agency, offering a team of speakers and pledging financial cover. Some of the ministers in town had welcomed the opportunity for a wider

74

Christian testimony; others saw in it opportunity for increasing their prestige and sphere of influence. The mayor would attend the opening session and other civic leaders would be represented. Advertising and organization were skilfully arranged but, significantly, there was no provision for the training of counsellors, and little spiritual emphasis in prayer preparation.

The first night we went along taking an assorted group of patients from the hospital — twenty of us all told in the Land-Rover, plus wheel chairs and crutches. A crowd of perhaps two thousand was seated on the school playground facing a large rostrum. The subsidiary speaker was an enthusiastic foreigner who rejoiced at the great opportunity and assured us we would see 'miracles'. The main speaker was an American Korean (ie Korean national now living in America with American citizenship). Fifteen minutes of good basic gospel outlines followed by 45 minutes on the theme of healing. Matthew 8.17 tells us, he said, that Jesus took our sicknesses on the cross. If we would only believe, our sicknesses would be healed. Unbelief hinders the miracles of God. Jesus is the same yesterday, today and forever. He healed then: He heals today. 'LORD! I BELIEVE' at high pitch close to the microphone. And so the meeting proceeded with progressively more frequent interjection of

LORD, I BELIEVE   LORD, I BELIEVE
chanted through the public address system like the cries of a football crowd in full-blooded support of the home team.

A dramatic break . . .

'Tonight we are going to lay hands on those who are deaf in one ear or both. Will all those who have difficulties with hearing please stand up.' — a smattering rose to their feet.

'Will stewards please stand alongside them . . . and now bring them to the front.' I saw a lad near me bundling a girl in high-school uniform who had hesitatingly risen to her feet towards the front.

One by one a dozen or so were led onto the platform. Hands laid on; fervent prayer; 'Can you hear better?' 'I think so.' 'Halleluyah! A miracle!'

My mind was in a turmoil as we left the meeting. We all too easily criticize, but was this the continuation of the healing ministry of Jesus? Secretly I was glad that none of the patients we had taken was deaf. We didn't go again and many of the local ministers were dismayed and brought strong pressure to bear to bring the emphasis back to gospel preaching. Next day I attended a ministers' meeting in connection with the crusade. I remonstrated privately with the previous night's speaker that Matthew 8.17 doesn't say anything about the cross. Indeed the quotation of Isaiah 53.4 by Matthew at this point shows that although much of Isaiah 53 *is* looking forward to the cross and the atonement, 'He took our infirmities and bore our diseases' refers more to the incarnation than to the crucifixion, to His life on earth rather than His death on earth. The speaker got angry and it would have been unprofitable to pursue the subject.

I asked a local Methodist minister who had been on the platform the previous evening if I could see some of those who had been 'healed', to validate what had happened and counsel with them. No names had been taken, and there was no means of follow-up. Later we were to search in vain for one person who had come into any of the churches through these meetings, though one of my patients, a Christian lady who had had multiple breast abscesses and septicaemia and had ended with a partly-paralysed left arm, was bitterly disappointed. She was self-critical at her own lack of faith, because although she had gone forward at a subsequent meeting, nothing had happened.

Why do I describe this caricature of Christian evangelism? Because it is happening up and down the length and breadth of Korea and in many other lands. Earnest but undiscerning believers are beguiled, hearts are seared, hopes dashed and the Lord's name dishonoured. Many patients who come to us have been to healing meetings, some within the fold of orthodox Christianity, some among the sects, some by animistic Shamans (mostly female) with no Christian affinities at all. A few hundred yards from the house where some OMF missionaries used to live is a large church, recently rebuilt with very ornate exterior work. This church has a well-known lady-healer associated with it and much of the funds for rebuilding the church came from the 'proceeds' of her ministry.

A few miles north of the same city is the mountain settlement of a Christian healing sect. We had a lady from there with spinal tuberculosis. She had spent years praying for the healing of her pus drainage — a quiet and earnest soul who loved her Bible. We were glad that with a few months of anti-tuberculosis drugs and clean dressings the drainage healed up and she left us.

The well-known minister of a large church in Seoul, many thousands strong, says his main calling is divine healing 'because I was raised up from my death-bed. I was suffering from tuberculosis and I made a pledge before the Lord that if He would ever raise me up I would pray for the sick.' He says that in his church about sixty percent of those he prays for are miraculously healed.

Stirred by the meetings described above and faced with many claims like this, I went back to the gospels to look for the principal elements in the healing ministry of Jesus that one should look for as authenticating a similar ministry today.

Looking especially at Matthew chapters eight and nine, I noted two strands:

(1) *The Power of Jesus.* Sick people undoubtedly got better (8.3, 13, 15, 16 (26), 32; 9.7, 22, 25, 30, 33, 35), but it was a power that was deliberately veiled. What happened was dramatic, but again and again Jesus takes steps to play down the sensational (8.4, 18, 24-25, 30).

(2) *The Compassion of Jesus.* Invested with power from on high (and this was no strange thing for the Son of God) (8.3, 7, 16, 32; 9.19, 22, 36). This, as one commentator has put it, was the clearest sign of His being the Christ. 'His miracles need not mean more than that He was "a great prophet", but it was a new thing that the poor whom the Greek despised and the Roman trampled on, and whom the priest and Levite left on one side, should be invited into the Kingdom of God.'[1]

A helpful rule of thumb thus seemed to be that wherever we saw genuine compassion for people in need, unmistakable results and deliberate self-effacement on the part of those involved, we were treading near the path of true discipleship. Where we saw play on the emotions, build-up of the sensational, strong boosting of the central figure, dubious results and the abuse of the individual in the interests of the programme, we should beware of the spurious. It had lessons for us in our own work.

Each year we chose a motto for the hospital. That year Mr Lee had proposed as motto:

'Something beautiful in the sight of God' unconsciously echoing Mother Teresa's phrase. We had already sought to apply this in our welcome of the poor and care of those that society had rejected. The studies in Matthew 8 and 9 gave added impetus.

Our friend Choi Oo Yong had not done well as an out-patient. He was discouraged. He had already had a year of treatment. Now we were in a position to accept adult in-patients as well. We persuaded him to sub-let his barber's shop to a friend for six months and come into hospital for treatment. He was a willing worker in hospital. Not only did he cut hair but he cleaned, he did carpentry jobs, he served food and at various times caught and reared a number of fledgling birds. But progress was slow, six months passed, another three. He was referred for surgery elsewhere. This was partially successful. He returned to us. More frustrating delays.

He attended the worship services we held and helped bring others for them, but never made clear profession of faith himself.

One night I was called at three am. Mr Jee, the driver, was on night duty. Mr Lee and I both went up to hospital where we found our friend lying in a drunken stupor on the carpenter's bench, with blood down one arm and the back of his neck. Things had become just too much and he had tried to cut his wrists. We ascertained that the injuries in fact were very superficial, and the staff urged me not to disturb him — they would deal with it. That was the last I saw of him for many months. In early dawn he made off in shame. Some days later Mr Jee found him, but he would not come back. Two months later when we had returned to the UK for furlough, he returned to the hospital and was re-admitted. He was referred for further surgery and then wrote to us in England as follows:

'Sir,

'In a deserted wilderness there was one lost sheep.

Everywhere he had wandered looking for his master. At your hospital he had found warmth and kindness and endless patience.

'That sheep is I, Oo Yong. I am lost in shame to know what to do. I can only cry to the Lord, walk in Christ's path and sing hymns of praise to Him. When you were here always you spoke the joyful words that if only we would seek the Lord He would pour grace upon us. Now I remember these. This weak and sinful Oo Yong is seeking to live carefully by the words of Scripture and, although my faith is weak, to seek God's glory. I am receiving successful treatment with a grateful heart from all the staff here and especially Mr Lee.

'I had a major operation in Soonchun on 18th February and now I am in a plaster cast on the bed here and dreaming of the day of glory when I can walk upright. This hope and expectation is I believe all by the abundance of the Lord's grace.'

Our hearts rejoiced. Perhaps we were not so far from the path of true discipleship.

Once a year we have had a visit from a senior surgical consultant from Britain. About the time that Oo Yong ran off this consultant was with us and in conversation with an embassy official in Seoul he said, 'There are patients there who all my training and experience tell me can't get better, but who seem to be recovering.' The grace of God through the careful use of modern medicine? The medicine of hope to the hopeless? The merciful finger of God beyond the limits of either? Who knows where one ceases and the other begins? If our concern is to be instruments of the Lord's compassion to the needy and to see incontrovertible results for their welfare, then it matters little and we are probably better not to know. It is our experience that God prefers to draw a veil of privacy over His most striking works of grace.

[1] Norval Geldenhuys, *The Gospel of Luke* (New London Commentaries, Marshall Morgan and Scolt) page 230, quoting Plummer, *the Gospel according to Luke* (ICC, T & T Clark).

When the crowds saw it, they were afraid . . .
. . . the crowd making a tumult.
. . . the crowds marvelled . . .
When He saw the crowds, He had compassion for them, because they were harassed and helpless, like sheep without a shepherd.
(Matthew 9.8, 23, 33, 36)

9

Crowds

Religion in Israel, in our Lord's day, was a thriving concern. It was the fabric of society. Many were earnest and zealous. Foremost among these, and held in high esteem by the people, were the Pharisees. In the face of our Lord's scathing condemnation of their practices and attitudes we all too easilly lose sight of their finer qualities. Zeal for the glory of God (*this man is blaspheming*, 9.3), concern for purity (*why does your teacher eat with tax collectors and sinners?* 9.11), strenuous efforts to draw near to God (*why do the Pharisees fast much, but your disciples do not fast?* 9.14), vigorous defence of orthodoxy (*the Pharisees said, 'He casts out demons by the prince of demons.'* 9.34).

Fine qualities all but, pursued without enlightenment, ones that led them into total conflict with the incarnate Son of God. *Go and learn what this means, 'I desire mercy, and not sacrifice'*, He had to say to them (9.13) and Paul could later bear witness concerning his own countrymen 'they have a zeal for God, but it is not enlightened.' (Romans 10.2.)

Repeatedly we come across Christians who have heard reports of phenomenal growth in the Christian church in Korea and others who have heard tell of the remarkable economic development. Both question why we are needed in Korea at all. They expect us to be apologetic as a sort of unnecessary anachronism.

We hear, they tell us, of churches several thousand strong, and growing; of Christians gathering for prayer meetings at dawn; of strict rules in the church concerning smoking and drinking; of the 'very, very much fasting and praying in Korea', as one Korean Christian leader said in an interview; of a strong reformed faith, and theological colleges several hundred strong; of highly-qualified theological teachers and deep concern for doctrinal orthodoxy.

True, all of it; as true as the thriving state of religion in Israel in our Lord's day.

Then others point out to us that there are medical schools and nursing schools in Seoul, Pusan and most provincial capitals — at least twelve medical schools in all; there are numerous highly-trained Korean doctors with post-graduate degrees and specialist skills. In Masan alone, with a population of four hundred thousand, there are probably more than two hundred doctors. Many Korean doctors and nurses have emigrated and are practising in North America, West Germany and other parts of the world. There are major mission (or ex-mission) hospitals in all the main cities, many of them with nursing schools attached and post-graduate training programmes for doctors. Some of these have been there more than fifty years, prestigious, well-equipped and providing medical service to a high standard. There are at least seven such institutions (both Protestant and Catholic) in Pusan alone. The country has its own thriving pharmaceutical industry, a network of government hospitals (half-a-dozen specialist ones in TB, leprosy, psychiatry — and city or provincial hospitals in each of the larger towns — 100,000 population upwards) and a government health centre in each county majoring in TB control and family planning.

With all these alternative facilities, it is said, are you really needed? Are there not far more needy areas of the world both spiritually and medically? I have never been greatly impressed with the arguments about relative need. They may be helpful as we seek to discover the place of God's choice for us in His service but, once this is established, they become largely irrelevant. However, the purpose of this chapter is to illustrate the work in which we have been involved and with it the reasons for which we regard it as right today that for Korea, too, we *pray the Lord of the harvest to send out labourers into His harvest.* (9.38)

- - - - - - - - - - - - - - - - - -

A ruler came in and knelt before Him saying, 'My daughter . . .'
Saturday afternoon. Opportunity for a bit of gardening. The dog barks, always the first indication of a visitor, and up the front steps comes a young policeman. *Please* would I come to his home and see his little girl. He carries a letter of introduction, too,

from the chief of police, to reinforce his request. Somewhat grudgingly I acceded to the request. Home time and family time is at a premium and I don't like forfeiting it. Arriving at the policeman's home — two little rooms in a back alley — I find his two-year-old daughter, watched by an elder sister and mother, struggling for breath with bronchiolitis and a tight wheezy chest. Yes, they had been to a doctor's clinic that morning: the child had had an injection and been told to return next day. The cost had amounted to a quarter of a month's salary: now she was worse. Hence their plea to me. A few simple drugs, some straight-forward advice, prayer and a gospel portion, and over the next few days the child made a good recovery.

Some two years later Dr Monica Hogben, OMF mission doctor, was visiting. We were just sitting down to supper when our 'early warning system' barked again. Once again the same policeman was at the door. Please would I come again. The same little girl was desperately ill again. Supper was laid aside and the doctors followed the policeman. This time our patient was more seriously ill. She had had measles and this had been followed by pneumonia. The child was very sick. We arranged for her admission to our wards, although we were ill-equipped to care for such a child. Lack of money precluded any other course. By the grace of God the little girl made a good recovery. Not long after, her mother came to see me. They were moving to Seoul shortly. She was attending church and the children Sunday School. They meant to look out for a church on their arrival in Seoul.

- - - - - - - - - - - - - - - - -

From 1969 until November of 1975 we operated out-patient clinics with only marginal involvement in the wards. During the last year of that period we extended our spread of clinics from the immediate neighbourhood to Pusan, Mokpo in the far South West, and later Taegu, capital city of the North Kyung Buk province. Much improved trunk roads meant that we could reach Pusan in little over an hour, Taegu in two hours, and Mokpo in about four hours. Patients from the nearer region could also reach us more easily and the spread of these clinics meant that we were beginning to draw patients from east coast to west across the southern third of the country — a population area of around fifteen million people.

In November 1975 the administration in the government sanatorium to which we are attached changed, and we were asked to take full control of the former children's wing building with authority to admit to its wards. At the same time we began to enrol adults as well as children. We had no extra staff for this venture. It meant that all staff had to take a rota of night and weekend duty, and that a team that was geared to out-patient work and regarded itself as tolerably busy in that had to readjust to carry responsibility for the wards as well. They responded magnificently.

One of the first patients we received at that time was a man in his late 30's from Pusan. A minor civil servant in Pusan city administration, Mr Kim was better educated and more sophisticated than the general run of our patients. He had suffered from tuberculosis of his lower spine for eighteen months before we saw him. In the early stages of the disease he had visited a university hospital, received correct diagnosis and been advised to have spinal surgery. The fees for this would have amounted to over £1000 ($25,000) Faced with this daunting bill and the natural fears of surgery, he had visited a local herb practitioner, who had prescribed medicines and required that he lay on his back continuously and took no other medicines during the course of this treatment. Nearly eighteen months of this had left him wasted, rigid and despairing. Even slight movements of most joints caused intense pain as they were nearly seized up through disuse. He arrived in the foyer of the hospital, carried by two strong relatives on a sponge mattress, groaning pitifully. He was our first serious adult patient. We wondered if we could cope.

It was four months before we got him on his feet, six before he left the hospital. Six months of hard work at physiotherapy, six months of instilling hope, six months of listening to the gospel on his part, discussing deeply with various members of staff, but never, as yet, reaching full conviction himself. He had read widely, including Luther and Plato. His wife's family had Roman Catholic connections. While he was with us he caught glimpses of genuine concern for his welfare, but still he remained uncommitted. During all his time with us, his wife stayed with him along with their six-year-old boy who used to run around the hospital and join in school lessons. His wife worked enormously hard in kitchens and laundry while we were establishing new patterns of work. As he recovered, Mr Kim himself took over handling the finances of food and heating for the wards. With that family we learned the enormous value to both patients and staff of encouraging self-help among the handicapped, rather than doing everything for them. We began to discover, too, an enormous area of need among adult chronic sick and disabled — need aggravated by the financial demands of long-term care and unthinking or ill-advised treatment from other sources.

First half-a-dozen patients, then ten. Then 'not more than twenty' as the limit. Soon, 'well, perhaps we can manage thirty'. 'We can't turn him away anyway, although we currently have 32 (we never have turned anyone away for lack of space, though occasionally people have had to wait a little if it will not affect them seriously). 'Perhaps we could borrow some more beds from the sanatorium and manage forty' . . . and all of a sudden we found ourselves with 55, children two in a bed, the occasional nine-year-old in a baby cot, and two beds run together for three teenage girls to sleep on. All this in the course of six months to a year. We never went over sixty patients, and eventually numbers settled down and fluctuated between forty and sixty. With our Peter going off to school in September 1976. Audrey began working mornings in the wards, but we never had more than the equivalent of our full-time staff in the wards. This would have been impossible with numbers of acutely-ill patients, but with the chronically sick and crippled with whom we were working, and with a strong emphasis on self-help, mutual help, and turning any visiting relatives to a task on hand, we were able to arrange a manageable (though large) work load for each.

Among those who came to us in the throng of expanding ward work, was Park Hay Sook, a thirty-year-old ship's hand in a fishing fleet off the east coast. He was unmarried (unusual) and came from a Seventh Day Adventist family. Although he joined in our worship services and had his own Bible and hymn book he showed few signs of personal faith. He was riddled with tuberculosis. Not only did he have it in the lung and spine, it had affected his left hip and also his left wrist (less common). It was fully six months before we were able to get him on his feet, and even then the deformity of his left wrist meant that he could not hold crutches very well. He was often despondent, sometimes smuggled drink into the hospital to drown his sorrows, and then would come with tears of remorse, asking for forgiveness and to be allowed to stay longer. Although not the poorest of the poor he was far less reliable about providing his money for food than most, and when he finally went home he left personal debts with other patients. It was sadly a recurrent finding that those with 'religious' background were more shifty and devious than the ordinary pagan poor, unless there was clear evidence of personal faith.

After he left we continued to see him as an out-patient and he steadily improved, though he and we realized that he would never be fully active. As I was writing this chapter a letter came from Mr Park, our staff member in Taegu, saying, 'I have some sad news. On 23rd March Park Hay Sook committed suicide by swallowing agricultural insecticide (a common method).' The reason: he went to the Christian hospital near his home for a medical certificate (needed for exemption from home guard training). The doctor had said to him, 'Your disease is completely incurable', or 'Your disease cannot be cured completely' — the wording would be the same in Korean with only a slight difference of emphasis. Hearing these words, he was so shocked that he went home and committed suicide!

Mr Park comments in his letter, 'How terribly important it is what the doctor says and does!'.

- - - - - - - - - - - - - - - - - -

One sunny Tuesday morning in June, among the throng of newcomers to the out-patients' clinic in Masan was a sixteen-year-old lad from the other side of town. 'I think you'd better come and see him outside,' said Mr Lee. Following him to the side door of the hospital I found a common push-cart with planks laid across it, and on top of them a pile of covers from amongst which appeared a sallow face with sunken, frightened eyes. Even before we lifted the covers the smell was repulsive. Removal of the covers revealed an emaciated body with dark discoloured skin engrained with dirt. His right thigh was grossly swollen and pouring pus. The slightest movement caused him to cry out with pain, but it was soon clear too that an area about the size of two hands on the back where he was lying was completely ulcerated as a large bed sore. Was it a cancer that had ulcerated and become infected? Was it grossly-infected osteomyelities (septic infection of the bone) that was the root cause? If it was the former, the kindest thing was to allow him to go home to die: if the latter, perhaps we could do something to help. X-ray was blurred and inconclusive. Again we questioned his frightened parents about the story.

Early in March he had developed pain and swelling in his right thigh. He had been admitted to a small 'Christian' hospital in town for ten days. The family had sold their two-roomed accommodation to pay the 370,000 won that this had cost, but then the doctor had told them that it was a septic infection of the bone and that an operation would be needed. Money had run out so they took him home. Nearly three months mouldering in the back room of the little noodle shop that his parents had managed to acquire, had led to the condition in which we found him. His parents had only heard of us the previous day.

We hesitated: could we really help him? Would it be kinder for him to return and die at home? Faced with the preceding history we felt we couldn't turn him away. We had to put him in a room by himself because of the smell. Audrey went twice a day to the room to turn him and dress him. We nursed him mostly naked with a mosquito net to keep the flies off. Although he cried pitiably every time we dressed his wounds, Chung Hyun showed great courage and, by the grace of God, the organisms that were invading him were sensitive to the antibiotics we had. Mr Lee spent hours working on his hips and knees to regain the movement of them, and little by little he regained strength. It was a joyful moment when we heard, after our return to Britain for furlough, that he had returned home on crutches.

Christian medicine is more than setting up an institution with a Christian name to it. It requires repeated heart-breaking decisions — heart-breaking because each fresh decision to attempt to rescue one of the crowd of 'harassed and helpless' requires fresh willingness on the part of all the staff to go the second mile. Heart-breaking, yes, but heart-warming, too, as one sees a team of young learners in the school of discipleship stepping out in the footsteps of the Master. 'Pray therefore the Lord of the harvest to send out labourers into His harvest.'

- - - - - - - - - - - - - - - - - -

Have mercy on us. (9.27)

Another young man who taxed our resources to the limit was Lee Chung Sook. He lived in Pusan with his married elder sister, both parents having died. In many Asian countries, when a girl marries she traditionally severs all ties and responsibilities in her own family and becomes part and parcel of her husband's family, so having this younger brother living with them was a concession on the husband's part and one that could not be pushed too far. He worked in a tailor's shop, but he began to develop recurrent bouts of abdominal pain. At the same time he began to lose weight, and eventually his sister took him to a large hospital. Tuberculous peritonitis (tuberculosis of the abdomen) was diagnosed, but all available finance was used in obtaining the diagnosis, with nothing left for treatment.

Over a period of eighteen months he continued to deteriorate without treatment. He could no longer work. He would lie awake at night groaning, and the husband was beginning to complain. At this point his sister brought him to one of our clinics in Pusan. The sight of this emaciated figure who could hardly stand filled us with dismay. We had never had a patient like this before. His chance of survival looked small. One of the complications of the disease was intestinal obstruction — and almost certain death. In such a case surgery would be imperative but very difficult — and costly. Where could we refer him? We could think of nowhere. In cases of emergency for short-term care we had various hospitals and doctor friends we could call on, but nowhere was geared to the long-term care of the chronic sick at economic rates.

His sister looked at us imploringly. Would Jesus have refused? We capitulated. We would try our best and if he improved we would send him on to missionary friends in Soonchun who ran a first-rate rest home for chest TB patients at very reasonable prices. They had no resident doctor so we could not send him on there until we were reasonably sure he was on the mend.

Driver Mr Jee looked flabbergasted. 'The doctor's really gone too far this time,' he said to himself (and later confessed to me!);

but we loaded him into the Land Rover and took him with us at the end of the day, groaning as he went.

The first few weeks were stormy. He wouldn't eat anything except sips of tinned fruit juice. He had bouts of intense abdominal pain from which we doubted if he could recover: but again, by the grace of God and the patient persistence of staff members who refused to let him die, he slowly improved. Shortly before we left Masan for furlough he returned to Pusan and his tailor's shop 15 kg heavier.

Have mercy on us, Son of David.

Do you believe that I am able to do this?

According to your faith be it done to you.

Such phrases take on new meaning in the light of pleading eyes, empty pockets and absence of alternative facilities. We have found the Lord leading us on in trembling faith with very basic medical tools to cooperate with Him, and again and again saying to us, *Go and learn what this means, 'I desire kindness . . .'* (9.13)

They brought to Him a paralytic . . . (9.2)

Kwang Soo was 24. He was an orphan, but had been adopted by an aged, childless couple (partly, no doubt, as insurance for their old age) living deep in the country north of Taegu. He came with his parents and a school-teacher relative who lived in Taegu. They had come four to five hours' journey, through the city of Taegu with its many prestigious medical institutions, Christian and other, to our small clinic on the south coast. Kwang Soo was paralysed. He had been so for six weeks due to spinal tuberculosis. Enquiries in Taegu had led to the suggestion of surgery and a frightening estimate of expense. So they had found their way to us.

He frightened us. In the right hands surgery would seem advisable, but we were not equipped for surgery, and neither he nor we had funds for referral elsewhere. He was totally paralysed and required more nursing care than most of our patients, but we found a place for him. For several months he appeared to make no progress. He was cheery and cooperating and joined in our weekly Bible study sessions in the ward, but secretly I was doubtful about his recovery. However, eventually recovery began and continued uninterrupted. At the first signs of recovery he wrote to us in England:

'Dear Superintendent,

'I don't know how to address you properly, so this is how I am writing. Sir, already the chilly winds are blowing here in Korea and leaves are flying everywhere. The beginning of winter is here.

'Sir, it is already more than a month since you left Korea. When you left I was very upset and, feeling that I had lost the one place of hope, I was very ill at ease.

However, now I am not the least afraid.

'The reason is that the Lord Himself is always with me. Furthermore under Mr Lee's leadership all the staff are running the hospital just the same as when you were here with us.

'A few days ago I began to move my toes. It is impossible to put into words my feelings at that time. Is it not all through the Lord's love and your kindness. From this time as a believer with deep faith I mean to become someone who can help those worse off than myself.

'I pray daily that the Lord will always be with you and that your plans will all be fulfilled.

May you have peace.

Im Kwang Soo.

26.11.77'

. . . take heart, my son, your sins are forgiven.

'There are major Christian hospitals (Protestant and Catholic) in all the main cities . . . prestigious, well-equipped and providing medical service to a high standard.'

'Christian medicine is more than setting up an institution with a Christian name to it.'

The early pioneers in missionary medicine in Korea, as in many other lands, did a magnificent job in extremely taxing conditions. Today among their successors are bands of outstanding men and women — outstanding doctors by any standards, and people of outstanding Christian calibre and compassion. However, not a few of these find themselves caught in a system that taxes their integrity. As one Canadian anaesthetist said in the annual medical missionary conference, 'It seems that the message we give all too often is, "God loves you if you have 100,000 won".'

Modern medicine is expensive, and in the altogether commendable drive for higher standards, it is all too easy to price the poor out of the hospitals. Some missionary doctors, conscious of the tension, have experimented with new schemes of community medicine. Some have given their whole attention to the fascination and satisfaction of specialist patient care among those who come to them. Others have returned home frustrated: yet others are still grappling with the issues of economics in missionary medicine. And all the time the message that comes over loud and clear in the churches and in the community at large is that Christianity has to do with that which is big, rich, powerful and prestigious. The Hospital Christian Fellowship (which also has a work among hospital staffs in Korea) rightly has as a slogan – 'More people pass through the hospitals of the world than its churches' and, whether we like it or not, in every pioneer situation in the last 150 years missionary medicine has had a very large part in shaping the image of what Christianity is all about. Young Christians with no traditions to build upon have seen in the hospitals the gospel at work. The influence of the hospitals has often been greater than that of the church in society at large because ordinary people are far more closely in contact with the hospitals than the churches.

In Korea, where church structure has developed very rapidly, the effect is catastrophic. The larger institutions are rightly handing over the leadership to well-qualified Korean Christian medicals, but many of these have inherited a dominant image of riches and prestige. Salary denotes prestige, so the newly-appointed medical superintendent of a large Christian hospital requires a salary of 30 million won per annum and department chiefs everywhere expect over a million won per month plus allowances. So prices escalate, and the effect is to erect a large notice outside the main entrance –

'The Poor are not admitted.'

(There is no such notice, of course, but the general effect on the ordinary poor is the same.)

Charity work is done, often twenty to thirty percent of the total budget – but the majority of this is for those with connections of one sort or another, or fees that could not be recovered being written off to 'charity'. Again and again we have had to emphasize to ourselves and our staff, 'You must not humiliate the poor; make them feel welcome, carry their bags, make sure they catch the bus home, and let those that come by taxi wait their turn.'

When He saw the crowds He had compassion for them, because they were harassed and helpless like sheep without a shepherd. Then He said to His disciples, The harvest is plentiful, but the labourers are few; pray therefore the Lord of the harvest to send out labourers into His harvest. The need is not so much medical labourers; the structure of medicine in Korea is such that it is rare and hard for a foreign doctor to find a satisfying niche. The task is not to substitute for local initiative, but to stimulate it. For that we need Bible teachers — men and women who will so handle God's Word and the portrait of Christ and His gospel therein that Korean men and women will be enthused with its demands and, rejecting the all-pervading preoccupation with power and prestige, will choose the narrow path of costly discipleship in medicine, education, the ministry and every walk of life. 'The harvest is plentiful. Such labourers are few, Lord . . .'

He called to Him His twelve disciples . . .
These twelve Jesus sent out . . . (Matthew 10.1, 5)

10

These twelve

Choosing a team is always a demanding occupation, whether it be a school football team or a government cabinet. Individual gifts have to be assessed, inter-relationships considered, team balance provided, and then the whole team forged into an efficient and harmonious unit. It is very hard to eliminate a misfit later without much heart-searching and often ill-feeling, and this accentuates the need for care in the initial choice. The same is true in Christian work. A team of missionaries has to be carefully chosen and then blended together. We have had fifteen in OMF in Korea, though never more than ten at one time. We shall be mentioning some of them in later chapters.

Between 1969 and 1974 we had had a small team of four or five Korean staff for our clinic work in Masan. From 1974 we were able to expand to a staff of twelve. In this chapter and the next we shall be meeting some of the twelve that have made up our hospital team since then — a fascinating group of people in their own right and each one representative of multitudes like them. Luke tells us that the Lord spent all night in prayer before calling His twelve (Luke 6.12). We found likewise a great need for care and prayer in their selection.

- - - - - - - - - - - - - - - -

We have already met *Mr Lee Chong Sup,* physiotheraphist, short of stature, strong in spirit, well-trained in patient-care under an excellent English nurse in the early 1960's before we came. He has provided continuity and backbone. Since his conversion in December 1970 a steadily-maturing faith has matched growing responsibilities and been expressed in continuing service. Now in

95

my frequent absences he largely runs the clinical side of the hospital. It is a joy to see him competently leading Sunday morning worship in the wards with a very clear understanding of the cross; and this with no training other than an open Bible and a praying heart. The patients hang on his words because they have seen the daily quality of his life. One of the hardest lessons for an able person is to learn to be self-effacing and 'in honour preferring one another.' This is doubly so in Korean society where the traditional image of leadership is cast in a strong feudal mould. The projection of this mould of leadership into the church has been one of the biggest pitfalls in Christian work in the country. Mr Lee could easily fall into this pattern. It is humbling to see him responding to the challenges of the pattern of leadership displayed by our Lord in the gospels and taught by His apostles.

Driver *Mr Jee* was our other long-standing member. You will remember the incident with the paraffin stove in chapter 3. Shortly afterwards another tragi-comic incident occurred that had a significant effect on his life. One Sunday afternoon we were out and, on our return, we discovered that we had had a burglary. However, nothing serious was missing — some sweets, a little money, some used postage stamps — it was apparent that the invaders had been children. Investigation revealed that two of the miscreants were Mr Jee's sons in company with two other lads (all between nine and thirteen years old). We were not unduly distressed, but Mr Jee was mortified. His self-respect was shattered. He disappeared for 48 hours. We feared we would never see him again, but he returned, sobered and crestfallen. We began a Sunday afternoon stamp-club and Bible class for the boys. Not long after, our missing stamps began appearing in the boys' stamp-albums!

Mr Jee was obviously thinking deeply. Around the middle of December Audrey asked me one day what I would like for Christmas and I replied without hesitation, 'Mr Jee'. We prayed much for him, and on Christmas morning he appeared at our door saying, 'I am coming to church with you.' We had never pressed for decision, still less for him to attend church. In a small village community such as we were in, a mile outside Masan city itself, to attend church casually would have been well-nigh impossible for Mr Jee. This was his public confession of new-found faith in Christ. We discovered later that he had prepared it carefully. At considerable cost he had laid the whole matter before his aging parents — parents cast in the traditional Confucian mould, whose religious aspirations were entirely Buddhist — and had won their grudging conset. Those who knew him better than we said, 'Once he's decided he'll never look back,' and they were right.

Mr Jee had left school at fifteen, but what he lacked in formal education he amply made up for in hard work and cheerful willingness to turn his hand to anything. When the staff began to take a rota of night duty in the wards, by universal consent Mr Jee was voted 'best night nurse', and it was a touching sight to see him changing the nappies in the baby ward. All of this was under-girded by a disciplined habit of morning prayer and Bible reading, whether at home or away. Waking from a night on an inn-floor on our monthly trips to Mokpo, it was always challenging and deeply encouraging to see Mr Jee cross-legged and poring over his Bible with SU notes open beside him. Always in staff Bible studies it was Mr Jee who was there promptly, and who had done his homework.

Mr Cho, who was the only Christian in our original Bible study group, was amazed at the change in Mr Lee and Mr Jee — and at first a little jealous. He soon recovered from that and rejoiced with us. After we had been continuing morning Bible studies for more than two years, he said to me one day, 'Now Bible reading is a part of my life. I could never be the same without it.' We knew that he had rarely and spasmodically opened his Bible before, and that now regularly at home with his wife as well as in our groups the Bible was an open book for him, and he was gaining spiritual sustenance from it. It was a pattern we were to find repeated almost universally. Active church members, ignorant of the value of Bible reading, neglected it, or read merely by rote. Typically it would take two to three years of training for a church-member to catch on to the riches of reading God's Word for fellowship with Christ and spiritual food.

It was fitting that in January 1973 John Wallis and Mr Yune, general secretary of the newly-launched Scripture Union, should suggest, on a visit to Masan, that Mr Cho should join them in the SU work in Seoul. Here was a man who had discovered the value of Bible reading for himself and therefore had one of the key qualifications for SU work. 'Go and ask him,' I said. They did. The invitation tied in with his own leading and inclination to move to Seoul, but he thought I would block it. In the Confucian pattern, a Korean leader would not let his 'disciples' go easily. We encouraged him and his wife to go. He was amazed.

'You are brave: what will you do in the hospital?' he asked.

'If we concern ourselves firstly with the welfare of others, whether our staff or other people's work, God will provide for us,' I said. It was a necessary lesson for us on many occasions, and it is in the hurly-burly of these sorts of decisions that Christian attitudes are instilled. Mr Cho spent two happy and profitable years in the SU office in Seoul and then emigrated to Canada with his family. We encouraged him in this move too. He joined three other brothers there and is active in a Korean church in Vancouver and in SU promotion there.

Mr Cho's departure to the SU office in Seoul was more by way of an exchange than merely a loss to us; Mr Yune proposed that we take on in the hospital *Mr Park,* who was currently working as office boy in the SU work in Seoul. We already knew him as young man (in his early twenties and unmarried) with a strong Christian faith and bags of energy. We were to get to know him much more closely in the years that followed as a close friend, fellow-worker and confidant. A native of North Korea, he had been brought to Pusan by his mother as a three-year-old boy along with his two elder sisters. That had been a hair-raising journey amongst the refugee columns in the turmoil of war in 1951. Father had been left in the north, never to be heard of since. Only his mother's courage, hard work and faith had held this little family together. High school was completed in spite of much financial hardship, and led to a job in a newspaper office.

Through all these years of hardship in Pusan, and later in Seoul, a real and deepening faith had sustained him. His story could be repeated endlessly by those who grew up with him in similar conditions. Sadly, all-too-often the end result has been hardness (preoccupation with self-preservation) or self-indulgence (absorption in enjoying the fruits of more affluent times). In Mr Park it bred a sensitivity to the needs of the poor that found a natural outlet in the ministry of our hospital. Many was the patient who had reason to thank God for Mr Park's championing his cause in a government office, or persuading the foreign doctor to find a corner for 'just one more.' Wherein lay the difference? For much of his youth his mother and he had been members of Pastor Yune's church (faither of SU's Mr Yune, introduced in Chapter 4). There they had learned to love God's Word and seen love in action. Its fruit was apparent. Just as his sensitivity to the poor found outlet in the hospital, so his love for God's Word found outlet in Scripture Union. After three and a half years in the out-patient work of the hospital based in Masan, Mr Park moved to Taegu to develop and administer our outreach to patients in that city of over a million and province of six million people. We shall meet him again.

During his first eighteen months with us Mr Park handled the administration and financial side of our work as well as the out-patients. However, when we returned from UK leave in April 1974 and the way was open to expand, it was apparent that we would need a business manager as a separate post. The position was a crucial one. Integrity was essential in financial dealings, poise was required in dealings with government officials, and Christian character was indispensable in view of the influence that one in charge of the office inevitably wielded among staff and patients. Traditionally in Korean society administrative responsibility carries with it status and power. Others are expected to conform to the wishes of the one who holds the keys and he has endless little bureaucratic tricks to ensure that his authority is enforced. We were to see this pattern repeated constantly and unthinkingly in churches and many Christian organizations as well as in the world at large. We were building a totally different form of administrative framework. It was essential that our business manager saw the issues and acceded, or at least could be led into new patterns. It was not that we were culturally different and we thought our cultural patterns better than Korean ones. Rather there was something essential to the gospel that would be missing if we did not teach leadership to serve. Thus we spent several weeks in prayer over the appointment, consulting closely with Messrs Lee, Jee and Park.

Among the names that came to mind was that of *Mr Kim Dong Suk*. I had first met him in 1970. He had had osteomyelitis in the thigh while in high-school and had one stiff leg. He had later been knocked down by a car, breaking the other leg, which had been inadequately treated, so he had consulted with us. We had been able to refer him to a surgeon for definitive care. Tall, good-looking and athletic in spite of his stiff leg, he had grown up in close association with the church in his native town of Chinhae, a small port city and naval base forty minutes from Masan. He had been active for a number of years in the leadership of students both in his own church and in a Christian student movement. He had had eighteen months at Bible College in Pusan, but had had to leave because of the traffic accident. was well-known in church circles and interested in the ministry himself, but, by a denominational ruling, his disability would probably debar him from ordination. We had kept in touch over the years, and he had helped in the early distribution of SU notes among students. On one occasion I had taken him to a tea-room (the usual place for serious discussion) and rebuked him as a brother over outstanding payments on Christian books. He had taken it well. 'Thank you very much,' he said. 'All these years I have worked for the church and never has anyone exercised pastoral care of this sort. I have been used, but not shepherded.' Now we were considering his name. We were well aware of the problems — Mr Kim was steeped in traditional Korean churchmanship with its weaknesses as well as its strengths. We knew he would be prey to temptation over money and the universal love of status, yet we were aware of his many fine gifts. We couldn't get away from his name.

At the crucial stage three things happened. I had a letter from him saying he was moving to Seoul to find work; Mr Jee independently, and not knowing we were considering his name, suggested him; and finally, on a journey to Seoul, I ran into him in the railway carriage. So he came to join us, bringing his young wife to live in Masan, and so began four years of partnership, not without its problems but fruitful nonetheless.

Introductions to the girls of the team must wait until the next chapter. One other incident relating to Mr Jee belongs to this.

- - - - - - - - - - - - - - - - - -

Do not think that I have come to bring peace on earth; I have not come to bring peace, but a sword. For I have come to set a man against his father, and a daughter against her mother, and a daughter-in-law against her mother-in-law; and a man's foes will be those of his own household. (Matthew 10.34-36)

Christmas Day in the year of Mr Jee's conversion was a Saturday. Next day, after Sunday church, the minister and several leading members of the local church went to Mr Jee's house for a service of prayer and dedication. Together with Mr Jee, his wife and four sons (the youngest not three months old), they sat round and sang and prayed in a simple but moving service of welcome. 'As the thread follows the needle,' said the pastor, 'so wife and family should follow the decision of the head of the house.' In the years that have followed his family have attended church fairly regularly, but we have never been able to have regular Bible study with Mrs Jee. After a few years they moved house to the other side of Masan. Disillusioned with the money problems in the church they have been attending, and lacking Bible teaching, Mrs Jee has tended to drift away. The end of the story is not yet.

Early in the following year, Mr Jee was faced with his first major trial of faith. One of the attractive features of Korean society is the cohesion and continuity of family life. As we discovered at the outset of our studies in Matthew's gospel, everyone knows his family tree and treasures his ancestry. Everyone knows his 'home-place' — where his family roots are and usually where his family grave-sites are. Even in today's cosmopolitan urban world, most city dwellers have roots somewhere out in the country. This is clearly seen at the two traditional annual festivals — *Chusok* or the autumn harvest festival (15th August by the lunar calendar — usually falling in late September), and lunar new year. These are traditional times for family gatherings, visiting the family graves and tending them. Every conceivable form of transport out of the cities is jammed with thronging crowds heading for their homelands. The reverse is true at the end of the holiday as city dwellers rush to be back in the office on Monday (or Tuesday) morning.

Great store is set by these family occasions and paying of respect to the ancestors (which underlines the plight of orphans and former refugees from North Korea). Confucianism teaches this respect, Buddhism adds a 'religious' framework to the ceremonies involved, and latent animistic beliefs are never far from the surface in the thoughts of the partakers.

Koreans do not have god-shelves in their houses like the Japanese or Chinese, nor, generally, do they have spirit houses in the garden as do the Thai (perhaps this is one reason for their receptiveness to the gospel), but they have another ceremony for the ancestors called *Jaesa,* which literally means 'offering' or 'sacrifice'. It is the responsibility of the eldest son to perform the ceremony on the anniversary of his father's death, in the home in the presence of other close family members, year after year. Strictly it should be after midnight, but this is often advanced because of the twelve-to-four curfew and other members' need to get home. Where a man dies without a son, the responsibility is commonly transferred to a younger son of a close branch of the family. Women are involved in the preparations but do not actually share in the ceremony. The connotations are manifold — simple pious remembrance of father, ceremonies expressive of family solidarity in a changing world, a welcoming back of the spirit of the deceased into the family home for his peace and to ensure protection in the coming year.

Christians have generally seen *Jaesa* as ancestor worship in which they cannot participate (though Roman Catholics have been less clear-cut over this), and this ceremony has been one of the chief stumbling blocks for young people coming to Christ — especially for eldest sons.

It was Mr Jee's night for *Jaesa.* He was not eldest son, but he had responsibility for another forbear. His elder brother would be leaving his dried fish and seaweed store in the market to come to the ceremony. Preparations were to be made. What should he do? He invited the local minister and us to join his family (for moral support, I think). His wife prepared the low table in the living room with a wide variety of cold foods — fruit, pre-cooked fish, vegetables, chopped meat. The deceased forbear's photograph stood in the middle of the table with a candle on either side. The elder Mr Jee was there, suave and charming as ever, but unyielding in his family loyalty. Another male relative whom we didn't know was also present. The minister took the lead.

'This is now a Christian house; your brother cannot bow to the photograph of a man.'

'These are the traditions of our family and our nation,' replied elder brother, 'it is not right to neglect them or abolish them.'

So the discussion opened and swung back and forth with point and counterpoint. Not uncommonly Christians hold a service of prayer and thanksgiving on the memorial day, without the connotation of ancestor-worship. But, no! Brother would not be budged. 'We are going ahead, anyway,' he declared, and so it was that we watched while elder brother and the other relative bowed low before the table with hands on the floor and face prostrated between the hands — two, three times. Mr Jee, likewise, sat at one side and watched without partaking. We could only begin to guess at what it cost him to opt out for conscience before God from the ceremonies that had been so much a part of him from boyhood and which were expressive of so much that he held dear.

Do not think that I have come to bring peace on earth; I have not come to bring peace, but a sword.

The issue was to recur in various forms subsequently, but never with such intensity, and Mr Jee stood firm. His brother remained outwardly charming and friendly, but we knew that an inescapable sword had come in that family. The cost of discipleship in every age and every culture has never been a small matter.

Come to Me all who labour and are heavy laden, and I will give you rest. Take My yoke upon you and learn from Me. (Matthew 11.28, 29)

11

Come to me

In the last chapter we met, besides others, the three men who belonged to that first Bible study group for hospital staff described in chapter 1. In this we shall meet *Miss Chang Young Ja,* who belonged to that group, and a succession of girls who have belonged to our hospital staff after her.

It was a cold January day in 1972. I was in Seoul for a periodic visit and, among other business, had arranged to meet Miss Chang. At that time government was promoting a scheme for girls with nurse or nurse-aide training to go to West Germany on a three-year contract with the German government. From the German side it provided staff for their hospitals, from the Korean it meant employment and interesting opportunity for a large group of girls, personal financial attraction, and an amassing of valuable foreign exchange for the country through the funds that these girls channelled back to their families at home.

Still dogged by the self-consciousness and sense of inferiority that her slight lip deformity produced in her circumscribed home community, Miss Chang was attracted. She had left us nearly a year before for training in Seoul prior to departure.

We met in front of her training school, a typical concrete block on a main thoroughfare. She led me round the corner, down numerous side alleys into a little cul-de-sac with a doorway at the end. Ducking through the tiny pedestrian door set into the main double doors, we found ourselves in the cramped courtyard of a typical lower-middle-class town house — the tiled roof sloping down over the open forecourt. A medley of plastic sheeting extending to the dividing walls of the adjacent houses provided cover from the rain over several corners. The enquiring eyes of the family in the main room before us, investigated the newcomer. Young Ja led round the side through an outside kitchen area sheltered only by the plastic roofing, into the tiny cubicle that was her rented room. We sat down with the door ajar.

Young Ja was lonely. Life in the big city had been hard and German more difficult than anticipated, and she longed for home. Before she had left us, she had made no clear commitment to Christ. She had stuck with the group to the end and been attracted by the teachings of Christ, but it had gone no further. Together we looked at Matthew 11.28-30 — *Come to Me, all who labour and are heavy laden* — it was so relevant to her need. Her heart warmed to former things lost in the hurly burly of city life. 'Would she like here and now to come to Him in prayer?'

Yes, she would.

It meant 'His yoke' — He must be Lord. It meant an ongoing learning of Him — there would be no growth without a persistent habit of Bible study and prayer.

Yes, she realized this, and wanted Him. We bowed our heads. She prayed. I prayed. The gentle peace of Christ filled that little room.

Later that year she left for Germany. Some excellent Christian groups existed among the Korean girls in German hospitals. We sought to link her up with these. For a time she attended: then she was posted elsewhere where there were no other Christians. Contact was spasmodic. Several years later she returned home for a visit — sophisticated and confident. Her hand was extended to greet me and I realized how greatly she had adapted to European culture. No Korean lady would initiate a handshake with a man. A polite bow is in order. Sophisticated and confident — but her Christian experience a thing of the past. The end is not yet.

Miss Chang was succeeded by *Miss Son*, another local lass from the village. Her parents were elderly, refugees from the North who had found a niche in Masan twenty years before; mother a Christian, father kindly but uncommitted. Son Ki Ock came from a very poor shack home on the hillside. Although highly intelligent she had completed no more than primary school because of financial stringency. A Sunday School teacher in the local church, she came to us with a clear and firm faith of her own. Above all, she was clear that when the time came for marriage, she wanted someone with a faith stronger than hers.

Although barely twenty years old she learned quickly on the job and soon assumed responsibility for the out-patient clinics, often doing serious burn dressings and other treatments on her own. We sometimes reckoned that if we had asked her to take out somebody's appendix she would have gone ahead without batting an eyelid (we never did!).

When we came back from leave in the UK at the end of April 1974 we found to our surprise that she had been married in a local church two weeks before. Husband was a former patient in the adjacent sanatorium who had made profession of faith and been baptized while in the sanatorium. From a country home between us and Pusan, he was feeling his way into a city job in Masan in television repairs. For the first year of their marriage they lived (unusually) in her parents' home in the village and she continued work with us.

Their first daughter was born that September, and after six weeks' leave she returned to work. A few weeks later when life had settled again into a routine, I hesitatingly broached the whole matter with her.

'You got married a bit late, didn't you?' I started. She knew immediately to what I was referring. We talked around it, leading through to the forgiveness and mercy of the Lord. She dissolved in tears. At the end of that time she said two things:

'Thank you for raising the subject,' and 'If you have opportunity, please warn the other young people in our church not to do what I have done. I don't want to be a bad influence on them.'

We learned several things from this incident. Sin that is covered and ignored comes as a barrier between people, shutting out real fellowship between them and even more, of course, towards God; but sin confessed, repented and forgiven is gone. Fellowship is restored — even when one may have to live with some of the long-term consequences. There had been no response from the leaders of the local church to Ki Ock's position. Her wedding had been a great local occasion. The birth of their child was welcomed and any eye-brows raised at the events had been courteously concealed. But *she* knew that fellowship had been marred and longed for healing. I broached the matter with the minister and leading deacon.

She wished to confess the matter formally and seek forgiveness, I said. A deputation of three or four leaders including some women should go to her for this purpose, I urged. They hesitated. Was this not too direct? It would hurt her. She needed some face-saving protection. No, I retorted, although this was acceptable culturally, it would destroy her spiritually. She longed for confession and absolution. I was reminded of the reports of scenes of seventy years earlier (see chapter 2) when, in the searchlight of the Spirit in revival power, 'face' was thrown to the winds and men cried out for mercy, confessing their sins. Here was something essential to the core of the gospel that we could not lightly cast aside in the name of cultural adaptations.

They yielded hesitatingly. We had a simple time of confession, prayer and admonition, not without embarrassment on the minister's part — though out on Ki Ock's. She was forgiven and restored. She still attends the church regularly, now with her two daughters, one on her back, one at her side, although she is now living in town five miles away, and her husband is at his busiest in the TV shop on Sunday morning.

There was one other sequel. A few weeks later I was asked to speak at Sunday evening service in the local church. Remembering Ki Ock's request, I let it be known in advance that I planned to speak on boy-girl relationships. There was obviously some apprehension on the part of the leadership. One deacon, a good friend and kindred spirit, came to me privately and urged, 'Do be careful what you say.' The subject had never been dealt with in churches. It was almost sacrilegious to raise it in the context of a worship service. Ki Ock stayed at home to pray. She was far from being alone among the young people of this small semi-rural church in the problems among which she had fallen. We looked together at John 8.1-11, seeking to establish a balance between 'Neither do I condemn you,' and 'Do not sin again.'

Come to Me all who labour and are heavy laden, and I will give you rest. Pastoral care is never an easy task and is full of pitfalls. This is doubly so when conducted in the context of an alien culture which one at best only partially understands. This is, however, no adequate reason for opting out.

- - - - - - - - - - - - - - - - - -

When Miss Son left us in the spring of 1976, our commitment to the care of ward patients was already expanding. We were under pressure from government authorities (quite rightly) to employ at least one qualified nurse. We approached the local Masan nursing school attached to the provincial hospital in the city. One of the teaching staff was a Christian and a friend. She recommended one of their graduating students — not a Christian, but competent and wishing to learn of spiritual things.

The nursing school has ninety students on a three-year course. The hospital to which it is attached, until recently at least, rarely had more than twenty in-patients and a smattering of daily out-patients. Not surprisingly its graduates had little more than theoretical knowledge of nursing. This was all to the good. It meant that we had new material to work with; there was no framework of bad habits to be unlearned before genuine patient care could be imbibed. *Miss Lee Kui Ock,* who came to us then, from being one of over a hundred nurses and students among a handful of patients found herself overnight in sole charge of twenty patients — a charge that rapidly grew to forty or fifty.

Over the ensuing year it was a delight to watch her growing competence, and emerging understanding of spiritual things. From time to time in our morning staff Bible studies a comment thrown in by Miss Lee would be like a shaft of light, and it was apparent that the Holy Spirit was gently illumining her heart.

Over the same period it was heart-warming to watch her growing relationship with Mr Park of our staff. So carefully handled was it that very few of the staff in a small community knew what was happening until a late stage. With great care they would avoid being seen setting out anywhere together. In returning, he would wait casually at the top of the hill while she returned alone. In discussing it with me, he was apologetic lest their relationship disturb harmony in the team, and that he might be removing a good worker not long after she had come. We encouraged them. Again and again we have found that as we have concerned ourselves primarily for the personal welfare of staff members, God has provided for the needs of the work. Her spiritual understanding blossomed, and they were married a week before Christmas that year in the local church. They were both insistent that I should conduct the ceremony. Never having done it before, I hesitated, but eventually was prevailed upon. By the grace of God all went smoothly, except at one point in the service where I addressed her as bridegroom — much to the amusement of all.

Now they live in an apartment block in Taegu, while Mr Park continues work for our patients in that area. Shortly after moving Miss Lee wrote, 'My time in Masan will always be remembered as a precious time of foundations for my life. Thank you for introducing me to our Lord Jesus Christ and allowing me to learn a pattern of compassion in His service.' Miss Lee has since been baptized, and they have one little girl. *Take My yoke upon you and learn from Me, for I am gentle and lowly in heart.*

- - - - - - - - - - - - - - - - - -

Miss Lee was on our staff for just one year. Again it was February, graduation time at the nursing school, and we were approached by various ministers on behalf of girls in their churches for the job. We also asked for a recommendation from the nursing school. We interviewed five girls. Several clearly had no conception of the job they were applying for. Said Mr Kim to one of them, 'Anybody in a city job enjoys going out in the fields for a day at rice-planting time, and coming home with muddy feet and an aching back. It's a welcome change; but how would you like that *every* day? That's what you'd be coming to here.' Her enthusiasm for the job waned visibly.

Three of the five who applied were Christian girls, but at the end of the interviews Mr Kim, Mr Lee and I were all united in the conviction that the most suitable girl for the job was *Miss Kim,* just graduating from the nursing school and a devout Roman Catholic.

This posed some problems. There was considerable Roman Catholic influence in the adjacent sanatorium and in town. The nuns were often devout, humble people with far more practical concern for the welfare of the needy then many of their Protestant counterparts, but we knew that in the small unit we had there was not room for both. We respected the conviction of any Roman Catholic patients who came to us (very few) and gave of our best to any referred to us by the priests or nuns without distinction, but a strong sectarian Roman Catholic influence from a staff member we knew would disrupt the team.

We discussed the matter with her before a decision was reached. She couldn't see the problem. 'Protestants.' she said (quite rightly) 'worked in the Roman Catholic hospital in town.' Why should there be problems with her, a Roman Catholic, working in a predominantly Protestant institution? It was not easy to make the issues clear, but we were very sure that there was a big difference between an institution that was Christian (whether RC or Protestant) because its charter was denominational and the name over the door a Christian one, and the sort of pattern we were working for. We were in government premises, our work was a secular one, but in its inner workings we were seeking the governance of God, the guidance of the Holy Spirit, the grace of Jesus Christ. This worked out at the practical level especially in the areas of patient care, inter-staff relationships, and finances. The patient must come first, and we were learning to trust the Lord step by step for His provision of staff and finance.

I don't think Miss Kim saw the issues fully at that stage, but she happily agreed to join our daily staff Bible studies and not to bring in outside Roman Catholic influence. In the early months not a few times she nearly gave up, overwhelmed with the load of work and weight of human suffering around. Not a few times the day closed in tears, but she weathered the early storms and grew to be a first-rate worker — swift, efficicent, and kindly. Our times of Bible study revealed an eager heart, but as yet no more than a nominal knowledge of Christ.

Come to Me, all who labour and are heavy laden, and I will give you rest. The end is not yet.

- - - - - - - - - - - - - - - - - -

Space forbids recounting in detail the stories of other staff members:

Miss Chang, younger sister of Young Ja who went to Germany. An efficient worker in the out-patients, but, 'I am very stubborn', has been her reply when faced with the claims of Christ.

Miss Kim her counterpart in the out-patient team — another local girl with a warm and loving heart that has blossomed in the sunshine of God's word, learned to love Christ and the patients, and to give unstinting service. But with marriage prospects looming ahead and strong family pressure, she has resisted the call for baptism. *My yoke is easy, and My burden is light* — yes, because borne by Him, but none the less costly in human terms.

'Little Miss Lee', as we called her, another local girl who joined us to assist in ward work. An earnest Christian with a faith strengthened by years of family antagonism, she yet had to learn that sometimes a little bustle was as much a part of serving the Lord as a 'holy stroll' down the corridors with a sanctified glitter in the eyes; that patients identified better with prayer using ordinary terms and an everyday voice than with glorified 'prayer language' poured forth in a high-pitched, pious voice; that ward services were not 'an altar where we offered sacrifices to the Lord', but more a fellowship of worship and learning of God's word; that being the first to carry bed-pans and clear up a baby that had been sick was more closely akin to the altar where we offered sacrifices to the Lord.

Mokpo Miss Kim, as she was dubbed — our staff member stationed at the clinic in Mokpo and responsible for patients in the far South West. She handled all our out-patients in that area single handed with monthly visits from us. Her visits to patients' houses often took her on ferry-boats to the islands, overnight stops in villages, a ride in the snow on a farm cart, and many other adventures. She brought a sturdy Christian character and a lot of courage to an often daunting task.

It was a mixed and predominantly young team — Mr Lee was in his early thirties; apart from driver Mr Jee and carpenter Mr Cho, none of the others was over thirty. Each in different ways was learning to follow the Lord's exhortation — *Take My yoke upon you and learn of Me; for I am gentle and lowly in heart, and you will find rest for your souls,* and God was forging us together, not without difficulties, into a united team in His service.

Look, your disciples are doing what is not lawful to do on the sabbath. If you had known what this means, 'I desire mercy, and not sacrifice', you would not have condemned the guiltless. (Matthew 12.2, 7)

12

Mercy or sacrifice?

General Assembly is a great occasion. Each year in the third week of September the leading ministers and elders (about half and half, delegates appointed by their presbyteries) meet for five days in one of the larger churches of the denomination. Each of the four main and a dozen or so minor Presbyterian denominations meets separately, generally on the same dates. Each claims the title, 'The Presbyterian Church in Korea' with the tacit assumption that 'we are the mainstream of Presbyterian life in the country. Others, however large or small, are breakaways.' The casual observer (if he understood Korean) would rarely detect any indication that there were other Presbyterians, or even other Christians, in the country beside those represented in the assembly. Methodists (in two separate conventions), Holiness Church and other denominations meet similarly about the same time.

The delegates generally sleep in nearby inns or the homes of friends. Lunch is served by the host church. Plastic attache cases, leaflets and souvenirs are distributed by a variety of publishing firms and businesses concerned with church furniture and other accessories of worship. A small cloud of reporters and photographers from Christian newspapers and journals hovers in the wings.

The assembly itself is an impressive affair. From earlier visits to many of the delegates in their home surroundings, one would expect to see a liberal sprinkling of grey hairs, but today it is a sea of jet black, broken only by the occasional bald pate and one or two rebels against the fads of fashion who are unashamed of 'hoar hairs'. Yes, a visit to the barber for grooming and fresh dying of the tell-tale grey to its original uniform Asian black is an essential part of preparation for Assembly. Not a few fresh-tailored suits are in evidence too. In all, if ever 'chic' and 'awesome' could be applied to the same scene Assembly would provide the scene.

Assembly is a place of conflict. This conflict can be overt but is more often subliminal. Like a succession of icebergs, each issue that surfaces in public confrontation on the floor has beneath it a far greater concealed body of lobbying, jockeying and verbal tussling for ascendancy. Interest on the first night focusses on the election of officers. The retiring moderator leads the opening worship and immediately his successor is appointed. Traditionally the retiring vice-moderator is appointed this year's moderator, so interest focusses more especially on the new vice-moderator's election. Then follows election of other officers and the various committee members — education, doctrine, finance, missions, business affairs, etc.

Assembly is a place of conflict for power. Assembly is also a place of conflict over doctrine. Here the traditions of the elders are established, and the course is charted for another year. Depending on how it is handled, such conflict can be creative or it can be immensely destructive.

Here are a few sample decisions reached at recent assemblies.
Family planning: God told Adam to be fruitful and multiply. Contraception is not permitted for the Christian.
Qualifications for the ordained ministry: men with a physical blemish are not to be admitted.
Saluting the national flag: Christian schoolboys and girls should dissociate themselves from the ceremony of saluting the national flag with hand on heart at school assembly (memories of bowing at Japanese Shinto shrines live on in the minds of older members).
Court cases among Christians: there are occasions where it is right to prosecute fellow-Christians when as officers of the church they have criminally abused their responsibilities.

Most of these have subsequently been challenged or reconsidered. Issues of Sabbath keeping and tithing have been thrashed out in former years and the official line fairly clearly demarcated.

The problem with such blanket rulings is that they tend towards spiritual eclecticism on the part of the few who can fulfil them (shades of the scribes and the Pharisees), provide levers for the ecclesiastical politicians in their quest for power (shades of the Sadducees), and load multitudes of intelligent and conscientious church members, who either disagree with the ruling or cannot apply it in their practical living, with a guilty conscience (shades of the sheep without a shepherd, harassed and helpless). *If you had known what this means, 'I desire mercy and not sacrifice,' you would not have condemned the guiltless.*

Whoever does the will of my Father in heaven is my brother and sister and mother (Matthew 12.50). The New Testament envisages an intelligent laity, reaching their own ethical decisions by a conscience illuminated by God's Word and guided by God's Spirit.

Assembly is furthermore a place of conflict between good and evil. For twenty years the separate denominations have had rather little interchange of ideas. More recently some of the best theological leadership — teachers in the theological seminaries in Seoul and Pusan who have theological doctorate degrees from America, Holland and elsewhere, men who have seen the growth of the gospel and the life of the church on a wider scale — these men have had a good measure of interchange and fellowship. Sometimes they have had to answer for it at assembly. Some of the best pastoral leadership of the church — older ministers and sometimes elders from rural churches — have had to join battle with those whose interests lie predominantly in the realm of power and influence. It is commonly this pastoral group that is unafraid to display its grey hairs.

Assembly is also an occasion of reports and greetings. On the morning of the first full day the 'fraternal delegates' from co-operating missions are allowed a word of greeting. Usually three or four such are present representing a dozen missionaries working in a framework encompassing over a million church members. Apart from ourselves, the other delegates have all been representatives from one of several Presbyterian denominations in the United States. In the denominations with which we have been associated, these links with American mission boards have produced only minimal financial contributions from the American church. This has been healthy, but would not necessarily be true of some of the other groupings. Our own position in OMF has been hard for many steeped in this strongly denominational tradition to understand. While we are officially related to two Presbyterian denominations, our interdenominational sympathies are wider than this. We include lay workers as well as ordained missionaries and most of us come from countries other

117

than North America. This is both our strength and weakness.

Events surrounding a recent General Assembly serve to illustrate some of the issues of doctrine, the inescapability of conflict, and the outcome. In the preceding summer vacation, a good friend was asked to lead three Bible Study sessions with college students at their summer camp. He took as his text the book of Malachi, using a mini-commentary originally produced by SU in Australia and recently produced in Korean. As is his custom, these sessions were conducted in a question-and-answer exploratory group Bible study framework. In the course of these studies the question of tithing came up and was considered in some detail.

Now it is common teaching in the Korean church that Malachi 3.10 clearly teaches that each individual church member should give one tenth of his income to his local church today. This is reinforced by Abraham's example before Melchizedek (Genesis 14.20), and Jacob's promise in Genesis 28.22. The Lord's words in Luke 11.42 are cited as New Testament endorsement of tithing. This very strong teaching discounts the fact that both incidents in Genesis are examples, not commands, and that the only other New Testament references to tithing are in Hebrews 7, where the context is that of abrogation of the Mosaic law (Hebrews 7.12).

Thus giving, which in the whole of Scripture is to be a glad and free-will activity, perhaps with the long-standing tradition of a tenth as a guide-post, becomes too easily a burdensome duty. Indeed in many churches in Korea today the tithe is a starting point. By the time weekly offerings, thank-offerings, building fund contributions and special occasion offerings have been added in, church members may be expected to contribute up to two-fifths of their income to the local church. In most cases only a small part of this will be used outside the church and only a nominal sum in charitable work. Sadly, today, under strong pressure to conform to the system, there are many who fall into the sin of Ananias and Sapphira (Acts 5). The strong application of Malachi 3.10 produces too often just the patterns of deceit over money against which Malachi was declaiming.

This teaching is commonly held, largely undisputed, but by no means universally applied. Consequently preaching is frequently an occasion for reminding the congregation of 'responsibilities' in this direction. Tithing in these terms is the hallmark of sincere

Christian faith, and many return home with guilty consciences unrelieved. Any challenge to this system, of course, is seen as a threat to the security of the congregation and the livelihood of its pastor. Money is always a highly-sensitive area of conflict.

In the study of Malachi 3 it was seen that a large part of the Lord's complaint against His people was 'against those who swear falsely, against those who oppress the hireling in his wages, the widow and the orphan, against those who thrust aside the sojourner and do not fear me' (3.5). In other words, the whole is set in the wider context of the godly man's use of money, and the emphasis is on integrity (Malachi 1.7-8) rather than on a fixed levy. This was then considered in the light of New Testament teaching on giving and the Lord's words, 'you tithe mint and dill and cummin, and have neglected the weightier matters of the law, justice and mercy and faith.' (Luke 11.42).

The students were greatly stirred. Discussion ranged over many related issues. As one said after returning home, 'I heard things there that I had never heard before.' Some went home to talk with their pastors. They had sensed something of the joyfulness of giving and of a life totally dedicated to God in all its parts, that contrasted sharply with the arid legalism of duty tithing which was the dominant impression left in their minds by the teaching they had received up to this date.

In the course of discussion afterwards, with a smaller group of students, the question of Sabbath-keeping arose. This is a dominant theme in the Korean church. The guidelines are clearly laid down. Sunday is the Lord's day. It is our duty to keep it as such. Public transport is banned, in theory (but not the employment of your driver to bring you to church and sleep in the car till you come out, if you are a prosperous city elder). Your time is available to the church and many elders and deacons see little of their families on Sunday. Indeed, the development of nuclear family life proceeds faster in secular society in the cities than it does in the churches. Work is barred for the shopkeeper, homework is banned for the schoolboy, but cooking is not barred for the elder's wife entertaining a visiting preacher!

In the course of discussion our friend sought to show the biblical themes on a thorny subject and to stimulate the students' thinking. The Sabbath was ordained as a reminder of creation (Exodus 20.11) and a reminder of redemption (Deuteronomy 5.15). The Christian believer has entered into Sabbath rest in

Christ (Hebrews 4.9, 10) and keeps the Lord's day as a day of rest, worship and good works as a token of faith and love, not as a burdensome duty. The issue at stake, which was the same issue that the Lord had with the Pharisees, and which has repeatedly arisen in Church history, was the same as that over tithing. Is my handling of money and of time a grudging parting with God's portion as a religious duty that I may keep the rest for myself, or is the whole of life a joyous surrender to God, and my attitude to giving and the Lord's day an expression of trust and love toward my Saviour and Lord? The question was a totally new one to most of the students present. It is hardly surprising that at least one somewhat confused student reported back to his minister, 'This man is teaching that we don't need to pay our tithes or keep the Lord's day.' Nor is it surprising that the reaction was sharp.

Our friend was already under fire in some quarters. Although highly qualified theologically, he is unordained. The previous year he had been invited by one minister friend to address a ministers' summer retreat on the subject, 'A layman's plea to the ministry'. Some had resented the invitation. What had a layman to teach the ordained ministry of the church? In the course of his address he had pleaded with the ordained leadership to resist the temptation to organize church for the benefit of church and its ministry, but to care for the sheep, entering into their real problems in living as Christians in a secular society; he appealed to the leaders that the church in its structure and leadership should be more concerned with ministering to its members the Word of Life; less concerned with extracting from them heavy commitment of time and money to the detriment of family and neglect of social responsibilities. Proper commitment of time and money would follow spontaneously from a proper attention to the ministry. The approach had been gracious, but forthright. He knew that he spoke for multitudes of younger people who were disillusioned with the church as 'ministers' business' and were leaving the fold of the Christian community for secular living. The response was disappointing. Privately many, especially younger ones, encouraged him to go on it the second and third talks and not to pull his punches. Publicly the leadership were nettled. A layman had no right to this sort of criticism of the ministry. As always in the conflict of good and evil, enemies were made and the smart not forgotten.

Now here was opportunity to hit back. This man was publicly teaching neglect of the sabbath. He should be disciplined. The general assembly requested the presbytery to look into the matter and report back. A presbytery committee was appointed and a lengthy session held. Foremost among the inquisitors was a man in his early 40's whom we had sadly watched as over ten years he stepped further and further down the road of ecclesiastical politics. An able man, we had seen him manoeuvre himself into the position of secretary to the assembly when the older man who had held the position was supplanted. We had seen him increasingly vocal on issues and in ways that boosted his own sphere of influence. He was a contemporary of our friend's; they had known each other over many years.

The issues were discussed at length. The opposing stance of a deep concern for truth and its pastoral implications on the one hand, and of ecclesiastical dogma and protection of personal power on the other could rarely have been better defined. A report was prepared. This was likely to be on the general assembly agenda. The normal procedure in such circumstances would be to prepare counter-measures, lobby among delegates and pull every available string to have the matter dropped or defeated. Our friend did none of these. He stayed away from general assembly (he was not a delegate, but could have gone as an observer), and committed the matter to the Lord.

The assembly was occupied with other matters and this question never arose. Three weeks later the chief protagonist, though still a young man, suffered a heart attack and was found dead in his bed one Sunday morning. 'It is a fearful thing to fall into the hands of the living God.'

- - - - - - - - - - - - - - - - - -

'I desire mercy and not sacrifice.' The issues at stake are no peripheral matter. They lie at the very heart of the gospel. It is essential that we know when and how to fight for gospel truth.

This people's heart has grown dull, and their ears are heavy of hearing, and their eyes they have closed, lest they should perceive with their eyes, and hear with their ears, and understand with their heart, and turn for Me to heal them. (Matthew 13.15)

13

Seed and soil

At the end of chapter 7 we traced the early beginnings of Scripture Union in Korea in association with an indigenous student movement. In chapter 6, however, we spoke of Mr Yune Zong Ha as general secretary of Korea Scripture Union. In this chapter we must trace how this change came about and see some of the issues we grappled with in charting the course for the first stages of Scripture Union's development in Korea as an independent movement in its own right. Many of these issues relate very closely to the underlying themes of Jesus' parables in Matthew chapter 13.

When we first worked with this student movement in Seoul in 1969/70 we were deeply attracted by the strong Bible emphasis, the careful attention to Scripture and the time given to its study and effort expended in seeking to apply it to life. This was all the more attractive in that it was in sharp contrast to much of what we found elsewhere. Here was a considerable body of intelligent young people from the best universities in Seoul being converted from a totally non-Christian background and built up in the faith — 'born anew . . . through the living and abiding Word of God' (I Peter 1.23). Certainly here was good soil (Matthew 13.8), and it was a pleasure to work in it. We had many opportunities for ministry among these students and delighted in them, but both by virtue of the basis of invitation on which we had entered the country and by conviction we saw our primary allegiance to the churches.

We sought to introduce the *Daily Bread* Bible reading notes that they were producing to the churches with which we had contact, and to encourage the students and especially the graduates to do the same. We had some success, but again and again ran into the problem that church leadership regarded these notes as the student movement's textbook and therefore unsuitable for general use in the churches. In our own country, people set considerable store by the publisher's label and by who wrote the foreword, in assessing the suitability of a Christian book before they ever examine the contents. This is doubly so in Asia and especially in Korea where group loyalties run very strong.

The American lady missionary who worked intimately with this movement from its start warned us of other problems. She was the epitome of what a missionary should be. Hard working and utterly dedicated, she had spent many years living in the simplest conditions with the students, often sharing her 8 x 10 foot room with one or two girl students. Previous to her work with students she had spent five years itinerating among the rural churches. She warned us that we would be utterly overwhelmed by the ignorance of Scripture, and the ears deaf to its voice that we would find. 'The Korean church,' she told us, as we were beginning to find our feet as new missionaries, 'has a glorious history of Bible-based growth, but that is all changed in the last twenty years. Our task is, like Isaac, to dig again the wells of water which had been dug in the days of Abraham, for the Philistines have stopped them and filled them with earth.' (Genesis 26.18, 15) We were loath to believe it.

As we became more involved with the churches we were unwillingly forced to concur in the diagnosis of tremendous need, but over the next two years of working together our differences of viewpoint became increasingly apparent. The student movement was becoming increasingly separatist in its position vis-a-vis the churches. This was understandable in view of the dominant characteristics of church life, and the fact that the majority of the movement's members had been converted from unchurched backgrounds and grown up in Christ outside the context of the churches. However, we were equally sure that for us the path was not withdrawal, but more intricate involvement. We were of one mind in our approach to Scripture and the vital place of God's Word in conversion and building up of Christian living; we differed in our understanding of church life; perhaps in the commission that was entrusted to us. Meanwhile, leadership of SU internationally in Asia was pressing for a more representative council of reference for SU in Korea as well as stressing

SU's essential ethos as an interdenominational work in and through the churches. For us and for SU, the commission was not within the circle of one student movement; it was to be in the context of the mainstream of Christian life in the churches at large. We had a focussed message regarding God's Word and its central place in church life. This was to be spread throughout the whole church, for all its shortcomings. This message was to be leaven leavening the whole lump (Matthew 13.33); we were to work in a field full of wheat and weeds, often not knowing which was which. *Let both grow together until the harvest* (13.30) could be applied to our pattern of work in the churches.

Parting from the student movement was painful, especially when we held so much in common. In the event a number of factors converged to make it relatively simple. The change was effected with the minimum of acrimony on both sides.

Late in June 1972 David Chan, East Asia regional secretary of Scripture Union, arrived in Seoul with a brief to get SU set up as a separate organization in Seoul. As well as his continuing discussions with the student movement, he contacted John Wallis and myself and Kim Heng Kwon, a friend of his from student days in America, now head of the trade and economics department at Koryo University in Seoul. Prof. Kim knew nothing of SU and none of us had met him before, but David Chan enthused him and he agreed to act as treasurer of the new movement. John Wallis and I introduced Yune Zong Ha as potential staff worker. We both knew him well by this stage, and the more we talked about SU the more we found his own personal convictions, independently formed, tied in with this ethos.

'How soon will you be able to start?' asked David Chan.

'Next week,' replied Mr Yune. Being self-employed and in the process of searching out the next steps for himself and his service of the Lord, he was ready for the opening which tied so closely with his own convictions. Here, it seemed, was a channel opening up through which he could make the sort of contribution to the church that he had always longed to do and which his convictions told him was so desperately needed.

So it was that within the space of a week, an office room was rented, a staff worker appointed, and a committee gathered to steer the newly-launched movement. The evening of June 30th 1972 saw a small gathering in this office room to celebrate the

125

birth of Korea Scripture Union — July 1st 1972. Mr Yune's father, old Pastor Yune, whom we met in chapter 4, gave the address. Committee members present included Professor Kim Heng Kwon (who later became chairman of council). Kim Young Jae who had followed our friend Kim Chin Kyung at Clifton Theological College in Bristol, Hong Chi Mo who had spent two years at the Bible Training Institute in Glasgow (these two had been students together with Yune Zong Ha and Kim Chin Kyung), Stephen Lee (whom we met in chapter 7), John Wallis and myself. Those who had been in Britain had some faint notions of what Scripture Union stood for, but we were all beginners, and it was an adventure of faith as we stepped out into the unknown. That unknown future was to contain many years of exploring, at the practical level, ways of applying the convictions that we held in common.

These convictions were threefold, though at the time we had not perhaps thought them out that clearly.

Firstly, the principal instrument in the hands of God and of His servants for the advance of the Kingdom, be it in the conversion of unbelievers, or the building up of the saints, is the Word of God. 'The seed is the Word of God' (Luke 8.11). Rightly taught, believed and obeyed, this Word had a tremendous power. We had seen this on a small scale in our Bible study groups among hospital staff in Masan. The principle could and should be applied very much more widely.

Secondly, that the church as a whole was in a perilous state. For all its growth and vigour and activity it was as though Scripture had been plucked out of the life of the church both at the personal and corporate level — and this not primarily due to the inroads of liberalism, but to an arid intellectual handling of the Word in the context of a strong human authority structure. The situation was very closely analagous to the state of religion in the days of our Lord. It could be said that there was an SU-shaped gap in the life of the church. This was a conviction not lightly reached, and was held not so much from the standpoint of judicial condemnation as of medical diagnosis with a view to treatment.

Thirdly, that our proper sphere of activity was primarily in the context of the churches. We were to work as closely as we could with the spiritual leadership of the church for the spiritual welfare and development of the church, not in isolation or competition with the existing structures. Our watchword became, 'Reformation and Revival through a return to the Scriptures.' The ensuing years have served only to deepen and strengthen these convictions.

A sower went out to sow, and as he sowed . . .
How did we set about the first stages of laying foundations for Korea Scripture Union and beginning to build on them? Although we were far from unconcerned with the area of youth evangelism, it was clear to us that the first steps needed to be in the area of Bible reading aids. More than that — using Bible reading notes as a tool, we were setting out to build a Bible reading movement within the life of the church at large. The emphasis needed to be on systematic, careful study of God's Word at the personal and small group level with emphasis on application to life. The Bible Reading notes needed to be fresh-written in the Korean context. English language notes from Australia were useful as reference material, but the application and cultural content was too geared to the western world to be suitable for direct translation.

For the remaining half of 1972 we produced two two-month booklets of undated readings, planning to launch dated notes in two series from January 1st 1973. The first of these undated booklets was an introductory series of New Testament readings for the young believer unfamiliar with Bible content. Mr Yune, John Wallis, myself and other council members wrote sections of these. I remember sweating over passages in Acts in totally inadequate Korean for the section entrusted to me. Mr Yune would then take these and rewrite them in good Korean. He said he frequently found the contribution from us missionaries easier to edit than those from other writers because, although he had to rephrase the Korean, they generally stuck to the text and contained practical application.

We were helped in planning a sizeable printing (5,000 copies) by a bulk order from the student movement of 2,000 copies for their membership. In spite of hitches we continued to supply bulk order of notes or reading cards for this group and for some others (Hospital Christian Fellowship, an Army Chaplains' Group, World Vision Orphanages, etc.) over the next two years, but became increasingly disenchanted with this method of work.

127

These bulk orders provided some financial stability in the early stages, but rarely did we find that more than a fraction of them had been used with understanding.

In the parable of the sower, perhaps part of the lesson is that no sower goes out to sow in this random fashion. He chooses his soil, prepares it carefully and plants his precious seed in it with minimum loss. The Lord had preached the message of the Kingdom far and wide, but had found much of the soil hard, rocky, and full of thorns. *This people's heart has grown dull, and their ears are heavy of hearing, and their eyes they have closed* (13.15). Now the emphasis would be on the selected good soil. *Blessed are your eyes for they see, and your ears, for they hear* (13.16).

Much of our early work with SU in Bible reading note distribution proved unfruitful (13.22). The soil was hard and unprepared. We prepared pastors' seminars, writers' seminars, readers' seminars, in various parts of the country. Mostly these were on a small scale, with twenty to thirty people at each. Feedback was mixed.

'We need more Bible reading in the church, but these notes are too simple.'

'The passages are too short. We read three chapters a day in our church.'

'Can I have the notes free?'

'You should provide some incentives; prizes for the most faithful readers.'

'Your vision is too small. Get them approved by the General Assembly Education Committee, authorized throughout the churches and you'll get hundreds of thousands sold.'

With the constant background pressure to make the accounts balance, and the demands to 'succeed' visibly, temptations were many, but it became increasingly clear that wide-scale blunderbuss distribution might produce large sales and financial success, but would not produce spiritual fruit. The soil was too unprepared. What we were emphasizing in our approach to Scripture was too unknown and revolutionary to take root immediately on a wide scale.

When anyone hears the word of the Kingdom and does not understand it . . . I remember Mr Yune in one of our readers' seminars contrasting the traditional presentation of the gospel in Korea ('Where do I go when I die?') with the questions being asked by today's young people ('How do I live here and now?'). Of course both were relevant questions for which the gospel provides answers, but the starting point must be at the place of felt need. Men of former years were predominantly asking the first question and the presentation of the gospel in those terms was relevant. The perpetuation of presentation of the gospel in these terms to today's young people has produced a generation who do not understand and no longer expect to. *You shall indeed hear, but never understand, and you shall indeed see but never perceive* (13.14). How easily the evil one comes and snatches away what is sown in the heart of such a man (13.19).

Group loyalty is very strong. If a Bible class leader urges the class to take SU notes, all will accede; yes, they will receive it with joy (13.20). But let one or another leave the confines of the group; let there be persecution on the personal level (family, etc.) and immediately he falls away. He has no root in himself. Mr Yune cites one after another of his classmates in school who were together in church. Today they live totally secular lives. The soil was rocky and shallow.

'Make money' is a phrase incorporated into Korean language. It expresses the prevailing ethos in the cities of an economically-booming nation. I remember one young church deacon who worked for the Korean sales office of Encyclopaedia Britannica, taking me aside after a meeting to pass on his recipe for success. He had listed his 'ten most successful men.' Howard Hughes was top of the list. I don't remember all the others, but it included Winston Churchill, and Billy Graham was listed 9th! (I doubt whether Dr Graham's own criteria of success would have qualified him for inclusion.) Yes, the cares of the world and the delight in riches choke the word and it proves unfruitful.

However, here and there we were to find good soil. A young minister in Masan who at our request had written some of the notes said 'I find the preparation of notes a real help in my sermon preparation.' Here was a pointer to a by-product of SU's emphasis to train local writers. Preaching, too, might become more biblical and expository. There was a Bible class leader, also in Masan: three years later we discovered that he had faithfully read the Bible and notes without missing a day. It was no accident that his Bible class members continued subscribing to the notes, and showed evidence of their effective use.

A leading doctor in Pusan said, 'I find the Adult series too difficult. I am using the New Testament readings designed for students.' Here was the answer to the unthinking dismissal of them as too facile. Here was a man prepared to go down deeply in his search for truth.

Seed and soil. Both are important to a good harvest. There is good soil in Korea today but there is much that is hard and rocky and sown with weeds. Robert Bruce, an Irish missionary in Persia, is quoted in *The Lion 'History of Christianity'* as saying, 'I am not reaping the harvest; I can scarcely claim to be sowing the seed; I am hardly ploughing the soil; but I am gathering out the stones. That too is missionary work; let it be supported by loving sympathy and fervent prayers.'

The hardness of Korea can scarcely be equated with that of a Muslim land, but yet our task approximates more closely to that than to the popular image of Korea as all rejoicing and revival. A large part of our task is land reclamation, and for this a team of ten is pitifully small. There is a work to be done in Korea today that no one else is doing.

As He went ashore He saw a great throng; and He had compassion on them and healed their sick . . . 'They need not go away; you give them something to eat.'
He said, 'Come' . . . 'O man of little faith, why did you doubt?'
(Matthew 14.14, 16, 29, 31)

14

People are precious

At the end of the last chapter we noted the sower's task of planting his seed carefully in the relatively small area of good soil, and the very much wider task of preparing the hard, rocky and weedy soil for planting. This reminds us of the perennial tension between concentrating on training a few in depth and seeking to meet the needs of the great crowds. That is the theme of this chapter, but before we take it up, the opening words of Matthew chapter 14 remind us of something else:

At that time Herod the tetrarch heard about the fame of Jesus (Matthew 14.1). Political and social issues of the day impinge upon the gospel narrative at various points, but Jesus never allows Himself to be deflected from the centrality of His spiritual ministry. Even in the context of the events of this chapter Jesus evades the popular demand to make Him King (John 6.15). While the gospel of the Kingdom would have immense impact upon politics and the social order, this was a secondary matter to be worked out by others. The gospel was set out and illustrated in terms of the everyday life of the people. The stark contrast with the religious framework of the day is drawn in the sharpest possible terms, but it is not set forth as a revolutionary alternative to the existing social and political order of the day. (The same could be said of Paul's missionary message and, for instance, his stance regarding slavery.)

The missionary does well to follow in the steps of His Master in this respect also. He is not unconcerned with the social and political ferment of the day. He seeks to relate himself and his message as closely as possible to the culture in which he is placed, but his message is a spiritual one. He learns to love the nation and people of his adoption, to respect their government, rejoice in their progress, and yearn with them in their problems. He is a spiritual revolutionary, not a social or political one. Given genuine spiritual regeneration, social and political change will follow where needed at the indigenous level. Among the thousand or more Protestant and Catholic missionaries in Korea, a very large number are involved in social and community works of various sorts, and not a few dabble in the political sphere seeking to impose solutions from their own cultural background on the social order. Once a missionary strays outside the sphere of his spiritual competence the pitfalls are numerous and not a few have plunged headlong into catastrophe or disillusionment. Sadly, the voice of such is most readily picked up by the mass media of the West and megaphoned through half the world.

When we were grappling with the first stages of Korean language study in the early part of 1967 in Seoul, the country was just emerging from the years of despair following the devastation of the Korean war (1950-53). The first pedestrian underpass in Seoul had just been opened. Old tram lines were being pulled up. Street corners and even buildings could easily be identified with old photographs of war-time Seoul. The vast sixteenth-century South Gate halfway between Seoul Station to the south and Seoul City Hall to the north stood out as a landmark. Ten years later all three are dwarfed by twenty-storey hotels and office blocks, and traffic flyovers, pedestrian bridges and underpasses abound. The expanding underground railway eases rush-hour congestion; everywhere business is booming and prosperity reaches a wide section of the community.

When we moved to provincial Masan in March 1967, the road to Pusan was the only paved one leading out of the city. Industry, such as it was, was limited to small family factories and one larger textiles firm; the road to our house and the hospital a mile out of town lay on a dusty rock-strewn route through a cleft in the mountains. Patients who missed the one bus a day, or who couldn't afford it, walked to the hospital. Today we go to town on a paved road with frequent buses. Very few among the poor cannot manage the bus fare. We may go out of town in five different directions on good paved roads. The population has doubled, and a thriving light industrial zone on land reclaimed from the sea provides work for tens of thousands of people, and much needed products for the export trade. In 1967 the journey from Seoul to Pusan by car was a hazardous two-day adventure, parts of it on unmade pot-holed roads. Today a fine dual carriageway links the two. Air-conditioned express buses leaving every five minutes through the day do the journey in five and a half hours.

In 1967 the first Korean-made saloon car was heralded as an achievement. It was a Japanese Toyota assembled in Korea with ten percent Korean-made parts. Ten years later the Hyundai Pony saloon car, entirely locally made, begins to compete on world markets.

In 1967 plans for Government-provided health services were little more than a skeleton. Ten years later the first stages of health insurance schemes herald large changes in the overall scene. We generally find it easier to work with government agencies in our medical work than with Christian ones because they often make more provision for the welfare of poor people than does the church.

Greatly improved communications mean that the gulf between city and rural life is minimized, and the increased prosperity is fed down to a wide cross-section of the community. In a small way this is mirrored in our own medical work. Where ten years ago we could cover only a radius of fifty miles, today that radius is two hundred miles.

Progressively we find ourselves entering into the joys and fears of the people with whom we live and work. When the Korean Women's table tennis team returns home with the world championship and all Seoul goes wild in its welcome, our hearts beat faster too. When the news is flashed across the country that the Korean Himalayan expedition has reached the top of Everest, our hearts swell with pride as much as the next. When a Korean fishing boat is abducted by a North Korean gunboat we feel the anguish along with our neighbours, and always the brooding apprehension of the North and its intentions is in the background of everyone's thinking. Almost every family is affected by military service or home guard training, and the united sense of purpose in resisting the pressure from the North is a refreshing aspect of society, in sharp contrast with the aimlessness and internal division of many of our western societies. All in all, it is an exciting atmosphere of change, and a society with whose aspirations it is not difficult to identify. Yet, in all of this one is brought back repeatedly to the primacy of our spiritual ministry. How may we most effectively convey the gospel of Jesus Christ and build His Kingdom within this social framework and in cooperation with the churches to which we are committed?

- - - - - - - - - - - - - - - - - -

I looked out over the vast sea of faces: 1500 girls of the Isabelle Girls' High School, a fine Christian school in Pusan, filling the newly-built auditorium in neat rows. It was the weekly morning chapel hour. One's heart could not but be moved by the sight of this throng of young faces. How may the Word of Truth most effectively be fed to this multitude? Lord! the task is too great: we have nothing to give. Please send them away. That sense of helplessness, of being swamped by too vast a need, that must have engulfed the disciples at that lakeside hovered as a cloud of fear. It was not the first time that I had spoken at this chapel hour. It was always a privilege, for one knew that here the senior staff were praying for the welfare of these girls, many of whom came from totally non-Christian homes and backgrounds. Here one felt supported as one of a team rather than merely a lone voice. We spoke on two-way communication with God through prayer and Bible Study: the need for communication first to be established through forgiveness at the Cross of Christ, then to be maintained through obedience and faith. A loose telephone in the rostrum, a doctor's white coat and stethoscope served as visual aids. The girls laughed and listened (usually the first is needed if the second is to be achieved). The seed was sown and then . . . and then . . . This sort of widescale ministry was clearly needed. Openings abounded: an army of missionaries could find more than enough to occupy them in this ministry. Yet, we knew that if this was where it ended, the harvest would be meagre.

- - - - - - - - - - - - - - - - - -

July 29th. The first day of the four-week summer holiday for schools (Korean schools have their long holiday in winter from the third week of December to the beginning of February, to save heating costs in the classrooms). A day conference had been organized by the chaplains of 27 different Christian schools, all within the city of Pusan. Two delegates from each school, Christian leaders among the students, were attending for a training day. I was asked to take a session on Bible study. Cecily Moar of OMF, only a year in the country and still buried in language study, accompanied me. The boys and girls enjoyed themselves that day, and I hope learned something. Our session included an introductory talk, a practical assignment on Bible study and a reports session. We were slowly leading them into an understanding of God's Word and how to feed upon it themselves. And yet — what can one convey to a group of fifty people of concepts entirely new to them, in an hour and a half?

- - - - - - - - - - - - - - - - - -

That same summer we experimented with a schoolgirls' camp. Cecily Moar and SU staff member Miss Gwon Chun Ja led the camp. A site was borrowed from a Christian student organization who had used it the previous week for their own summer camp with 500 students present. The camp we planned was for twenty girls. A boat was laid on, for the site was a beach side and rough mountain slope on an island off Masan. The student organization lent some tents. Arrangements were made with a Christian school in Masan, who found it hard to understand why we set an upper limit of twenty (this actually became 24). Fifty or sixty was their suggestion.

The camp, like all pioneering ventures, was hard going: torrential rain, confusion, lengthy sermons with a flow of words reminiscent of the rain from one speaker, little visible response from the girls. Thinking of established, prayerful, well-organized camps at home, Cecily felt ashamed to call it an SU camp. Was this the way? Clearly, if camping was to be an effective means of work, very much more training of camp officers was needed. That camp should be fun; that talks should be short; that time at the personal level was vital — all these concepts were totally new. Truly, we were pioneering at a very much more basic level than we had envisaged.

A year later Cecily Moar moved to Pusan and, sharing a flat with Miss Gwon, began work in that city. Among other openings, the Isabelle Girls' School invited them to take a lunch-hour Bible club in the school. School authorities wished to 'volunteer' sixty girls — one class — for the meeting. Cecily insisted that it should be truly voluntary, and wanted no more than twenty. Through various ups and downs the group continued for two years. Often people came and went. Was anything of the Word of God penetrating, or was the soil all hard, rocky, choked with weeds? Only when two of them came and spent a long evening at the flat, and began to share some of the problems they were facing at home (where would the money for school fees come from?) and school (I am so tired I can't concentrate, let alone read the Bible regularly), did Cecily and Miss Gwon begin to feel they were digging down to good soil.

This was further borne out in the often exhausting, lengthy evenings with an open Bible on the floor of the flat, and young people in ones and twos, sometimes fives and sixes, who were attracted by warm friendship and personal interest as bees are to the honeysuckle. Among those who came were two from that first camp. One at least showed evidence of spiritual rebirth. Others are still friendly. Three years later, Cecily could write: 'A friend met one of the girls who went to our 1975 camp in the street the other day, who asked if I was still around, and then she phoned the following week. Last week she came to tea, and I think she will come again. I'm really thrilled to see her as she is the lass I really felt drawn to and have continued to pray for even though she didn't reply to my letters. I don't think she has much interest in Christianity, but please pray for our future contact with her.'

The crowds or the few? Jesus was faced with this issue. His heart went out to the many (*I have compassion on the crowd ... I am unwilling to send them away hungry*, 15.32), but increasingly He gave His time to the few (*Take heart; it is I; have no fear ... Lord, if it is you, bid me come ... Come.* 14.28-29), so that through them, in due course, He might also reach the many (*they need not go away; you give them something to eat* 14.16). It is not either/or. It is both/and. More especially it is through the few to the many. Amidst the burgeoning numbers of seekers after truth in Korea there is no shortage of preachers on the grand scale. There is a vast barren wilderness of need on the personal level, and almost no one seeking to meet it. On this level truly the harvest is plenteous: the labourers are few. *Pray therefore the Lord of the harvest* . . .

For the sake of your tradition you have made void the Word of God. Do you know that the Pharisees were offended?
Behold, a Canaanite woman . . . I was sent only to the lost sheep of the house of Israel.
Great crowds came to Him, bringing with them the lame, the maimed, the blind, the dumb, and many others.
Then Jesus called His disciples to Him. (Matthew 15.6, 12, 22, 24, 30, 32)

15

Priortities

Missionary life is full of distractions. Some of these concern doctrine; others arise from relationships. The young missionary needs to have his priorities before him and to be sifting these all the time if he is not to be swept off course by the currents of temptation to conform in various ways. The Lord Himself, and His servants before and since, have always faced similar temptations. In the present chapter we shall look at some of these, firstly in the doctrinal area, and then in the personal.

Why do your disciples transgress the tradition of the elders? For they do not wash their hands when they eat. (15.2)
We go for holiday in Korea to one of a group of ten holiday cabins in the mountains. This entails four hours' walk up mountain trails, but it is cool, quiet and beautiful, and worth the climb. The early part of the trail is an upward path through fields of rice, vegetables and sweet potatoes. As we sat resting in the shade of a group of trees at the head of this section, a granny returning from her fields stopped to admire the children and pass the time of day. A roughly-made cigarette hung from her lips, her gnarled hands were ingrained with good, honest dirt, and the wrinkles around her eyes spoke of years of screwing them up in smoky kitchens as she had crouched feeding dry grass, twigs and leaves into the fire under the wash-pot. Handing her a tract, we asked her if she had attended the church in the village at the foot of the hill.

'Well,' she said, 'I am getting old, and I would like to go to heaven, but I'm too old to give this up.' She waved her cigarette in front of us. 'Christians don't smoke and Christians don't drink, and I can't go there unless I give this up.' Sadly, we watched her make her way back through the fields to her smoky kitchen.

She had verbalized the hidden attitude of very many people in Korea, both sophisticated and simple, towards the Christian gospel. The first criterion of a Christian is that he neither smokes nor drinks. This is respected, but reckoned unattainable by many honest-hearted men and women. Now there are strong practical reasons for Christians refraining from drinking and smoking; this is doubly so in a country like Korea where the commonly-accepted purpose of drinking is to get drunk, where those who smoke very often chain-smoke, and where, for all but a very few, family finances are constantly stretched beyond the limit. Furthermore, drinking and smoking are traditionally and commonly associated with gambling. Yes, the reasons are cogent, and it was with the wisdom of the Spirit that the early leaders in the Korean church established the pattern of restraint. Woe betide the missionary who does either and expects to find acceptance with the Korean church. However, when a helpful pattern of life becomes exalted as an article of faith and prerequisite of acceptance before God — when a tradition of the elders becomes an essential element of ceremonial cleanness — priorities have become distorted. In the same way there are, of course, strong practical reasons for washing hands before meals, but these do not have to do with ceremonial purity and acceptance before God. To exalt them as such deflects attention from the cardinal points of the gospel and 'weightier matters of the law.'

For the sake of your tradition, you have made void the Word of God, says the Lord (15.6), and immediately brings the issue back to the central authority of the Word of God and the central issue of human sinfulness of heart (15.19) that defiles a man (15.20).

You say, 'If any one tells his father or his mother, "What you would have gained from me is given to God," he need not honour his father.' (15.5) We have become familiar in the West with the effect on families of the Moonies (followers of the Unification Church of Sun Myung Moon) who originated in Korea, as well as of other sects. These sects often demand total loyalty, total surrender of personal possessions, and severing of family ties. The result can be catastrophic. Christ does demand such loyalty to

Himself (Matthew 10.37), and sometimes the implications in a non-Christian family can be intensely painful; but the will of God is for mercy and not sacrifice. It includes a loving concern for family, a proper respect for parents. When the demands of the religious group impinge upon this, that group is in danger of establishing the traditions of its elders over the authority of God's Word. We see this in sharp focus in the sects.

It can happen, too, within the fold of orthodox Christianity. When church life is structured for the financial benefit of the group and its organizations rather than the spiritual benefit of the people; when the demands upon the people, bolstered by group pressure, are such as to impinge on other rightful personal responsibilities; then danger signals are flashing. We have seen church elders selling their houses to fulfil their quota for a church building project, women neglecting the family breakfast to attend dawn prayer meetings, students abandoning their studies to work the church duplicator, churches failing to meet their contract deadlines on payment to a Christian building contractor with the cover that 'It is for the Lord, and you won't mind the sacrifice.' Yes, only careful attention to the Word of God will keep a missionary and the people among whom he ministers clear on their priorities among the many ethical and social issues of the day.

- - - - - - - - - - - - - - - - -

I was sent only to the lost sheep of the house of Israel (15.24). Priorities concern doctrines; priorities also concern people (and time available to devote to them). The westerner in Asia is something of a rarity except in a few cosmopolitan cities, and foreigners naturally tend to associate together. This is doubly so in a monochrome society like Korea where there is one language, one race, one culture — and the foreigner, however well adapted he is to the local culture, is for ever an outsider. We see the same natural pattern of association among immigrant groups in our own country. The missionary, by virtue of his calling to a ministry among the people of his adoption, is not infrequently placed in awkward situations with respect to his fellow-country-men, or other western nationals in the same country. He is required to live very much more deeply immersed in the local culture; proficiency in local language is essential, and generally he

143

is at a lower standard of living than other foreigners. All this is outward indication of a heart attitude that has identified to a considerable degree with the life and aspirations of the people among whom he works.

For foreigners in other walks of life, many of whom are only there for two or three years and work in an English language medium, it is almost impossible to enter into the emotional and psychological pressures that the missionary faces in relating both to them and to the people of the land. In spite of commendably deep interest in local culture on the part of many foreigners, in the very nature of things the majority cannot acquire more than a veneer of local understanding; this inevitably places many temptations in the path of the young missionary. He needs to walk warily, keeping his priorities very clear yet maintaining, as did the Lord, flexibility in individual cases. More often than not it is a matter of time. How much time do I devote to this area of my life, and how much to that? The missionary is also, not infrequently, faced with the temptation to sponge on those whose standard of living is better than his own. Casual remarks picked up in business, diplomatic and other professional circles reveal that this is the commonly-held image of the missionary. 'Of course, he'll be going round with the hat when he comes home. They all do.'

It is a matter of honour before God to maintain the highest standards of integrity in this matter. We are abundantly provided for by the living God and have no need to beg. There are many occasions when we have been deeply grateful for the spontaneous kindness and generosity of those in other walks of life, and have accepted it as such, but in all our relationships we are here to give, not to get.

The ensuing selection of incidents reveals something of the variety of relationships with which a missionary is faced, and through which his life is enriched.

- - - - - - - - - - - - - - - - - -

The professional supervision of the research side of our medical work has entailed visits from medical consultants in Britain, usually twice a year. The ability of these to adapt from the sophisticated facilities of a British teaching hospital to the limitations of basic medical care with few ancillary aids has never ceased to amaze us. We have gained much from their professional expertise, their approach to patients, their kindness to our children, and their ability to mingle with our staff and communicate with them. I recall us seated cross-legged on the floor of a local Masan restaurant with the hospital staff, the upper portion of the room thick with smoke from the beef braised on a charcoal fire in the centre of the table; or alone in the dining room of a provincial tourist hotel while the waiter watched us watching a rat scurrying across the floor; or again at the spotless table of the Nine Gates Dining Room in the plush Chosun Hotel in Seoul. I can see us seated with the Minister of Health in his reception room, discussing the problems of British miners; or standing in the yard of the country home of one of our patients while we counted the remaining drugs, and then walking the last two miles home after the second puncture that day.

- - - - - - - - - - - - - - - - -

Visitors to hospital have been many and varied. The day the British Ambassador's wife came, Mr Jee had to chauffeur her in our hospital Land Rover from Pusan. From the outskirts of Masan he was provided with a police motor-cycle escort, and enjoyed a few moments' glory driving through town with headlights blazing while the other traffic courteously gave way. The incident almost ended in a catastrophic loss of face when the police motor-cyclist stalled his bike in a pot-hole on the rough road out to the hospital, but all ended well. It was good to be on the side of the cops rather than the robbers on the roads for once.

On visits to Seoul, many has been the occasion when generous invitations by embassy staff to a meal or the offer of a night's hospitality, have had to be declined for pressure of other essential business — a quiet evening with a new missionary family; an SU council meeting; a late night with Mr Yune talking, praying, planning, thinking, dreaming of the future development of SU till one or two in the morning, and then a short night on the floor of his house (the normal sleeping place) — but there have been occasions too when it has been possible to accept such invitations.

Less than an hour from Masan is the smaller port city of Chinhae. Headquarters of the Korean navy, it also has a small American naval advisory group based there. We have had a number of interesting associations with them over the years. The clinic provided all our children with their basic immunizations. The dentist has cared for our teeth. 'You're a dental cripple: you need full-mouth rehabilitation,' said the forthright Mormon dentist from Salt Lake City; and then set about providing it. On occasion we have enjoyed their swimming pool and snack bar; the series of chaplains of a variety of theological persuasions have been our friends, and the doctors our associates. One such hosted us to a meal followed by what turned out to be a blue-film show (I don't think he realized this in advance, and was somewhat embarrassed at inflicting it on the missionary and his wife). Another of the doctors (generally there was only one at a time on a two-year assignment) proved the most mature Christian of any of the personnel we met there over the years. It was great refreshment to have real fellowship with a family living in a totally different milieu from ourselves, yet at one spiritually.

In recent years the Women's Welfare Committee from the American base have been more and more generous in financial help and gifts in kind to the hospital. Just when our work was expanding and our needs greatest they chose to make our hospital a fresh focus of their giving. God has His angels in many guises.

From time to time British and Commonwealth ships call at Chinhae on courtesy visits. Sometimes we are invited to these. One such was HMS Antrim. A launch to the ship's side, a tour of the decks, and afternoon tea in the mess-room. It could almost have been Portsmouth. That night we were invited to a dinner hosted by the resident American captain. Yes, ladies would be present, we were assured, but Audrey found herself the only lady among a dozen of the senior officers of the Antrim and the American captain. Had we misunderstood the innuendos of American culture the way we so often do Korean?

Paul was one of the earliest of American businessmen coming as consultants to the developing industrial zones of Masan. In fact 'business-man' was hardly a suitable title. A sensitive and quiet-spoken man in his mid-thirties, he had opted out of the rat-race of business in Los Angeles, sold up and come to Korea on contract with a firm building quality ferro-concrete pleasure yachts. The first would be his, and he planned to cruise the world for a few years with his family seeking, as he said, to find out

146

what life is all about. Of Jewish background, he had left his wife and two young school-age daughters at home for this period. Clearly they were a warm and united family, and he was terribly lonely. Often he would come to our home, play with our children, and talk of many things.

When he left we lost a friend; we gave him a Bible to take home, and he wrote later of the joy of sitting on board with his family reading the story of the Exodus together as the sun set over the Pacific. May God's Word lead him on to greater entry into life in Christ.

- - - - - - - - - - - - - - - - -

The American Peace Corps is a flourishing organization. For more than ten years they have sent team upon team of fine young people to work in Korea; the majority of whom have been involved in English teaching in schools and colleges. More recent teams have also been involved in health programmes in leprosy and tuberculosis. At most times there have been between three and eight Peace Corps volunteers in Masan. We have known many of them as friends. Mostly they have been a selected group of soft-spoken Americans of conservative habits and liberal views. All highly motivated and with high ideals, they have contributed much in often intensely frustrating situations. It would seem that they have been selected from among those who do not hold political or religious views so strongly that they might cause friction. We have found very few evangelical Christians among them. One married couple used often to come to our house in early days, and we had many long talks together as they were seeking a meaningful basis of life. It was great joy to receive a letter from them after their return to the States telling of their conversion to Christ.

- - - - - - - - - - - - - - - - -

Another group of dedicated young Americans is the Mormons. At any one time there are over a hundred Mormon missionaries in Korea — young 'elders' working in twos for a two-year period. They generally achieve a remarkable facility in language in that short time, and can often be seen in the streets with smart suits, close-cropped hair, and neat black attaché cases. Masan has been a training ground for their recruits, generally with eight of them in the town at a time. One of these became friendly for a time with one of our hospital staff and began visiting the hospital. I arranged an interview with him, expecting a pitched battle. I found a sensitive young man, lonely and confused. After an hour's talk I asked him, 'But, do you know the Lord?'

He paused.

'No,' he said, 'but I wish I did.'

A sad commentary on Mormonism, and incidentally one that could be applied to much that comes within the bracket of orthodox Christian faith in Korea.

Yet another group of young people has been the OMF 'SPOT' (Summer Programme of Overseas Training) workers. These, mostly college students, have come for about two months during their summer vacation, lived and worked with us, laughed, cried, criticized and co-operated. From Glasgow and Los Angeles. Ontario and London they have been varied and stimulating. Above all, they have underlined to us, and to themselves, the vast differences in culture that exist between West and East (and between the two sides of the Atlantic), and the cost involved if one is seeking to cross those boundaries with the gospel of Christ for more than a transitory period of one's life.

One could multiply examples — the British agricultural engineer who fitted the heater in our Land Rover, working two evenings until midnight to complete it; or the elderly American businessman who phoned from the Crystal Hotel (new twelve-storey pride of Masan) with colicky pains. He emptied his wallet of US$20 and 4000 won in gratitude for my visit, and thus was provided food money for one of our patients for a month.

I haven't spoken of fellow-missionaries, both Protestant and Catholic, with whom we cross paths — some with whom we enjoy fellowship at a deep level; others with whom we differ sharply. There have been only a handful altogether in Masan, rarely more than six Protestant and Catholic combined, but with both medical and Scripture Union work spanning the width of the country we meet many others further afield.

Neither have I spoken of the other visitors from overseas, some mission representatives, some family or friends, some friends of friends, some self-invited; mostly thoughtful and generous; occasionally like the Australian supporter of another mission who quite unconsciously assumed that his long-term support of the mission entitled him to free hospitality and chauffeuring by the missionaries in all the countries of East Asia that he visited. Most are necessarily dependent, for lack of language and knowledge of local lore; some eminently adventurous, like Hayden Melsop of OMF in South Africa, who presented himself on our doorstep one evening, having arrived unexpectedly in Seoul, found his way to Masan, and from there to our house beyond the outskirts (this last part being the most difficult). He had not been in China for nothing. Later, when we returned to Seoul together, found our train stranded in floods, and spent half the night in a police station for being out after curfew, he regaled us with stories of the Japanese police tactics in occupied China – just to reassure us!

Yes, diversions are many, some frustrating, most delightful; some necessary, most needing to be carefully disciplined. It might be thought from this catalogue that precious little time can be left for the job in hand. This is provincial Masan. In Seoul the problem is multiplied! The foreigners' church; inter-mission meetings; the social round; Christian women's lunches; passing visitors – all take their toll, and the conscientious missionary needs courteous courage to sift out the important from the trivial, the necessary from the needless, the appointed tasks from the distractions. *I was sent only to the lost sheep of the house of Israel* . . . and yet *O woman, great is your faith! Be it done for you as you desire.*

Yes, priorities were important for the Lord. Priorities are important for His servant today.

You are the Christ, the Son of the living God.
*If any man would come after Me, let him deny himself, and take
up his cross and follow Me.* (Matthew 16.16, 24)

16

The Christ and the cross

Chapter 16 is the watershed of Matthew's gospel because in it the disciples, headed by Peter, most clearly understand the Person of their Master. 'You are the Christ, the Son of the living God.' It is not the first time that such confession has been wrung from their lips (Cf 14.33), but it marks the climax of their understanding of His Person.

It is also the watershed because here most clearly the pathway to the cross opens before them. *Jesus began to show His disciples that He must go to Jerusalem and suffer many things . . . and be killed, and on the third day be raised.*

The disciples recoil in horror at the prospect, but just as they have been strictly charged not to make Him known as yet (16.20), so they are strictly taught that there is no bypassing of the cross, either for the Master or His disciples.

The chapter is also important because these two themes are set against a backcloth of the prevalent religious attitudes of the day. The Pharisees and Sadducees ask for a sign (16.1). The disciples are warned against the leaven of the Pharisees and Sadducees (16.6).

It is at the hands of the elders and chief priests and scribes that the Son of Man will suffer (16.21). The conflict with these forces will become inescapably dominant in the ensuing chapters.

In laying the foundations for Scripture Union in Korea these two major themes — the Christ and the Cross — have recurred again and again. To understand the complex nature of the task involved in steering a new venture on course it is essential, too, to understand the prevailing climate of religious assumptions. Without knowing the wind and the tides it is impossible to keep on course and avoid the many shoals and rocks awaiting the unwary.

Korea has borrowed from the Chinese language a number of epigrammatic phrases that neatly sum up human actions and attitudes. Mostly constructed of four Chinese characters, they are revelations of human behaviour, and warnings to the alert. One such is the phrase *Yoo Ah Dok Jon,* the meaning of which could be paraphrased, 'I alone am worthy of exclusive respect.' An attitude by no means confined to the Orient, it is nonetheless greatly enhanced by Confucian traditions. The traditional picture of the Confucian teacher is of a man of wisdom and authority with his disciples seated at his feet. They are *his* disciples. They hang on his words, and the more accurately they can repeat them back to him, the more perfect their discipleship.

There is much that is attractive in Confucianism; it produces a stability in society and in the family that is to be envied in today'd world. But at heart it is a feudal system — relationships are strictly vertical

     King and Subject
     Teacher and Disciple
     Husband and Wife
     Father and Son

The head is an autocrat: the place of the underling is unquestioning subservience. Where you have a strictly pyramidical society with no deviations the whole hangs together admirably, and in this lies much of the traditional stability of society in China, Japan and Korea in bygone centuries. But in the complex interrelations of cosmopolitan society today the stability is less easy to maintain.

The corollary of being one man's unquestioning disciple is that the disciple cannot easily change his master or have more than one teacher. The corollary of expecting total personal loyalty from disciples is that they need constant watching lest some other teacher should steal them. Nowhere is this tendency more clearly revealed than in the religious sphere. Beneath many of the splits within the church, the rivalry between leaders, the difficulty of co-operating across denominational barriers, lie deep roots of Confucian thinking.

Perhaps, among other things, something of this lies behind the Lord's exchange with His disciples over leaven and bread.

Beware of the leaven of the Pharisees and Sadducees, says the Lord.

'We forgot the bread. He is telling us that just as the Pharisees wouldn't be beholden to common men for "unclean" food, so we should dissociate ourselves from them. Don't borrow bread from a Pharisee and don't have anything to do with them. We are to switch sides from them as our teacher,' they conclude among themselves.

'No, no, no!' replies the Lord, 'stop fussing about externals. I want you to be delivered entirely from this partisan spirit of whose disciples you are. This sort of teaching, this sort of human discipleship is destructive of true spirituality.'

And then He gently leads them on to that wonderful point of inspired confession — *You are the Christ, the Son of the living God.* Yes, they are to be His disciples, not as one teacher among many human teachers, but as standing over all human teachers. 'In Him all things consist. He is the head of the body the church . . . that in everything He might be pre-eminent' (Colossians 1.17, 18). The point was made, but the problem would recur many times within His own lifetime, in the early church, and ever since. 'The Practice of the Pre-eminence of God is at a Premium.' It was essential that from the very start of Scripture Union in Korea we should establish this priority. Over what sort of issues did the problem arise?

One of the earliest matters was the question of membership. In most countries Scripture Union has a membership — a loose affiliation of those who are committed to a daily habit of personal Bible reading, generally following the Scripture Union plan. We found it advisable to avoid the term 'membership' completely in Korea. 'Membership' here carries strong connotations of exclusive loyalty. If I am, then, a Scripture Union 'member,' it is questionable whether I can be a 'member' of my local church in the full sense. My loyalties will be divided. The term carried too many false connotations for the potential 'member' himself, and for the leadership of the churches ever on guard against fragmentation and extra-church groups eroding their authority. Membership was dropped.

One of the first things we did in Scripture Union (and still do) was to issue an annual reading card. In some ways we regard this as even more basic to the Bible reading programme than the notes. It contains the essence of it all — consecutive daily readings of a length suitable to the average lay reader, a planned balance of Old Testament and New Testament, the stimulus to cultivate a disciplined daily habit, the reading method outlined. This last we regarded as crucial, for it emphasizes at a practical level that authority is ultimately vested in Christ and not in some human interpreter of Him, in the Holy Spirit speaking through Scripture and not in some human system of theology. It stresses that the medium of Scripture is God's appointed way of our knowing His Son, and not just that the content of Scripture is propositionally accurate concerning religion. The four steps of the SU reading method enshrine SU's approach to Bible reading and, as we were at pains to point out, enshrine at the same time the basic steps of biblical interpretation that had been amplified and developed in a multitude of theological works on hermeneutics. They are:

1. Prayer before reading, for the Holy Spirit is the Interpreter of the Holy Word.
2. Careful reading of the text, and seeking to understand its context, and meaning.
3. Application to life with the help of simple questions that emphasize the two purposes of Scripture
   (a) What does this passage reveal to me of God?
   (b) What does this passage reveal to me of God's will for my life and for men in general?
4. Prayer again, applying the lessons learned into today's life.

The readings' card enshrined the essence of our message, and was less open to abuse by those who would read only the notes and not the Bible text, or attack by those who would dispute the content of notes or see them as sectarian or 'unsound.'

For two consecutive years a readings' card was published jointly with the Bible Society following SU's reading plan and incorporating SU's reading method. Internationally in Asia SU and the Bible Societies enjoy close co-operation, and this sort of joint venture had been done in a number of countries. The Korean Bible Society is a long-standing and well-established organization with a fine modern headquarters on one of the main streets of Seoul. When Mr Yune and I called on the Society's

154

general secretary to discuss production of a joint readings card we waited first in the ante-room with his secretary, and then were ushered into the spacious office — expansive desk at one side, and comfy chairs either side of a coffee table, with a presiding chair at the head. Seating ourselves in these, having come straight from the cramped SU office with three standard desks and a borrowed table, we felt a little like schoolboys in the headmaster's study, but the general secretary was charming and friendly, and soon arrangements were in hand for a joint production of the following year's reading card. This was worked out in detail by Mr Yune and a member of Bible Society staff. It worked well for two years, but then foundered. It is easier and more comfortable to work within the confines of one's own organization. It is hard to develop that interchange that betokens true Christian fellowship under the overall Lordship of Christ.

There were problems in relationship with other organizations and the churches. Confidence had to be won; suspicion had to be allayed. Even more important was the internal development of leadership in SU staff, council and committees. Beginning from scratch with almost no one with any first-hand experience of SU or understanding of the ethos behind it, it was vital that those who would be in positions of leadership should understand the pre-eminence of Christ and the practice of faith at a deep and practical level. We shall take up the theme of the practice of faith in the path of the cross in the next chapter, but our present subject concerns the pre-eminence of Christ. In seeking to put this into practice it was essential that all who would be involved in leadership should understand the centrality of Scripture, and the nature of spiritual leadership. From the days of SU's association with the student movement there was a legacy of autocratic leadership centred in one Bible teacher (which later led to splintering within that movement). This we wanted to avoid at all costs.

No one leader was dominant within Scripture Union. Mr Yune was staff worker and subsequently General Secretary. Much of the initiative and hard work of development was in his hands, but he was answerable to the advisory committee that later became the national council. John Wallis was first chairman of that council, succeeded by me, and later by Professor Kim Heng Kwon (the first treasurer). Note-writing and translation of other materials was farmed out as widely as possible. Besides Mr Yune, Council members Mr Hong Chi Mo, Mr Stephen Lee and Mr Choi Nak Jae as well as a wide group of others were involved in writing. Subsequently, regional committees operated largely autonomously, with visits and a guiding hand from Mr Yune.

Right from the start, work was developed by Mr Yune in Seoul, John Wallis in the Cholla provinces of the south west, and ourselves from Masan in the south east. We deliberately sought to avoid concentrating everything in one Seoul office. This had the advantage that no one person could easily dominate the whole. Almost every other Christian organization in the country could immediately be identified with the person of its dominant leader. This we sought assiduously to avoid. Christ must be, and must be seen to be, the dominant Head over all, uniting a tenuous but widespread work and blending into harmony the personalities and contributions of the different people involved.

This was particularly important in the delicacy of relationships between local and missionary personnel. So often we had seen unhappy trends in the development in Korea of movements with international links. Either the work was run entirely by the foreigner, in which case the Korean personnel were employees of the foreign boss and often deeply unhappy at the mistakes made by this boss who was too proud or aloof to listen to the advice of people who understood the local culture intimately: or, conversely, the work was entirely in Korean hands and run largely on traditional Confucian lines. Then the foreigner served as a supply of finance and a front behind which an organization grew up, the inner workings of which he had only the faintest inkling. It was not necessarily that these workings were corrupt, though sometimes they were; rather they were according to a system that basically ran counter to the gospel, for it gave pre-eminence to a man and not to the Christ. These situations usually ended in frustration, and the foreign missionary returning home just at the point when he should have been at his most productive. If he did understand the inconsistencies within the movement, he felt himself powerless to correct them.

We were working for a structure within which Korean leadership could express itself, foreign missionary contribution could be creative and catalytic, and the whole actively under the Lordship of Christ. To this end it was essential that the Bible should be an open book for staff, council and committee members. Just as the unity and motivation of our hospital staff in Masan was built around group Bible study at the start of each day, so the two or three members of staff in the SU office would gather at the start of each day to read the day's portion and discuss it together. Many were the times when John Wallis, on one of his frequent visits to Seoul from provincial Soonchun, would alight from the night train at six am, eat his breakfast at the all-night restaurant of one of the central hotels, and then begin the day's work by joining the little gathering — patiently, slowly, progressively, together submitting to the authority of God's Word. From the start of our monthly council meetings in Seoul we established the pattern of beginning with study of the day's portion and prayer together arising from it. Sometimes it seemed barren; sometimes it would go on for forty minutes or more — but always the goal was before us. 'If we are to establish a real Bible reading movement, we as a council must be subject to God's Word.' It was a new approach for many of the council members. Although among them were theologians, university lecturers and businessmen, rarely had they had opportunity together to seek light from God's Word without a dominant expositor who would hold the stage while the remainder assumed the position of a silent audience.

Beginning in the latter part of 1975, we began to gather together regional committees for the promotion of Scripture Union. The function of these was to draw together those interested or potentially interested in the work, stimulate promotion and initiative at the local level, and subsequently support local distribution workers.

One of the first of these was in Pusan. A distinguished group of people gathered. Our friend Kim Chin Kyung, whom we had first met on his way to study at Bristol back in 1960, took the first initiative by introducing us to Mrs Yoo, an outstanding Christian lady and headmistress of the large Isabelle Girls' High School. She brought several lady friends, among them a university teacher and the wife of the chairman of a large plywood factory. The chairman's wife, Mrs Cho, moved in a sphere of cultured affluence, yet maintained a humble Christian heart. One of our finest meetings was in her home. As we sat in her spacious lounge in plush leather chairs with a thick carpet before us, and multiple works of art and beauty around, we read Psalm 34 together. As we went round the room, each had some contribution, some verse that had lit up for them, some thought from the text that was relevant to daily living. 45 minutes later, there was not much time left for committee discussion, but the Lord had been among us and we had been nourished. It was this sort of feeding upon God's Word that we wanted to multiply among rich or poor up and down the country.

Headmistress Mrs Yoo, herself a mature Christian and a very able person, yet confessed to us shortly afterwards that SU had become such a help to her personally. She had always known that she should read the Bible regularly, but somehow the pressure of life and lack of a plan, had meant that very often it had been missed. Now, with this simple tool, she was finding herself able to apply it consistently, even in the midst of a very busy life, and it was proving a blessing to her. We longed to see this kind of testimony multiplied among all sorts of men and women throughout the land. The pathway would be slow and hard, and the pitfalls many. We shall look at some of them in the next chapter.

Why could we not cast it out?
Because of your little faith. For truly, I say to you, if you have faith as a grain of mustard seed, you will say to this mountain, 'Move from here to there,' and it will move; and nothing will be impossible to you. (Matthew 17.19-20)

17

Faith

'God's work done in God's way will never lack God's supplies.'
(J. Hudson Taylor)

Chapter 17 of Matthew's gospel is in many ways an amplification of the two major themes we noted from chapter 16. While Peter, James and John receive vivid reinforcement of their understanding of the sole supremacy of Christ on the mountain (*This is My beloved Son ... listen to Him*), the remaining disciples are humiliated by their failure to cast out the demon. When asking why, they are told, *because of your little faith.*

We are often taught, and rightly so, that the opposite of faith is fear, or the opposite of faith is unbelief. But there is another and perhaps commoner opposite of faith. Faith is reliance upon God; the opposite of faith is self-reliance. This may be personal self-sufficiency over which, perhaps, the disciples stumbled ('we can manage this one'), or it may take a wider form of reliance upon human structures, personal links, and string-pulling, and the whole framework of human life organized without reference to God.

Hudson Taylor was led to establish the 'faith basis' of the China Inland Mission for two reasons. Firstly, he didn't want to compete or to appear to be competing with other existing organizations. Secondly, in the prevailing atmosphere of the churches of 19th-century Britain, a clear testimony to the faithfulness of God in practical living was desperately needed. In this he followed in the footsteps of George Müller of Bristol. For the same reasons, the same testimony is vitally needed in Korea today.

One important aspect of the cross, shown here in the preparation for it that the Lord was giving His disciples (Matthew 17.12,

22-3) and His emphasis to them of the necessity of cross-bearing on their part (16.24) was just this. The cross expressed, more clearly and fully than any other event, utter dependence upon God over against self-reliance or reliance upon the human structures of religion. This reliance upon God, of course, is in the context of faith that, *He will be raised on the third day.* Such reliance is never completely learned in this life; lapses are frequent and the patience of the Lord amazing, but opportunities to exercise the faith that 'God's work done in God's way will not lack God's supplies' abound in a host of minor matters as well as bigger ones. Perhaps the amusing little incident at the end of Matthew 17 (24-27) is meant to make this point. Nowhere is this principle of faith more important than in laying the foundation for a new work, and the present chapter seeks to record some of the incidents involved.

- - - - - - - - - - - - - - - - - -

When Scripture Union was launched in mid-1972, money was put down for rent of the office room, and Mr Yune's salary as staff-worker was underwritten by the Council of Scripture Union's ANZEA (Australia, New Zealand, East Asia) region. It was projected that there would be an annual grant from ANZEA funds, declining over five years, after which time Korea Scripture Union should be self-sufficient.

The system of rental employed in Korea is an original one. Generally the tenant pays down a substantial lump sum (up to half the outright purchase price), and the owner gathers his rental from the interest on this sum — generally let out on private loan at rates of interest considerably higher than those offered by the banks. Sometimes this may be partially remitted and the balance paid in monthly rental calculated at three percent per month of the lump sum remitted. Not infrequently in purchasing a property a prospective owner will count on the 'key money,' as the tenant's deposit is called, to pay for the property. Then, as he lets out part of it, he repays his debts to the previous owner. The lump sum rental deposit is returnable on departure of the tenant, but it can readily be seen that the owner does not always have the substantial sums to hand. Thus rental is always something of an adventure of faith. Furthermore, as prices (and property values) rise every six months or so, the landlord may demand further key-money deposit to keep pace with the current value of the property.

For these and other reasons the Scripture Union office in Seoul has occupied at least six different premises in the course of its first six years. Ultimately the aim is to purchase permanent office premises, but in the meantime the insecurity and frequent upheavals have been a necessary school of faith for staff and council. Never has God abandoned us homeless.

From the first noisy room rented from the guitar school, the office moved to a back room of business premises operated by a friend of Mr Yune's. His boss, coming in from the provincial factories of the firm, objected, and a move was precipitated. In a generous gesture of fellowship and faith, the Hospital Christian Fellowship of Korea, who had recently rented premises too large for their current needs, made room for Scripture Union. Eighteen months of happy co-operation with them followed. Then mounting costs meant that they had to contemplate a move. Our presence was clearly an embarrassment, although they didn't complain. Yet again, time to move.

Narrow accommodation was secured in a four-storey building on a wide thoroughfare in Central Seoul. The building was owned by a Korean herb doctor, who lived on the top floor and operated his clinic at ground level. The other two floors were let out to tenants. Scripture Union acquired space on the first floor, and for nearly two years this L-shaped room, and later slightly larger accommodation on the second floor, housed the headquarters of SU in Korea. As I came up the cement steps after the six-hour train journey from Masan, the pungent smell of Korean herb medicines drying on the landings would greet my nose. Inside, Mr Cho would look up from his desk and greet me with a cheery smile. (You will remember that he had moved from work in our hospital in Masan to the SU offices in Seoul.) Then the cheery smile would fade as he would recount the shortage of funds.

'I don't know where salaries will come from this month.'

'We haven't paid the printer for the last lot of notes yet.'

'The landlord is asking for more key money and more monthly rent.'

Yes, Mr Cho handled the accounts. There had never been any money to spare in the hospital. Now there seemed to be less than ever. Again and again we had to pinch and scrape, pray and wait, and encourage each other once more that 'God's work done in God's way will not lack God's supplies.' Many were the opportunities for the exercise of faith and, although we were never affluent, we always had enough. We look forward to the day of more settled things — permanent office, steady income, stable finances — and that day will come, but we tremble lest this should herald a weakening of active trust in the living God. Now is the time to strengthen the habits of faith. Now is the time to prove to ourselves and to others that 'God is faithful.'

During the time that we were in those premises over the herb doctor's clinic another crisis arose. It was found that to be within the law we had to have a publishing licence for dated materials in the same way that the publishers of a monthly or quarterly magazine or journal needed one. That was in April 1974. Paper for printing was in short supply, and the government licensing authorities were necessarily being very cautious about issuing new licences. We applied to the relevant government body, and we also applied to God in prayer for His overruling. In former times, an appropriate 'gift' to the officials concerned would have been the normally-accepted means of achieving the desired end. In recent years, much of this has been eliminated, and by a judicious balancing of improved civil servant pay scales with severe punishment of sample offenders at every level, the habit and necessity of 'oiling the wheels' has very largely been removed. Nonetheless, old habits die slowly. The temptation was there. Perhaps a token gift — not money, that would be too blatant — but perhaps an attractive book or some of the fancy cakes that Seoul bakery shops make up in gift boxes. But no! If government was set on eliminating this form of favour-seeking, then it was incumbent upon us from Christian conscience to support the policy in letter and in spirit. We would make application courteously 'through the usual channels', and commit our cause to God.

The wheels of government turn slowly anywhere. Early June approached. Material was in hand for the next series of notes beginning July 1st. Mid-June drew on: still no answer. A courteous enquiry drew blank. The material was sent to the printers . . . the type was set . . . and still no word. Further delay would mean late distribution, disruption of the habit of reading so newly established, loss of readership.

The morning of June 21st came; only one working week left to print, bind, and distribute the new series of notes. The phone rang. Mr Cho lifted the receiver to answer the call.

'This is the publishing licences section of the ministry. You may come and collect your licence this morning.'

Thus quietly, almost casually, the situation was relieved. The doors were open, and gladly we went forward. That licence still hangs framed on the office wall. Our publishing licence, yes, but more than that, certificate of the faithfulness of God: certificate that it is not in vain to apply to the living God in time of need. We learned subsequently that seven similar applications had been filed by different businesses at that time. Ours, and one other, were the only ones granted.

The timing of this licence was dramatic, but the resolution of the problem so quiet and unostentatious. We were to find this again and again. Occasionally there would be dramatic incidents of the Lord's provision. More commonly, the eye of faith had to trace the goodness of God in humdrum daily life.

Two other areas became spheres of opportunity for the exercise of faith: leadership and finance. We have touched on the first of these in so far as it concerns the pre-eminence of Christ over against the dominance of human leadership. It has been, and still is, a challenge to the daily walk of faith to maintain the stance that self-effacing leadership giving room to the Lordship of Christ is the most glorifying to God and the most closely aligned to our aims of a biblically structured movement promoting the effective use of the Bible.

One day some members of the Pusan Committee of SU said to me, 'We like the devotional emphasis of SU, but we wish we had more dynamic leadership.' This was partly criticism levelled at Mr Yune, partly at the whole framework that was growing up. If there was leadership with more personal charisma, so the argument went, young people would be more readily attracted; the movement would take off, and have sweeping results. The argument is a common one and, as we have seen, almost every movement in the country has its dynamic personifications at the head — general secretary, president, director, or whatever he may be termed. The movement then revolves around him and his teachings, and the end result is a structure not unlike that of Mr Moon's Unification Church. Again and again within the fold of doctrinally orthodox Christianity, or among the sects, we were to see this kind of Christian leadership emerging, and we were very sure that we wanted to avoid it.

The friends in Pusan saw the point, but it is terribly easy for even mature Christians to be carried away in the tide of enthusiasm surrounding a dominant and attractive personality. Self-effacement does not mean weakness or lack of purpose. Deliberate avoidance of publicity (*Tell no one the vision, until the Son of man is raised from the dead*) is not a sign of petty thinking, content only with little things, but it does require the continued exercise of faith that God, in His own time and way, will vindicate His Name and do a deep and lasting work among His people.

Finance was the other area for the exercise of faith. One day Mr Yune and I were travelling together by comfortable express bus on the new highway across the south coast of Korea. We were going to strengthen the links with friends in Soonchun — friends that John Wallis had made during the eighteen months he was there. He had won wide acceptance and laid the foundations for a wide influence of SU in the churches; but now we had no one to take his place, and these tenuous links had to be strengthened by visits from Mr Yune and myself as well as others as time allowed.

'I wish,' said Mr Yune, 'we could adopt OMF's approach to finance in SU.' My heart sang as he went on to explain what he meant. Current attitudes to fund-raising in the churches and other Christian organizations are so competitive, so preoccupied with human effort; leave so little room for the activity of God. What Mr Yune was seeking to avoid was the competitive spirit inherent in much self-advertisement in the Christian world (much of it a carry-over from commercial advertising), and self-centred attitudes preoccupied with 'getting' rather than 'giving'. '*You* should give to *me,* because (implied) what I am doing is more important than what you are doing.' Thus, what Mr Yune was advocating was not a theoretical stance that so-called 'faith principles' are more God-honouring than others, but that the realities of the situation in which we found ourselves demanded the sort of avoidance of self-advertisement that Hudson Taylor had found himself forced to adopt. He was not advocating a slavish copy of Hudson Taylor or of OMF, but rather that the

166

same conditions prevailed, and similar answers were needed. Perhaps a glimpse at current practice in Korea may help to clarify the matter.

I think of a church in the provinces with a plan to build a church hall. Plans were drawn up, a budget set, and then broken down to how much each elder and each deacon should contribute. No account was taken of personal circumstances and no opportunity given to dissent, except in a powerfully-controlled public meeting at which public dissent would have been a courageous matter, or earned scorn as 'mean' or 'unsacrificial'.

I think of another church not far from us, where the pastor spent weeks of his time travelling the country, calling upon fellow-pastors and acquaintances in business to elicit promises of donations for their building project. I think of a women's group where, in the course of fund-raising for a certain project, the names of donors and the amounts given were read out in the gathering amidst mounting applause for the larger donors, irrespective of private means.

I think of another church in a different city involved in rebuilding, where the figure of a million won per head set for an elder's contribution involved at least one elder in selling his house — by no means an isolated case.

I think of a student work in which the leadership moved on from a healthy biblical emphasis on sacrificial giving, to turning on the screws to wring contributions beyond their means from students. I think of two representatives of that group calling on a missionary friend of mine to solicit donations for the Christmas project of helping the poor in Chicago. (It was a healthy sign to see money flowing the opposite way across the Pacific, but not a little pride and nationalism was intermixed in the whole project, and a fanfare of publicity accompanied the presentation of the $8,000 cheque to an American organization.) The representatives castigated my missionary friend for his unwillingness to contribute handsomely, nor could they accept his further plea that for him, anyway, Christian giving was a family matter, and he was not at liberty arbitrarily to divert funds without family consultation.

In this prevailing atmosphere of hard business in the matter of Christian finance, it can more readily be seen why Mr Yune was attracted to a fresh approach.

Scripture Union and OMF are of one mind in their dependence

167

upon God in financial matters, but the detailed outworking of this has not been identical. OMF's lines are clear-cut. Financial need is made known to God alone in prayer, and only to man in answer to specific enquiry when this could not be construed as solicitation. SU has felt it right to make known publicly, in a restrained way, the financial needs of the movement generally and in specific projects. It is not a question of one method being more 'right' or more 'spiritual' than the other; merely that methodology is slightly different within a general framework of restraint and prayerfulness. OMF missionaries involved in work with SU or other organisations, in order to be consistent with OMF's 'no solicitation' policy, cannot be involved in 'fund-raising' for other organizations. For us, it is clear-cut and there-fore easier, but we stand on the sidelines, as it were, and see our Korean brethren grappling with the problems.

SU in Korea has not adopted OMF principles wholesale. Needs are made known when it is deemed appropriate, but it is an exciting and sometimes tantalizing experience to see the Korean leadership (council and general secretary) battling its way through to a common mind in financial outlook. Said someone in council one day, after several hours had been spent in facing up to the financial problems, 'Well, we can't go round begging for funds.' This just summed up the consensus, and the council as a whole brought matters before God in prayer.

There are two offshoots of this matter of finance that we must mention before the chapter closes, one international and the other internal. Both demand a response of faith.

Because SU is still little known in Korea, local giving to SU is sluggish. The publishing of notes and other material is basically self-supporting, but overheads, salaries and especially expansion have to come largely from donated funds. Whenever money is tight the temptation is to look overseas for funds. Money *has* come from overseas — from ANZEA council of SU, from International Council of SU, from donors in Britain, Germany, Switzerland, Australia and other lands — and this has been grate-fully received. However, the goal constantly before us is that SU in Korea should be self-supporting. There is money available in Korea today, and plenty of it in Christian hands. Our prayer and goal is that God should direct as much as He sees fit towards us, and that this, too, should demonstrate on the local scene the faithfulness of God. The input from overseas needs to be restricted. It is not so much that local self-sufficiency is the acme of Christian maturity (it can be merely the goal of local pride). International sharing has been a mark of Christian brotherhood from the earliest days of the church (Romans 15.20), but such giving must stimulate local initative, not substitute for it. Too often we have seen the fresh green shoots of practical faith buried under a cartload of generosity from overseas.

Secondly, in the development of the work there is a conflict of interest between fund-producing projects and faith-producing projects — or perhaps, more accurately, between fund-producing motives and faith-producing motives, for that which is effective in producing true faith will generally also produce feedback of funds in the long term. We shall see more of this later, but it affects the selection of publishing goals (Is it needed? Will it sell well?), young people's evangelism (heavy on staff: light on material rewards), and geographical expansion (travel and communication costs much less if all is concentrated in Seoul). In all of these we have sought practical submission to God's Word in the confidence that 'God's work done in God's way will not lack God's supplies.'

If you have faith . . . nothing will be impossible to you.

Who is the greatest in the kingdom of heaven?
Whoever humbles himself like this child, he is the greatest in the
kingdom of heaven.
Truly I say to you, whatever you bind on earth shall be bound in
heaven, and whatever you loose on earth shall be loosed in
heaven. (Matthew 18.1, 4, 18)

18

Colony of heaven

Part of the biblical understanding of the church is that she is a colony of heaven planted upon earth. Those who truly belong to her have their citizenship in heaven, and she is to portray the hallmarks of heaven in the context of earth. As the gospel story moves on relentlessly to its climax the Lord seems to take every opportunity of impressing upon His disciples the qualities that should characterise this colony of heaven —

Self-effacement (4)
Kindness and caring (5, 12)
Sensitivity to others (6-7)
A tender conscience (8-9)
A love for little ones and for the lost (10-14)
Reality in personal relationships (15-20)
and especially Forgiveness (21-35)

The disciples, all too preoccupied with the quest for greatness (1), and limited by the world's standards of forgiveness (21), are not quick to learn. The pattern is repeated in every growing church today. It is no easy thing to plant upon earth a colony of heaven that significantly reflects the qualities of heaven.

In this chapter and the next we shall be looking at one church and its struggles as representative of the whole.

The city of Masan lies on the south coast of Korea curved around the northern and western shore of a deep inlet from the sea. This inlet is some two to three miles wide. Fifteen miles to the south it opens into the sea after passing numerous islands. The northern and eastern end of the city is the newest, with large industrial zones in process of development. This area contributes much of the recent growth of population which has doubled the inhabitants of Masan in ten years to a current figure of over 400,000. The city contains some sixty churches of all denominations.

Down the western shore of the bay, the city is older and quieter. From the city bus terminus at the south-eastern end of the town a smaller road winds round the hilly coast between the power station and steel smelting works on the coastward side and the military tuberculosis hospital to landward. After a steep climb it emerges from a cleft in the rocky hills and descends into a quiet wooded valley with the government tuberculosis sanatorium below it on the left, and our clinic above it to the right. Passing these, another quarter of a mile brings you out into the valley stretching down to the western coast of the Masan inlet — a few paddy fields in the centre and, away to the left, a cluster of houses climbing the hillside from the water's edge.

Standing on a bluff at the entrance to the village is a simple whitewashed church clearly in view for anyone passing on the road. This is Kapo church, and Kapo village has been home to us for the last ten years. Continuing on that road as it winds off to the right further down the coast, you pass the fine white buildings of the Masan College on the right hand hillside, and the beach resort on the coastward side (no swimming allowed here any longer due to pollution); a mile further on the road ends at another village also included in the term Kapo. Here the houses are older, the community largely farming and fishing, the whole atmosphere traditional and rural. There is no church. Both villages come within Masan city boundary, but ours is semi-rural and combines many of the attractions of rural life with the amenities of city life. In referring to Kapo we shall be speaking of this village rather than the further rural one.

Kapo church reflects the semi-rural nature of the village. By and large the city churches are large and prosperous — at least after the initial pioneering struggles. The country churches are mostly smaller, less prosperous, and, like the countryside around them, suffer a constant drain of their best people to the cities. None the less we often find the rural churches spiritually stronger. Life is harder; temptations are fewer; there is less about which to boast, and the muscles of faith are exercised. Kapo church is a half-way house. It has been our home church for these years. We have worked in it (seeking to keep our contribution limited so as to stimulate local initiative rather than swamp it). We have learned to love its members as our friends and neighbours, and most of our hospital staff have worshipped here for some part of their lives. In a village community of little over a thousand people, with a fairly static population, neighbours get to know each other pretty well and the church as a colony of heaven, for all its failings, serves as light and salt in the community.

When we first came to Masan, the church was meeting in one half of a small L-shaped building. The other line of the L was the evangelist's house. Fifteen years previously the village community had been swollen by the influx of refugees from North Korea in the trails of war. Among these had been a church elder, Mr Kim. Himself a tuberculosis patient, he spent some years in the sanatorium, founded a church there for the patients, and, when he moved to live in the village, founded this village church. The present evangelist was himself a refugee from the North from the same period. The evangelist had little education, but great energy and real faith. Week by week thirty or so would gather on the floor of the little building for worship. Sunday School would meet at nine am in the same space, and several local girls were engaged in teaching at this. It was to the evangelist's credit that when, a few years later, the Presbytery placed an ordained minister in the church, he stepped down gracefully and remained in the congregation as a deacon, teaching Sunday School and occasionally preaching. Many would have moved.

In 1970 plans were laid for a new church building. Permission was obtained to build on the adjacent land (the whole valley belonged to the Ministry of Health), and early in 1971 a simple attractive building was erected with maximum seating capacity of about 200. The total cost was about 3½ million won and nearly all of this was contributed by the local congregation. A joyous and triumphant dedication service crowned the endeavour, with many of the village community joining in the occasion. It was an exemplary pattern of church development. Since that time the church has grown step by step until at the present time some seventy to a hundred gather on Sunday morning. How far has this 'colony of heaven' manifested the qualities of leaven' within itself and to the community around?

We were returning one day from a walk with the children on the path leading round the promontory above Kapo village. Struggling up the rough track below us was a hawker from town, his handcart laden with briquette coal; and coming up behind him, with his characteristic fast, springing, businesslike pace was Mr Han, the government-appointed village head, and a leading deacon in the church. We watched from above as Mr Han stopped, his slightly balding head bowed, and the shoulder of his dapper wind-cheater jacket was put to that cart to help it up the hill. As he reached the place where we stood at the top of the hill, the hawker stopped for a rest, and Mr Han went on his way. 'Who was that?' asked the hawker, turning to us.

'The village head,' we replied. A look of amazement spread over the man's face. This was in total contrast to his conception of the role of a village head.

Yes, Mr Han is highly esteemed, not only in the village but in the city as a whole, as an exemplary government servant and sincere Christian. Kindness counts.

Shortly after New Year 1972 the church organized special evangelistic meetings. Not being able to afford to invite a visiting evangelist, they asked me to take the meetings. They wanted to advertise them as 'Great Revival Meetings'. We stuck out for the more simple 'Evangelistic Rally'. There were three morning Bible Readings on Romans for the Christians and four evening rallies of which I took three. We took straightforward themes of the gospel —
  — Creation and the fall;
  — The Person of Christ;
  — Sin and redemption;
  — The Cross and Faith.
There were more non-Christians than Christians at most of the meetings. At the end of the meetings fourteen heads of families, as well as some others, indicated a desire to believe or to know more. Mostly these were unlettered, labouring men, able to read but largely having lost the habit. For the most part there was a genuine desire to seek the Lord, as far as we could judge. We had one follow-up meeting for them at our house, but were anxious

that the church itself should take on the responsibility for discipling them. Sadly we watched as one by one they fell away. No special teaching was arranged for them. The standard church services were too 'difficult' for them to assimilate, and they received too little teaching to nurture them. They had no resources to deal with the pull of drink and society around them. One lasted longer than most. He had a keen Christian daughter. However, he too was sucked back. Later his daughter became pregnant by a man who had left his first wife; then she married him, thus entering on a miserable life with a bullying, dominant man.

Another who lasted fitfully was the father of Miss Son of our hospital staff; but the most significant convert of those meetings was Mrs Ma, mother-in-law of Mr Cho, our hospital clerk. Mrs Ma was Japanese, though married to a Korean. For some years she had been closely associated with a Buddhist sect related to the Japanese Sokka Gakkai. This flourishes particularly among women in the villages. They meet in houses and chant *Nam Yuh Horang Keki,* facing to the east. They claim a wide variety of healings from rheumatic pains, varicose veins and other ailments, and they also had a little shrine in the village. Mrs Ma was the leader of the village group, equipped with books, vestments, rosary and images. Mr Cho and his wife were praying especially for her. On the Wednesday evening of our evangelistic rallies, I dropped in on their meeting before ours (somewhat to their consternation), and invited anyone to attend. Mrs Ma came. Next night she came again without further invitation, and Friday night she was there once again for the final meeting. On Saturday morning she asked Mr Cho to come round, handed him all her accoutrements, asked him to take them away and burn them (she was afraid to do it herself) and declared that she would follow the Jesus way. The ladies in the church gathered her up. She never looked back in faithful attendance at church, but we sometimes wonder how much *real* understanding of the faith she has. Lack of on-going teaching in the church means that it is hard for her to grow spiritually, and it is difficult to tell if she really knows the Lord, or if she has merely exchanged one religious framework for another.

As well as the daughter who was Mr Cho's wife, Mrs Ma had a younger daughter, Ae Ja, a Sunday School teacher contemporary with Miss Son and Miss Kim, the labourer's daughter mentioned above. Both Miss Son and Miss Kim married unbelievers, but Ae Ja chose differently. Against considerable family pressure she married a delightful Christian young man, the son of a watch-repairer and church elder in a nearby town. The family's complaint was that the young man had one leg weakened from childhood polio, and walked with a limp. Ae Ja (like the Lord Himself) looked on the heart and not on the outward appearance, and it was a delight to see them visiting from time to time afterwards — a happily united couple, with a great delight in their children.

The church continued to suffer from lack of teaching, but weakness in the pastoral ministry had a counter-balancing benefit. The church did not suffer from the inertia of the dominant one-man-band type of leadership. Lack of strong leadership on the part of the ministry threw the initiative back on to lay leadership, and tended towards more of a family fellowship with a number of men and women sharing the decisions and work. Mr Han was prominent in this, and his hand was strengthened by the coming of Mr Chung, a young and active church elder. He was a primary school teacher, and was posted to the Kapo school. One day Mr Han said somewhat wistfully to us, 'What can the sheep do when the shepherd is asleep?' 'Go direct to the Good Shepherd,' was our reply. 'He neither slumbers nor sleeps.' These laymen were beginning to learn the reality of communication with God.

We tended to exercise our influence by occasional preaching ministry when invited, and more especially through our hospital staff members who were also members of the church. If I were to make suggestions, it was all too easy for them to accede without real understanding. Our staff members were younger than the church leadership. If their suggestions were adopted, it would only be as a result of real conviction. Physiotherapist Mr Lee, and Mr Park, were the most influential in this. Through them we saw SU reading adopted by twenty or thirty families in the church (with varying degrees of success). Through them we saw the Friday night house meetings taking on a new form. Instead of being merely informal hymn sandwich and sermonette, they slowly became discussion Bible studies, based on the SU readings. Progress was slow. It was a new concept. Some who had been in the church for decades didn't know the most elementary aspects of the Bible. One vainly searched for Psalms in the New Testament. People were shy to open their mouths. Having been bred in the habit of silent listening (or perhaps just silence), they were terrified of making a mistake or revealing their ignorance; but slowly it improved. Mr Park was especially adept at getting people to relax, contribute, and laugh. Fellowship was beginning.

There is still a long way to go. A colony of heaven is so easily engulfed, and only solid, persistent, patient teaching of God's Word will arm it to show forth the qualities of heaven down here on earth.

They are no longer two but one flesh. What therefore God has joined together, let not man put asunder.

Let the children come to Me, and do not hinder them; for to such belongs the kingdom of heaven.

Go, sell what you possess and give to the poor, and you will have treasure in heaven; and come, follow Me. (Matthew 19.6, 14, 21)

19

Family of God

Associated with the Lord's strong view of the sanctity of marriage, especially in the present context of teaching related to the kingdom of heaven, is also, perhaps, the thought of the family as a picture of the church, and vice versa (developed by Paul in Ephesians 5). In both, the basis of mutual trust based on mutual faithfulness is sacrosanct. To mar this is a terrible thing. Certainly in Kapo church and village we have seen the vicissitudes of family life working to the building up of the family of God — and to the undermining of it also. In the present chapter we shall be looking at some of these, but first a glance at family structures in a world of change, and how they are reflected in church teaching.

Traditional Confucian family structures still play a major part in the life of a community such as Kapo village. Age is all-important. Husband and father play the dominant role. Generally, marriages are still partially arranged by parents (or at least parental approval is expected). A new daughter-in-law spends many years subservient to mother-in-law, the latter often a domineering personality. So long as each member submits to the system, it provides a secure framework for life. Individual members are cushioned against hardship and calamity by a caring wider family; stability and continuity are maintained. The price is submission, and many today are not prepared to pay it. The independent nuclear family strongly portrayed in immigrant western culture is very attractive, and many opt for it. But not a few find that the price of independence is higher than that of traditional interdependence.

The two strands can also be traced in church life. The extremes of modern individualistic decision evangelism appeal to young and old alike. Many respond, but for many decision for Christ is like a marriage of convenience, later to be dropped, leaving a sourness and sadness. Happily, by the grace of God, there are many fine Christians who are the only ones in their family, but generally we find it is those who have the support of a Christian family behind them who are the most stable.

Covenant theology, with its emphasis on solidarity in the people of God, fits the traditional mould very naturally, and Calvinism is the dominant theological force in the church. Sadly, when twentieth century change is modifying the extremes of rigid Confucianism in family life, it is all too common to see trends in the church pushing beyond the extremes of covenant theology. Thus it is commonly assumed not only that the children of Christian parents are included with the covenant but that, whatever their profession in adult life, they are necessarily Christians. We have frequently met in Kapo church enquirers who are taught that regular attendance at Sunday worship betokens inclusion among the people of God, and therefore within the covenant. After six months' attendance, they are enrolled for baptism, and after another six months they are baptized on minimal confession, whether they have any real understanding of the gospel or not.

This line of thought can be projected in a high church direction until it becomes almost indistinguishable from Roman Catholic theology. The church is the ark of salvation. Inclusion within her betokens membership of the kingdom of heaven. The church building is the temple of God (rather than the building within which the living temple of God meets), so it is important to expend considerable funds on the beautification of the building. The pulpit (central according to common Presbyterian practice) is termed an altar at which the minister (? priest) offers sacrifices in the name of the people (there is a subtle interplay and overlap of terms here that make it easy to slide in a sacerdotal direction). Alternatively, the communion table at which the offerings are received is an altar on which we lay our sacrifices while the choir sings

All to Jesus I surrender . . .

The attention is on the monetary offering rather than the heart's dedication of which it is a token. The trend is there in Kapo. It is much more pronounced in larger city churches. It seems an inevitable trend unless the corrective of careful biblical teaching is constantly applied.

The Lord, and Scripture as a whole, is intensely concerned with the individual: *It is not the will of My Father that one of these little ones should perish* (18.14).

Jesus said to him, 'Go — sell — give — come — follow.' (19.21)
Jesus stopped and called them saying, 'What do you want Me to do for you?' (20.32)

but all is set in the continuing solidarity of the people of God. The emphasis is on the kingdom of heaven (which is mentioned eight times in chapters 18-20) and membership of the community of God's people.

- - - - - - - - - - - - - - - - - -

Marriage. In the last chapter we saw some of the pitfalls into which some of the girls in Kapo church fell. Miss Son's husband came from a traditional country family near Pusan. They wanted him to bring his wife home, where she would be subject to mother-in-law and he would work the family fields. Much of the incentive to go in for television repairs in Masan arose from the desire of both of them to escape this sort of life.

Miss Cha was another girl of the same age. She attended staff Bible studies for a number of months although she worked in the adult sanatorium rather than with us. She clearly wanted to believe, but was held back by family pressure. She had a domineering mother, one of the strongest personalities in the village. To this mother, if her daughter became a Christian she would be limited to choosing a Christian for a husband. This must be opposed. Sadly, Miss Cha complied, withdrew from the group, and later was married to a man she hardly knew, who already had a strong taste for drink. It is sad to see the choice parents will make avowedly in their children's best interests.

Miss Chung was in the same group of girls. Although we knew her well over many years, she steadfastly refused to have anything to do with the gospel. She had reached this decision while still in high school, and stuck by it. She worked for several years as superintendent's receptionist in the sanatorium, and enjoyed the independence of a nine-to-five job and personal income. Like many girls her age, she liked to dress smartly in western clothes. Then came marriage into a traditional family in

Masan. Three months after her wedding she came to see us one day. It was the first time she had been allowed out of the house on her own. Her face told the story of the trauma of this transformation.

Miss Kim is a few years younger, one of our nurse-aides. An attractive, kind-hearted and hard-working girl, she has warmed to the gospel in the context of staff Bible studies, and shows obvious understanding and a believing heart. Of her own volition she has attended Kapo church regularly, but baulks at the step of baptism.

Why?

Marriage.

Hers is a kindly and united family in the village. Perhaps this makes it all the harder to step outside the bounds of parental choices and, in committing herself to Christ, commit herself also to marrying only a Christian. The battle still goes on. How hard it is to build the family of God here upon earth.

Happily, not all is tragedy. We described in chapter ten Mr Park's marriage to our nurse, Miss Lee. Hers was a traditional family. Her father was just retiring from a lifetime in the office of a country primary school. They were gentle and kindly parents. Mr Park was not a good marriage prospect as he had no father (lost in North Korea) nor any close senior male relatives. He had a regular income, but no capital. Miss Lee's father was happy to accede to his daughter's wishes, but her elder brother thought otherwise. He was serving in the army on the border with North Korea, but obtained compassionate leave and came all the way down south to deal with this young man who was leading off his young sister. Mr Park is forthright and often headstrong. The scene was set for an ugly clash, and he asked us to pray as he went to meet this brother in a tea-room that night. 'A soft answer turns away wrath.' Mr Park was so friendly and unruffled that the wind was quite taken out of the brother's sails. Eventually, he left without a word to say in opposition to the match. The grace of God had prevailed, and it is in the hurly-burly of life like this that spiritual maturity is developed. The brother returned half-way through the wedding, half-drunk, and tried to make a disturbance, but he was dealt with by other friends and neither Miss Lee nor her parents knew anything about it at the time.

And how does marriage work out? Mr Lee, of our staff, was married just about the time we first arrived in Masan in 1967. His wife, a country girl from simple background, had definite aspirations to luxury. As Mr Lee's skills developed and his salary increased, she had endless plans for house improvement. When he repented and trusted the Lord, she thought he had gone mad. Voluntarily to confess to pilfering was bad enough. To repay it from salary was total insanity. She was not antagonistic to the gospel — just totally immersed in a different system of values. They were not rich, but for rich or poor it is only the foolishness of faith that will count treasure in heaven greater riches than treasure on earth. Later, when Mr Lee would give generously from his salary not only to the church but also to Scripture Union and to individual patients in need, she would again find it impossible to understand.

Mr Lee worked patiently at his marriage. He made no bones about his faith and sought to give her every opportunity of teaching. On many occasions, where we had house meetings or there was some other activity, he would offer to stay at home with the children so that she could go (a Christian, but definitely not a Korean, attitude to adopt).

The family in the house next to them had many problems. Granny ruled the roost. Old grandpa slaved away in the fields. Father worked fitfully in the sanatorium. Mother (granny's daughter-in-law) was granny's slave. They had one little girl, but granny desperately wanted a grandson to continue the family line. It was not surprising that in this situation quarrels broke out, and not infrequently these arose between Mr Lee's wife and the neighbours during Mr Lee's absence. Occasionally he would have to hurry home at lunch time to a flurry of screaming women tearing each other's hair out. Not unnaturally, Mrs Lee expected her husband to stand up for her unconditionally. It was a situation in which Mr Lee developed the Christian art of forgiveness. He would work for peace and harmony, see the faults on both sides and work at reconciliation. The approach was Christ-taught, totally foreign to all that either family knew of relationships with neighbours.

No sudden miracles were wrought, but gradually things improved. Now Mrs Lee attends church regularly and is preparing for baptism. Their four children are growing up in an atmosphere of increasing harmony and tenderness. The family next door are also attending church, perhaps touched by kindness, more of which we shall see later.

Self-effacement
Kindness and caring
Sensitivity to others
A tender conscience
A love for little ones and for the lost
Reality in personal relationships
Forgiveness.

These qualities mark out the colony of heaven, the family of God. They do not come readily. Patient teaching of biblical standards, the response of faith, and a liberal dose of the grace of God, make up the ingredients. Mr Lee has set standards that others in the church are stirred to emulate.

- - - - - - - - - - - - - - - - - -

Birth. It is early dawn. The dog barks vigorously and we awake with a start. It could only mean someone on the front steps. A call from outside. This time it is not the hospital but Grandpa Koh, a neighbour of Mr Lee's. Please would the doctor's wife come quickly. Daughter-in-law is about to give birth. Granny has sent for help (a rare occurrence probably induced by panic in this instance).

Audrey hastily dresses and hurries down to the house. Some three hours later she returns for a late breakfast.

Yes, safely delivered, and it was a boy — but very jaundiced. Would I go and see? There had been no ante-natal care, and careful investigation led us to the sad but inescapable conclusion that this was congenital syphilis, a legacy of father's navy days which he had passed on to his wife. Treatment was instigated, but ten days later a panting and distraught mother arrived at the hospital at lunch-time with a bundle in her arms. Mrs Noh had run the quarter-mile uphill from her home, but it was too late. The long-awaited son was dead.

This incident led Audrey into ante-natal clinics for village mothers, with helpful organization from Mr Han, the village head. He would tramp round the houses letting it be known, and rejoiced in the opportunity of practical Christian ministry. He was a joy to work with. Nonetheless, attendance was fitful, and a sudden summons in the final stages of labour was still more common than preparation throughout pregnancy. Sometimes there would be two or three deliveries in a month; sometimes months with none. There were many obstetric hospitals in town, but prices were high and transport to town difficult at night. Audrey encouraged those who could afford it to go to town, but always there were some who would be having the baby at home, anyway, with help from granny or a neighbour. We were horrified at the high incidence of abnormal deliveries — two others with congenital syphilis, a face presentation in the Cha household with battle-axe Granny Cha staring in horror at the bloated lips of the new baby. I think she thought it was our fault that the baby looked like that, but our stock with her rose visibly when we confidently assured her that the swelling would subside within 24 hours, and the prediction came true. Another lost their baby through delay in the second stage of labour before Audrey was called. Another to whom Audrey was summoned lay in pools of blood, having haemorrhaged severely after giving birth to twins unexpectedly. They said that the sea ran red when the cloths had been rinsed out. The family only paid for one pint of blood to transfuse the mother, although we recommended two and she needed four. Both twins were girls, and the poor young mother hadn't the heart or strength to rear both. In spite of all we did to encourage her, one baby died ten days later. The other survived.

Audrey's ante-natal work revealed a host of problems among the women. Family planning was strongly advocated by government, and many women had had intra-uterine loops. Most of these loops had come out, or become infected, and not many women persisted with them. A few better-off ones used the pill, but for most the accepted method of family planning was recurrent abortion. There was hardly a married woman in the village who had not had an abortion, and many had had five or six. This applied to the Christians as much as to the non-Christians, and there was almost no Christian conscience in the matter. Only the Roman Catholics (and the Protestant missionaries) took a strong stand about it. We were disturbed, but merely saying 'tut-tut' was no answer. We have not really got any further in this yet.

Some of Audrey's deliveries in a Christian family were a

delight, where it was possible to pray with the family with real understanding. Others seemed shrouded in superstition and a darkness that the surface beauty and friendliness of the village generally concealed. A few began to attend church and seek the things of the Lord. All in all, a ministry of kindness was appreciated and became a part of the overall testimony of the family of God. The incidents of these last two chapters, both successes and failures, could be repeated in churches up and down the length of the country. They make up the substance of Christian living, the testimony of a colony of heaven, the family of God, in a world that is estranged from both.

Go into the vineyard . . . and whatever is right I will give you.
Behold, we are going up to Jerusalem; and the Son of man will be
. . . mocked and scourged and crucified.
You know that the rulers of the Gentiles lord it over them . . .
It shall not be so among you, but whoever would be great among
you must be your servant.
Two blind men . . . Jesus, in pity, touched their eyes. (Matthew
20.4, 18-19, 25-26, 30, 34)

20

Servants of Christ

In this chapter Jesus is still concerned with teaching the qualities that characterize the kingdom of heaven. In particular, He demonstrates to His disciples the qualifications for service and leadership in the kingdom. Peter had asked, *Lo, we have left everything and followed You. What then shall we have?* (19.27) The reply indicates that service in the kingdom should be concerned with service rather than rewards. It is enough to trust the generosity and fairness of the Master for remuneration. He underlines once again for them the inescapable imminence of the cross, and the importance of self-effacing inter-relationships. He then demonstrates for them, at the end of the chapter, the place of personal concern for insignificant people.

All of these things we have been learning with our hospital staff. Some of them have rubbed off on the life of Kapo church, through their influence. It is an approach to service that, rightly maintained, bears the fragrance of heaven, and one that is constantly eroded by the pressures of earth. Only by careful attention to the Word of God, a sensitive conscience toward Christ, and mutual forgiveness and encouragement in failure, can progress be made. The incidents that follow illustrate some of the tussles involved in the context of our work in Masan.

As we have seen earlier, Mr Park came to us in February 1973 to replace Mr Cho who moved to the SU office in Seoul. That was only three months before we were due to leave for nearly a year's furlough in Britain. Mr Park took on the administration and handled the finances of the hospital clinic. He was only 25 at the time, young, energetic and headstrong — something of a Peter by character. Both Mr Lee and Mr Jee, besides having been longer in the job, were considerably older. Humanly it was a recipe for friction, especially in our absence, but we felt this was the way God had led us, and that He would use the tensions of the situation to develop the character of those involved. This, indeed, happened in a variety of ways.

Mr Park carried the self-assurance of youth ('You can't do it that way,' he roundly declared to me within a few weeks of arriving, but later understood why we had come to 'do it that way'), but he was genuine, hardworking, and intensely honest. He learned to work within the limits of others' points of view. He learned to work for harmony, rather than bulldoze his way through. He was out on frequent trips with driver Mr Jee in the hospital land-cruiser (Toyota equivalent of Land Rover) up and down the dusty roads of mountainous, rural Korea, visiting the homes of patients, tracing those who had failed to return, checking on drug-taking, explaining to relatives the plan of treatment. The normal relationship between the two in secular society would be that of master and servant. The driver is there to serve: the administrator to dictate. These two learned, not without difficulty, to develop a teamwork relationship. Mr Jee, besides being older, was experienced, knew the roads, knew many of the patients and, although himself also hardworking and very willing, knew when to stop. He took a fatherly interest in Mr Park and, while respecting his wider education and position in the hospital, was able to mellow and mature him. It is a beautiful and precious thing when fellow-servants learn to serve and care for one another.

On several occasions we found that strife erupted just before we returned from a period away (maybe holiday or, as on this occasion, a longer period away in Britain). This time it was between Mr Lee and Mr Park. Mr Lee, struggling with shortage of dressings materials among the ward patients, appropriated some from the out-patient dressing room that were not being used. Mr Park, who was responsible for out-patient supplies, accused him of stealing. Angry words were exchanged. These led to mutual accusations and blows and, although Mr Jee had tried to pour oil on troubled waters, when we returned the two were not on speaking terms. As far as we could see there was no serious wrong on either side, but rather a situation mishandled, relationships marred and, behind it, an unspoken jostling for supremacy ('Why should *I* consult with *you* about *that*?') — truly the devil's mixture. Matthew 18.20, 24 reflects the situation, and the Lord's answers were intensely relevant. We worked hard with both toward apology and forgiveness, and eventually Mr Park apoligized for striking Mr Lee and Mr Lee apologized for not consulting Mr Park. Forgiveness was at first grudging, but ultimately full. A valuable lesson had been learned, and real fellowship became progressively easier in the years that followed.

Between the years 1974 and 1977, salaries for government servants in Korea went up about thirty percent a year, with additional benefits adding another ten to fifteen percent. (This was in conjunction with a continuing and largely successful anti-corruption drive.) Salaries in other jobs reflected this rise. Our hospital staff salaries were provided through a research grant and, as we worked in close association with a government hospital, were closely tied to salaries in equivalent government jobs. The aim was to provide a good salary for the job at the going rate. Although the decisions on salary scale were not technically mine, the staff knew that I had a large say in them, and in practice much of it devolved upon me. It was a delicate situation. People are sensitive about money anywhere in the world. We wanted a fair wage scale. The staff were technically in secular employment, and there was no cause to expect them to be content with a 'sacrificial level of income' for the sake of Christ. If there was to be sacrifice, it would be in the area of willingness to go the second mile for individual patients, or of voluntary giving out of salary. Yet it was important to develop the sense of trust — not just of me or of the institution, but of God. *Whatever is right I will give you.*

From time to time, when salaries were reviewed, we held a staff meeting for discussion, airing of grievances, suggestions, and so on. At one of these Mr Park established himself as spokesman and champion of the rest, and took the bit between his teeth in a style that would have done credit to the most militant of union leaders. The atmosphere stiffened. One sensed the uneasiness of the others. It was not that the demands were unjustified. It was the attitude that was wrong. Trust was giving way to hard bargaining, harmony degenerating into strife. It was necessary to rebuke him publicly, but to go along with most of the requests that were being made because they were right. Once again, the hard-won and easily-shattered peace was restored. This genuine harmony in the service of Christ is a precious and fragile treasure.

Shortly after Mr Park arrived in Masan, I was amazed to

discover that he had a list of the birthdays of each of the children in the Sunday School class he had taught in Seoul. Koreans don't set a lot of store by birthdays (except the first and sixtieth which is rather a long gap for most people), but here was a man who cared enough for this little group of a dozen children to know their birthdays and write to them individually when the time came. Here was pastoral potential. He had not been in Masan long before Kapo church asked him to take over the high-school group — at that time about fifteen boys and girls between thirteen and eighteen. Mr Park visited every home in the village that had a high-schooler in it, invited them to his own home, loved them, played with them and spent time with them, besides teaching the Sunday class. Before long the class was forty strong, and there was hardly a high-schooler in the village who was not attending. Quite a few of these fell off subsequently, but it was indicative of the impact that genuine caring could have upon young people. They were not merely being herded into a class for religious instruction. Here was someone who cared for them.

While we were away in 1973/74, Mr Park extended this work to embrace a united fellowship of high-school groups from nearly all the churches in town. He won the confidence of ministers and youth leaders, and they arranged a monthly Sunday afternoon rally. In the summer Mr Park, almost single-handed with the help of some of the Kapo group, organized a two-day conference for them, using our house and lawn as a venue (in our absence!). The opening day dawned threatening rain. Mr Park told later how he went to the church alone early to pray, setting himself to pray for several hours that the weather would hold for outdoor meetings. He had only been there a few minutes when he sensed it would be unbelieving and rude to plead with God any more. His prayer was heard and answered. The weather held until just after the close of the meetings. So is faith strengthened, and the reality of prayer learned in the context of service.

While employed at the hospital Mr Park, still a bachelor, used most of his spare time in this work with the high-schoolers, and in developing SU work in the churches locally. He was deeply convinced of the need for an SU approach to Bible reading among the young people and in the churches. He gave much time to talking to ministers about SU for their churches. He handled the distribution of notes and collection of payment, not only for the immediate area, but for the whole province, for Pusan, and later, when John and Kathleen Wallis had left Soonchun and our hospital outreach spread into the south west, for the whole of the Chunnam province as well. It was a vast area — ten million people, nearly two thousand churches. We were barely scratching the surface, but locally in Masan Mr Park had links in almost every one of the fifty churches in town. The fact that he was not employed to do this work and received no remuneration for it added strength to his influence. The fact that there was no big organization behind him and he was manifestly seeking to assist the ministers in their pastoral work, to contribute to the life of the church rather than detract from it, won him acceptance. He was labouring in the Lord's vineyard, and there was no other incentive but that the Lord had said, *You go* . . .

This was a start, but clearly if the work was to develop, more hands were needed. In 1975 Mr Park pushed us into taking on Miss Jae as SU worker in Masan. At first there was no visible basis for her salary, but gradually we gathered a committee in Masan to support her, and several members of hospital staff contributed regularly to her support. In 1976 Australian OMFer Cecily Moar completed basic language study and moved to Pusan with Miss Gwon, who had already been working for SU for two years. It was then possible to pass the care of SU work in Pusan to them.

At about the same time, two other workers in the south west region came forward in a voluntary capacity. One of these, in Soonchun, was an ex-patient. Cho Il Sun had come to us in 1968 as a teenage orphan boy with very far advanced chest tuberculosis. After several months' treatment with us, we had passed him on to rest-home care in Soonchun. There are two excellent medical works in Soonchun run by American missionaries, with whom we have co-operated closely. One is a leprosy and orthopaedic service based at the Ae Yang Won leprosy colony, made famous by Pastor Song Yang Won (central figure of the IVP books *The Seed Must Die* and *The Triumph of Pastor Son,* both excellent accounts of the life of one of the finest fruits of the Korean church). The other is a tuberculosis treatment service with two associated rest homes for long-term and 'incurable' patients. These two homes were distinguished by the somewhat euphemistic descriptions of the 'not-so-bads' and the 'not-so-goods'.

Cho Il Sun was written off by most of the doctors as hopeless. But through the next six or seven years he gradually won over

193

the disease, and although not strong he is today active and hard-working, and is attending a Bible School with a view to the ministry. Through his years of hardship he kept in touch with us, received SU notes regularly, and grew in faith. Today, as a sideline to his studies, he acts as SU agent for the area, enthusi-astically recommending and circulating the notes.

In 1976 further development was possible and Mr Park moved to Taegu, but before that we had to face a serious crisis together. A new senior doctor had come to the adjacent sanatorium. Our relationships there were always delicate, and we could not exist and operate satisfactorily without their goodwill. If this evaporated there were a thousand and one little ways of hamper-ing us, none of them big enough in itself to take issue over, but collectively enough to render our unit inoperable. Before returning from furlough, I had preached at one supporting church from 2 Thessalonians 3.1-2, 'Brethren, pray for us . . . that we may be delivered from wicked and evil men; for not all have faith.' Now we were to see the force of it and of the ensuing words, 'The Lord is faithful.'

This man set himself to oppose all that we were doing. For him a hospital existed for the comfort and benefit of its staff. Patients were an unfortunately-necessary means to that end. For us, the patient must come first, and if his rights and needs were infringed, we had to fight. Over the course of several months the issues were clarified. We would not fight for ourselves and our 'rights', but we had to stand up for our patients. The world says, 'God helps those who help themselves.' Faith says, 'God helps those who help others.' We would not engage in human strife, but we couldn't run away from the cross. Gradually the crisis rolled on to its climax. Increasingly we were hampered and misrepresented. Relationships with the adjacent sanatorium staff were poisoned, but this served only to draw our own team closer together, and incidentally to draw out some others to risk their necks in standing up for us. How grateful we were for that.

One morning, Mr Park, Mr Lee, Mr Kim and myself were discussing the problem and how to resolve it. It seemed a brick wall. We turned to Psalm 37:

'Fret not yourself because of the wicked, . . . they will soon fade like the grass

Trust in the Lord and do good; so you will dwell in the land and enjoy security . . .

Commit your way to the Lord; trust in Him and He will act.
He will bring forth your vindication as the light . . .
Be still before the Lord, and wait patiently for Him: fret not
yourself over the man who carries out evil devices!
Refrain from anger (how hard this was!)
Fret not yourself; it tends only to evil.
Yet a little while and the wicked will be no more; though you
look well at his place, he will not be there.
The meek shall possess the land . . .
The wicked draw the sword and bend their bows to bring
down the poor and needy, to slay those who walk uprightly.
Their sword shall enter their own heart.'

As Mr Kim read the words to us, we found ourselves, four
grown men, reduced to tears before the Lord — tears of helpless
frustration, yet tears of gratitude at the goodness and promises of
God.

Not long after, the Lord sent a new superintendent to the
sanatorium, an upright Christian man. This enemy's power was
curbed, and then he was posted elsewhere. We are grateful that
that sort of man is the exception. As an outcome of all this, a far
wider door was opened to us to admit adult patients and to care
for ward patients. It is not possible to escape the cross in the
service of the Lord, and we had learned valuable lessons.

When Mr Park moved to Taegu, besides his hospital work in
caring for our patients who came from that large province of six
million people he developed excellent relationships with
government health authorities. He established a framework of
referrals from their workers of the bone tuberculosis patients
that we were treating, and commended our work and His Master
widely in government circles. Much of his spare time was again
given to developing SU work in the churches, and this is still
taking shape. While there he was in fairly close contact with
several other Christian agencies in the medical field. Two things
he noted that he had learned in Masan and longed to see more of
elsewhere. One was patient-centred care — so easily lost sight of
in the mechanics of a larger institution. The other was genuine
fellowship between staff, which is so easily lost in a hierarchical
system if the senior administrators lose sight of, or have never
learned, the cardinal principle of Christian service that *whoever
would be great among you must be your servant.*

This chapter must close, as Matthew 20 does, with a little

story of a needy soul.

One day in out-patient clinic, the hubbub outside the examination room had risen so much above the normal level that I went out to investigate. I found on the steps of the hospital a poor spastic lady in her mid-thirties. She had been crippled from infancy, and was intensely ugly in the weird contortions of her face and arms, yet there was something appealing about her eyes. She was surrounded by a crowd of fellow-patients, some jeering, most just watching or giggling, while two members of staff were trying to explain to her that we didn't treat her sort of case, and that she should go home. She had spent a lot of money coming and had come to stay, she declared roundly in her slurred speech.

Bringing her out of the melée outside into the quiet of the examination room, we found a woman mentally quite normal under the outward ugliness. She lived in Chung Moo, a small port city two hours away, with her husband, a man crippled with polio. She attended church when she could, and they had recommended her to come to us. There was little we could do medically, but we could give her a rest and TLC (tender loving care — excellent treatment for a multiplicity of ailments) so, to the consternation of some staff, I said we'd have her in for ten days. Out-patient nurse-aide Miss Kim, leapt for joy and exclaimed, 'Oh good, Jesus would have welcomed her.' Scoffing is infectious, and so is kindness. She settled gratefully in the wards and returned home happily ten days later.

The story had a sequel when the lady returned a year later for another short stay in hospital. Our new nurse, Miss Kim (different from the above), had only just come. She looked at this new arrival with obvious misgiving. I said she needed a large dose of TLC. A few days later, going down the wards, I was delighted to see Miss Kim sitting on the lady's bed beside her (even the best of nursing rules are better broken sometimes) looking at her wedding photos. Of such is the kingdom of heaven.

If anyone says anything to you, you shall say, 'The Lord has need of them;' and he will send them immediately.

Hosanna to the Son of David! Blessed is He who comes in the name of the Lord.

He overturned the tables of the money-changers, and the seats of those who sold pigeons.

The blind and the lame came to Him in the temple; and He healed them.

The chief priests and the scribes . . . were indignant.

By what authority are you doing these things, and who gave you this authority?

The tax collectors and the harlots go into the kingdom of God before you.

The kingdom of God will be taken away from you and given to a nation producing the fruits of it. (Matthew 21.3, 9, 12, 14, 15-16, 23, 31, 43)

21

By what authority?

September 1968. We were coming to the end of our two-year spell in secular employment in Masan, and had been able to take a holiday in Hong Kong. We were exploring the channels for return as missionaries, and asking ourselves, 'Is it worth it?' 'Can we contribute anything?' Now with one small child and another on the way, was it wise to pursue a course of work in Korea? Would it not be 'safer' to settle at home again? Language was limited; we still had only the vaguest ideas of the problems in the church, and whether we could contribute anything.

My mind went back to that night when Audrey went into labour for our first child ... summoning Mr Jee to help us ... the two-and-a-half hour journey to Pusan ... the kindly and efficient Australian maternity hospital ... the apprehensiveness brought on by necessary curfew breaking, apprehensiveness relieved when the police at the check-point at the entry to Pusan, after a word from Mr Jee, hurried us on. Yes, apprehension — generally quite unfounded, but easily brought on by being a foreigner, and therefore never quite 'au fait' with etiquette or protocol. This contributed much to fear of the future and desire to go home. Beatrix Potter expresses it beautifully in *Pigling Bland.* Dutiful Pigling, in the midst of his adventures on the way to market, exclaims, 'I just want to go home and grow potatoes.' The dash to Pusan would soon need to be repeated, and Pigling's heart-cry was somehow symbolic of the deep-seated longing for a more congenial and settled life.

But, as we entered church that Sunday morning in Hong Kong, my eye caught words written into a cement block at the side of the path —

The Lord has need of you.

They expressed beautifully the conviction of our hearts, from which we could not escape. We were to be just a family of donkeys bearing the Master. Is it worth it? What can you contribute? *If anyone says anything . . .* It was enough that the Lord should say, *I have need of you,* and the rest could be entrusted to Him. Yes, the colts would have their place too — a family of donkeys, but privileged to bear the Master. It was a conviction that was to stand us in good stead when we returned nearly a year later, a small OMF team of five adults with four children under three between us.

July 1969. Joining John and Kathleen Wallis and Margaret Robertson in Singapore after six months in UK, we spent six weeks together preparing for our return. When Mr Arnold Lea, the Overseas Director, spoke to us of the hardships of missionary life, the spiritual conflict and the path of victory, some of us were tempted to ask, 'Why be so negative and pessimistic?' We were setting out on a new adventure, and it was exciting and challenging. We were to learn that the spirit of adventure is an ephemeral thing. The spirit of discipleship lasts.

However, for the present adventure lay ahead. Most of us had heavy baggage, and after a demanding spell in tropical Singapore, we all wanted to go by sea to Korea rather than by air, if a passage could be obtained at competitive rates. Nothing materialized.

Then one morning John Wallis, coming down to breakfast and browsing through the paper, noted in the shipping news:

MS Vega, Korea Shipping Corporation, sailing August 13th Singapore — Pusan.

Time was running short, and he had prayed that day that if it was right to go by sea, there might be something available. Enquiries revealed that it was a 7,000-ton cargo ship on its home run to Pusan after several calls in South-east Asia. The fare was very reasonable (later we discovered why), and the timing perfect. We were all of one mind that this was God's provision, and this was endorsed by the mission's administration office. The man in the booking office looked a little doubtful at our application for passage, but finally acceded. They took up to a dozen passengers, but had never had Europeans on board before.

In the closing hours of our time in Singapore, John and I dashed to the market to buy two big sticks of cheap miniature Singapore bananas, and a roll of wire netting. These were to prove our lifelines.

As we gathered on the quayside for farewells, one of the Singapore staff prayed for a 'quiet and restful' journey (amidst sniggers from the mothers, who could see no prospect of quiet or rest on this journey with four small children).

So started a week of steaming in the cabins, freezing in the dining room (ultra-powerful air conditioning), and dashing for small children before they disappeared overboard. The ship's rail was adequate for adults, but offered little protection against inquisitive toddlers. The wire netting served to fence off a portion of deck in which we placed the children like so many young pullets in a hen run, while one stood guard.

Supper the first night was cold rice, with cold raw cabbage, and a few dried fish. Supper the next night was the same — and the next, and so on until we reached Pusan a week later. For breakfast they sought to accommodate to the Westerners.

First morning: Cold fried eggs,
so, 'please may we have boiled eggs?'
2nd morning: Cold, hard-boiled eggs.
so, 'please may we cook our own eggs?'
3rd morning: Cold, hard-boiled eggs.
('Sorry, the cook forgot!')
after that, we had them to taste until the bread ran out and breakfast reverted to rice and fish soup. The bananas were our lifeline. The crew were very kind, but totally ignorant of a foreigner's likes and dislikes.

John spent a good bit of time on the bridge, and the officers would show him on the chart how there were typhoons all around, but we hardly met even a ripple. I think they regarded us as sort of Jonahs in reverse. After we had sailed past the steep eastern seaboard of Taiwan and sighted the first of Korea's off-shore islands, we slowly nosed our way into Pusan's beautiful harbour in the late afternoon of August 20th. Only then were we to discover that the ship was heavily overladen. As we drew away in a launch toward shore and looked back with a faint nostalgia (but little regret) to our MS Vega, we saw the rail only very little above the water line. If we had met a bad typhoon, we could have been in real danger. How graciously the Lord withholds things that might trouble fearful hearts, but afterwards allows us to see His loving hand.

We were greeted by loving friends in Pusan, and in the weeks that followed we somehow managed to clear our baggage, move to Seoul, get residence papers completed, the children settled, and a routine of language study established. The oft-repeated inner questionings, 'Why did we come back? Why live in this fog of apprehension born of only half understanding what's going on? What can we contribute?' were met again and again with the unadorned answer, 'The Lord has need of you.'

- - - - - - - - - - - - - - - - - -

The blind and the lame came to Him in the temple and He healed them. (21.14)

It is noteworthy how, in the midst of mounting controversy, the Lord maintained His ministry to ordinary people in need. The focus is not on that, but the fact was there (19.2, 20.33, 21.14). As we set about establishing our missionary role in relation to the churches, the continuing medical work was a needed and satisfying sphere of service.

During the week after that arrival in August 1969, several of us went on one of the regular clinic visits to Chung Moo, two hours away on the coast to the south west of Masan. On this occasion, or a similar one shortly afterwards, we were taken past a motley of barbed wire and oil storage tanks to a little shack of a house on a disused wharf by the seaside. There, on a makeshift bed, we found a lad in his middle teens lying on his back. Pale and wasted, he was none the less cheery. We discovered that eighteen months previously he had had a septic infection of both hips which had only been partly treated (money ran out). Since that time, he had been lying on his back with his legs splayed in a frog position, and pus discharging from both thighs. The cause was not tuberculosis in this case and, strictly speaking, he did not come within our province, but we admitted a number like this whom we thought we could help and for whom there was no other provision. He made slow progress over a number of months, and the discharge dried up, but his hips remained fixed in this useless position. Later, he would join in the joke of watching himself trying to waddle across the ward with crutches, with both hips fixed and splayed out sideways. His legs were spread so wide that he could only be got through a door sideways.

He was one of the cases for whom we were grateful for good co-operation with the American Presbyterian orthopaedic unit in

Soonchun. Besides being technically excellent, their prices were deliberately geared to the ordinary poor, being one-fifth to one-tenth of the price charged in other hospitals. Sung Yuli had one hip fixed straight and the other replaced with an artifical hip, with excellent results. Several years later, on another visit to Chung Moo, we heard a shout from the hillside and Sung Yuli came bounding down with just one crutch.

I last saw him once more in Soonchun; this time on a one-year course in tailoring in a small house training school set up in association with the hospital there for former patients. Now a tall and good-looking young man with only a slight limp and a clear and grateful faith in Christ, he was a delight to see; it is good to know that still today, the lame come to Him, and He heals them.

- - - - - - - - - - - - - - - - -

By what authority are you doing these things, and who gave you this authority? (21.23)

When we moved to Seoul at the end of August 1969 for language study, it was Dr John Kim who met us at the station with some of his students (see chapter 7). He was now teaching Church History in one of the Presbyterian seminaries in Seoul. He was very kind in helping us settle in, and welcomed John and Kathleen Wallis to his church, a pioneer venture in first-floor rooms of an office block in central Seoul. He introduced John to the seminary for a weekly English language lecture (they took Dr Packer's *Fundamentalism and the Word of God* as a text book).

We were also welcomed by a number of denominational leaders, who arranged a reception for us. This reception took the form of a sumptuous meal at Korea House, a cultural centre and tourist attraction. As young missionaries, we were flattered and humbled to be welcomed thus by these senior men — old warriors, all of them. After the meal the president, in the name of all, welcomed us formally. In the course of his remarks, he was at pains to explain why his denomination was the continuing stream of the formerly-united Korean Presbyterian Church. The other Presbyterian denominations were breakaways, but theirs stood in true line of descent from the original Presbyterian seminary in Pyung Yang (now capital of North Korea). It was the same story that we had heard from church leaders of another denomination concerning *their* position. We were to hear it repeated, either verbally or implicity, by the representatives of at least two other Presbyterian denominations. It was confusing to the newcomer, to say the least. *By what authority?* Wherein lay the truth?

Also in the course of his remarks, he stressed the Calvinism and reformed faith by which they stood. In the course of replying (by interpretation), I thanked him for his welcome and remarks, and commented that the faith by which we stood went back further than the reformers. It was the faith of the Apostles and was based upon the New Testament. The matter was not taken further at that stage, but it was the seed of an important distinction. By what authority? Ultimate authority is vested in Christ. Christ Himself was at pains to bring the religious leaders of His day face to face with the impact of this (*What do you think of the Christ? Whose Son is He?* 22.42). We were to find, as we have stated before, that 'the practice of the pre-eminence of God was at a premium.'

How is this authority transmitted to us? It is transmitted to us in Scripture, Scripture that reveals to us both the face of Christ and the will of God. It is transmitted to us in Scripture, and not through an ecclesiastical hierarchy. It is transmitted to us in Scripture, and not in some framework of systematic theology. If we were Calvinists, we were so because Calvin was biblical, and the Bible was Calvinistic. We were biblical Calvinists, rather than propositional ones. If we embraced reformed theology, we did so because it most clearly approximated to the apostles' understanding of God not because, in itself, it was the hallmark of orthodoxy. The distinction may appear as hair-splitting. At that stage we were content to accept the status quo, but we had inadvertently put our finger on an important distinction that was one part of the Lord's contention with the Pharisees. It was also a large part of the reformation battle-cry, and we saw the loss of this distinction as a danger imminently threatening to engulf the Korean church.

The following words written about the reformers and the convictions that motivated them in the 1520's summarize very aptly the conclusions we were reaching in Korea in the 1970's — 'The Reformers did not feel that they were handling and interpreting Scripture; but that God was handling them through Scripture. Beliefs and church practice could not be justified if

they were other than, outside of, or apart from the Word of God
... The Roman church, too, accepted the authority of Scripture,
but in practice claimed that both the Bible and tradition were
sources and rules of faith' (How often we were to hear the
explanation, 'Oh, that's Korean custom' to cover a wide variety
of practices that we found surprising.) 'The Roman church also
made tradition, as it was expressed in the decrees of popes and
councils, the only permissible, legitimate and infallible interpreter
of the Bible. Roman Catholics appealed to Scripture to support
views and positions arrived at on other grounds. The Bible was
hardly ever read ... Medieval theologians had tended to put the
church between the believer and his Bible.'[1]

All of this we were to find valid criticism in the Protestant,
strongly reformed, Calvinistic Presbyterian churches of Korea.

It was six or seven years later that, with Mr Yune of Scripture
Union and several other Korean theologians, we put this into
schematic form as follows for ease of understanding:

Christges   is the Head of the Church

|

The Church is His body.

How does He communicate Himself to His people?

'Sola Scriptura' — by the Word of God:

Christ

|

The Word ⟵   The minister of the Word.

|

The Church

He is the Minister of Christ ('Him we proclaim' Col. 1.28).

He is a minister of the church (Col. 1.24-5). He stands at one
side, as it were, to bring Christ and His people into close
communion by the ministry of the Word. He is to 'make the
Word of God fully known' (Col. 1.25). This is basic reformation
theology. Authority is vested in Christ through His Word, and
not in ecclesiastical hierarchy or traditions of interpretation.

Now, various aberrations of this scheme can creep in. The first
and most subtle is to reverse the role of minister and word:

Christ

|

His minister — *the Word*
|

The church

Here the minister still believes and teaches the Word, but does so in such a way as to reinforce his own authority rather than that of Christ and His Word. The response sought, and often obtained, is, 'My minister says . . .' rather than 'Christ says . . .' or 'the Bible says . . .'

From here, it is only a step to drop the Word and we have:

Christ
|

His minister
|

The Church.

This is an issue that is totally unrelated to theological liberalism. Liberalism is an issue in the Korean church, as we shall see in the next chapter, but this trend towards ecclesiastic authority can continue in the context of the most stringent criteria of doctrinal orthodoxy. The Pharisees were doctrinal purists: the Roman church of the sixteenth century stood squarely on the authority of Scripture. Eventually human authority obtrudes so strongly on the vision of Christ that the end result looks like this:

Christ that the end result looks like this:

The minister
|

his church

At this stage it is irrelevant whether the minister is a doctrinal conservative or liberal. The church is dead. It needs reformation and revival through a return to the Scriptures.

At no point in history is every church in a country identical. Individual churches differ; individual ministers differ, but over the last ten years in Korea we have seen the church as a whole sliding progressively in this direction. It is to the correction of this trend that we are committed, principally through the ministries of Scripture Union.

Ten years ago, on that church pathway in Hong Kong, the Lord spoke to us through those words in a concrete block:

The Lord has need of you.

He says it still to others of like mind. Is there a place for you in this ministry today?

The Lord has need of you.

1   James Atkinson: *Lion 'History of Christianity'* (pp 364, 366)

Everything is ready; come to the marriage feast.
They made light of it and went off, one to his farm, another to his business.
The Pharisees sent their disciples to Him, along with the Herodians, saying, '... Tell us what you think. Is it lawful to pay taxes to Caesar or not?
The same day Sadducees came to Him saying, 'Teacher, Moses said ...'
You are wrong, because you know neither the scriptures, nor the power of God ... have you not read what was said to you by God?
Teacher, which is the great commandment in the law?
You shall love the Lord your God with all your heart.
You shall love your neighbour as yourself.
Jesus asked them a question, 'What do you think of the Christ? Whose son is he?' (Matthew 22.4-5, 15-17, 23-24, 29, 31, 36-39, 41-42)

22

Distractions

It was Toynbee who said that there have been two great Christian heresies in history. The first, Islam, was a response to neglect of the first commandment, *You shall love the Lord your God with all your heart.* The second, Communism, is a response to neglect of the second commandment, *You shall love your neighbour as yourself.*

Neither Islam nor Communism is a force in Korea today, but the neglect of the two great commandments poses serious threats for the future of the church. In this and the three chapters that follow, we shall be examining some of these threats. The treatment may appear critical, but it is by nature of critique rather than criticism; diagnosis with a view to treatment. We are told to discern the times and this we seek to do, trying to understand why it is so hard to be a faithful minister of the Word and true pastor; why it is so hard to be a maturing Christian in the context of the Korean church. It is not our province to assign guilt. That is for God. (Perhaps the very strength of the words used by our Lord concerning the religion of His day in Matthew 21-25 is in itself an indirect claim to divine authority).

In saying that neither Islam nor Communism is a force in Korea today, we must remember, of course, that North Korea has one of the most hard-line Communist regimes in the world, and anti-communism is an equally potent force in the south. Islam has never had any roots in Korea (although it had in N.W. China), but recently the development of economic links with Middle Eastern countries — Korean nurses in Kuwait, Korean engineers in Saudi Arabia, regular Korean Air Lines flights to Bahrein — has led to the opening of a mosque in Seoul. This is mostly for Arab expatriates, but a few Koreans have embraced

Islam. The converse is also true. There are Korean churches for Korean expatriates in Middle Eastern countries and, hopefully, some Christian Korean technicians in these countries could act as non-professional missionaries in Muslim lands.

- - - - - - - - - - - - - - - - - -

You shall love the Lord your God with all your heart, and with all your soul, and with all your mind.
'The practice of the pre-eminence of God is at a premium.'

What are some of the distractions that lead people's thoughts away from the centrality of God?

In Matthew 22, we see the Pharisees, the Herodians, and the Sadducees. *Party spirit* is nothing new, and the problem is by no means confined to Korea; but here it is one on which much energy has been expended, and which has taken a severe toll on godliness.

Until 1945, the Korean church was united. Presbyterians were the largest group, all within the fold of one denomination. Methodists and Holiness Churches (the latter the fruit of the Oriental Missionary Society's work) made up the majority of the remainder. These co-existed happily, with commity arrangements for evangelism of different provinces.

In the wake of the liberation from Japan, the first splits occurred among the Presbyterians, as we saw in chapter 3. A relatively small group of those who had not given way to Japanese Shinto shrine worship reorganized themselves as a separate assembly and denomination based in Pusan. At the other end of the scale, a smallish group of theological liberals separated themselves. The main body of the church remained together.

Ten years later, this main body was split over the issue of linking with the World Council of Churches. Feelings ran high. Missionaries working with the churches threw their weight on one side or the other according to their personal convictions. Undercurrents of rivalry between leaders helped to confuse the issues. The outcome was an acrimonious split into two approximately equal church groups. One joined the WCC. The other remained non-aligned. The majority of Presbyterian missionaries (American and Australian) were associated with the former, because their home churches were WCC-linked. The two groups were known respectively as the *Dong hap* and *Hap dong*. It will

210

be seen that the two words are the same with the syllables reversed. Both mean 'United!'

Another ten years on, in the late 60's when OMF first came to Korea, we were invited by the *Hap dong* (non-WCC-linked), and the *Koryo Pa* (Pusan-based group mentioned above, also not WCC-linked), on the understanding that we would have no formal relationship with WCC-linked groups. 'We are the hope of the Korean church,' roundly declared one Pusan leader to us in early days.

Feelings ran high, and there was still almost no exchange between the two sides. Another name for the WCC party was the 'Cal' party, from the last syllable of the English word 'ecumenical'. One suspected that understanding of the issues at stake was sometimes about as extensive as the depth of meaning carried in that isolated syllable.

The missionaries with whom we found ourselves associated in the orbit of the *Hap dong* and *Koryo Pa* churches were American Presbyterians of the Orthodox and Reformed Presbyterian churches in America (never more than six couples), more recently joined by several couples of the Presbyterian Church in America — a recent off-shoot of the American Southern Presbyterians. They were warm in fellowship, kindness itself, and had among them missionaries of a very high calibre. Coming, however, from a strongly denominational background in the American church scene, they often found our interdenominational stance hard to understand. It is to their lasting credit that they have borne with us so patiently.

Other forces, too, from the world scene were at work on the Korean church, from the extreme separatist groups, such as the Bible Presbyterians of Dr Carl MacIntyre (ICCC), to the extreme liberals, sponsoring Bultmann for a lecture tour in Seoul. The American Southern Baptists founded the Korean Baptist church in the 1940's, and many smaller groups from America began their own work. Thus, today, there are probably a dozen separate Presbyterian denominations, two large Methodist conferences, two Holiness churches, two Baptist, three or more Pentecostal, and a host of smaller denominations.

Ripples from the American and world scene have cast up some of these, but for many, that is no more than a pretext. The real causes that have precipitated fragmentation and strife locally are far more to do with personalities and rivalry between leaders. As we were considering in the last chapter, where the basic church structure of

$$\begin{array}{ccc} \text{Christ} & : & \text{the Head} \\ & | & \\ & \text{His Word} & \\ & | & \\ \text{The Church} & : & \text{His body} \end{array}$$

becomes replaced by a structure of

$$\begin{array}{c} \text{The Minister} \\ | \\ \text{his disciples} \end{array}$$

there is bound to be rivalry for the leadership. The head is no longer One. Perhaps this is in part why the Lord, having faced a variety of party leaders, faced them with the question: *what do you think of the Christ? Whose son is he?*

It has been an encouragement over the ten years that we have been associated with the churches in Korea to see this harsh sectarianism considerably mollified. Various activities have been sponsored across denominational boundaries. Joint support for the Billy Graham meetings of 1973 and Campus Crusade's Explo '74; united Easter morning services on Nan San mountain in Seoul, and at other centres; a prayer rally and declaration supported by 19 different denominations on the 30th anniversary of liberation from the Japanese (15th August 1975); increasing academic exchange between leading theologians of the different denominations — all these things have helped towards greater interchange and mutual understanding.

However, the basic problem of authority structure in the church (which reflects deep-rooted Confucianism) has not been resolved, and has increasingly revealed itself in another form.

'Big is beautiful' is the spirit of our commercial age dominated by economics. Where the church is booming, it is all too easily applied in the spiritual sphere. Leadership of a large, growing, prosperous organization is an attractive goal for those with a taste for power. I remember visiting, on furlough, a Free Church minister in a small rural community in the highlands of Scotland. After a few initial exchanges, he turned to me and said — 'And how goes it with the gospel in Korea?' It was a heart-warming question. As we parted, I thought ruefully that if the roles had been reversed, and this man had been visiting in Korea, the most

likely first question of a Korean minister would be, 'How many do you have in your church?' If it was not in three figures — maybe four figures, or even five — he would lose interest.

Speaking one day with a student in Masan, convert of an independent student group, I was urging on him the importance of belonging to a local church. 'Church,' he said scornfully, 'Oh, that's just minister's business.' The thrust of his comment was not so much that church is all right if you want to be ordained — 'go into the church' as used to be said. Rather, it was that church is organized in the same way as a small private business is organized — for the commercial profit of the proprietor. The comment was painfully close to the mark. The message that Christians are interested in power and money, which we noted from the growth of medical and other institutions, comes home to roost.

Churches are springing up everywhere in Korea. New churches are planted in new housing areas, and in hitherto unchurched rural areas too. The *Hap dong* denomination alone plans to expand from around three thousand churches at the end of 1976, to ten thousand in 1984. To date, it is ahead of schedule. Other denominations have similar plans. Existing churches, too, are growing rapidly, but at the head of too many of them is one who dreams of standing before a congregation of hundreds or thousands (depending on the extent of his ambitions), respected by all, on a pinnacle of success.

A recent highly-favourable article in a British Christian magazine revealed this underlying preoccupation with bigness, power and money. Under the title 'Korea's Mighty Church', it was a summary of an interview with the senior pastor of a Seoul congregation 50,000 strong. One little paragraph summed it up: 'I have plenty of time, because I delegate all of my work. I do not go out and tire myself to death visiting homes and so on. I study. I pray, and I only take the big things.'

This is where every ambitious young man in the ministry aspires to be. It is an atmosphere in which it is hard to be a faithful pastor and minister of the Word.

They made light of it and went off, one to his farm, another to his business. These words were said by the Lord in the context of critique of the religious leaders of His day.

What do you think of the Christ? It is an important call to return to centre.

Render to Caesar the things that are Caesar's, and to God the things that are God's.

The Pharisees (religious zealots) and Herodians (collaborators with Imperial Rome) — strange bed-fellows — were seeking how to entangle Jesus and to bring upon Him the wrath of Rome. They chose a sensitive political issue — taxation. The Lord effectively refused to be drawn. In a country under tension, such as Korea, there are bound to be a multiplicity of such sensitive issues. It is not an easy matter, either for the Korean Christian or the foreign missionary, to determine his stance.

This is not a new matter. Following the annexation of Korea by Japan in 1910, it was the Christians who provided the backbone of resistance — not armed resistance, nor even resistance to the colonial government per se (although feelings of antipathy ran high), but resistance to the Japanization of the country and especially to Shinto shrine worship. The Japanese held this to be a ceremony of national loyalty and solidarity. Many of the Korean Christians saw it also as a bowing to idols in which, as worshippers of the living God, they could not partake. It was exactly akin to the dilemma of the early Christians in Rome. Although under relentless pressure many ultimately gave way, the majority conscience rejected the ceremonies as unacceptable for the Christian — on religious grounds, not political.

On 1st March 1919, Christians were prominent among those who organized a non-violent protest movement against the excesses of the colonial government. It was vigorously repressed, and heralded particular pressure upon the church from the Japanese authorities.

More recently, Korean Christians have been to the forefront in anti-Communist activity, and it is no secret that every Christian leader is listed for annihilation on North Korean files, should opportunity arise. The book *The Triumph of Pastor Son* (IVP) gives a classic account of one man's sufferings for his faith both under the Japanese and the Communists. It is questionable whether much of present-day anti-Communist campaigning on the part of Christian leaders is of the same spiritual calibre. The attractions of a popular cause, fear of the future, desire to save one's own skin, plus the lure of possible sponsored travel overseas to international conferences, are all powerful motives. A return to centre, *What do you think of the Christ?* is greatly needed.

Government sees in the church, of course, a powerful anti-Communist force and is not slow to make use of it. Behind the reports of widespread conversion of Christianity in the armed forces lies a government drive for moral fibre in the forces. Religion (be it Buddhist, Roman Catholic or Protestant) was rightly seen as a powerful anti-Communist force and the army chaplains (predominantly Protestant Christians) were not slow to seize the opportunity. Undoubtedly large numbers of young men in the forces have found Christ, and the army chaplains are some of the finest Christian ministers in the country, but behind the reports of mass baptisms in the army lies also group pressure to conform. Large numbers have submitted to baptism, some of them without even understanding the barest essentials of the gospel.

More controversial have been issues over so-called 'human rights', and clashes between government and a few Christian leaders and missionaries. In this confused situation it is easy to draw false conclusions about the general state of the country from isolated incidents blown up out of all proportion. The gospel, inescapably, has deep implications for society, but it is so easy to be swept off centre by the winds of fashionable thought.

We have sought to operate along the following guide-lines.

One has a duty of thinking deeply on every issue affecting human life, but one only has a right to speak or campaign publicly in those spheres in which one is personally involved and accountable. Some of those who have been most vocal politically have been strangely silent about ills in the church.

Acting on these principles, we have found no conflict of loyalties with political authorities. In the medical sphere, in which we are intimately involved, we have been outspoken over the excesses of private medicine organized for the financial advantage of the practitioner rather than the welfare of the patient. In so doing, we have found ourselves not infrequently in the same camp as a government which is concerned for the welfare of its people, concerned to feed down the benefits of a booming economy to as wide a section of the population as possible. However, this is accidental rather than intentional. We render to Caesar the things that are Caesar's, but we render to God the things that are God's in seeking to lead all kinds of men to face the question, *What do you think of the Christ?*

215

Distractions. Yes, there are others. Theological liberalism is an important one. One Australian missionary, teaching in a Seoul seminary, was asked to leave shortly before we returned in 1969. The complaint was that he had taught that the story of Jonah was myth, not fact. However, a number on the staff of that seminary today (Korean professors) are Barthian[1] in their view of Scripture.

The Korean church, as a whole, from its strongly Bible-based background, is traditionally conservative, but in recent years the Christian Literature Society (with subsidy from World Council of Churches agencies — one side-product of WCC affiliation) has produced a wide range of liberal theological works. After a period of majoring on extreme radical works — Robinson, Tillich, Bultmann — they found that there was a poor market for these, and redirected their policies towards more acceptable (but none the less clearly liberal) works. The inroads of liberalism (boosted by scholarships to liberal theological courses in the States and elsewhere, as well as by publishing grants) have tended to produce an over-reaction of extreme sensitivity over doctrine on the conservative side. Calvin and the reformers are the hallmark of orthodoxy. To label someone 'Barthian', or 'Neo-orthodox', or 'Neo-evangelical' on the basis of some isolated or tentative remark is to rule them out of court.

It will readily be seen that in the sort of authority structure that we have described, where rival leaders vie for supremacy in the power struggle, theological orthodoxy can be a weapon in this struggle. On the surface, the issues are doctrinal. Underneath, these are merely tools in the game of ecclesiastical power politics. If I can discredit my rival, I may usurp his power. Dr John Kim suffered much from this sort of in-fighting, and it was a major factor in his departure to Los Angeles to pastor a Korean congregation there.

An encouraging sign on the theological front has been the establishing of the Asian Centre for Theological Studies (ACTS) in Seoul. This is an international venture with wide support, and has brought together theological leaders from a variety of backgrounds in Korea. The aim is to provide post-graduate theological training for Asian leaders (not just Koreans), and the basic medium is English. A wide representation of visiting lecturers has added to the locally-based teaching. Besides its central aim of advanced theological training, it has provided a forum for theological exchange within Korea itself. This has been much needed in an academic atmosphere stifled by fear of mutual heresy hunting.

Discussion of the rarefied atmosphere of the advanced theological world (thank God for those who give themselves to this work and are forerunners in the intellectual advance of the church!) leads on to mention of the distraction of intellectualism. The Sadducees were theological liberals (*who say that there is no resurrection*). Their question (designed to ridicule the doctrine of resurrection) was also an academic distraction. The Lord saw it as such, and corrected them: *You are wrong, because you know neither the Scriptures, nor the power of God.* (22.29)

It is hard to realize in the West the pressure there is on pastors and teachers in a country like Korea to obtain advanced degrees for the sake of respectability. Advanced study to equip oneself better as a teacher is one thing. Advanced qualification for the sake of status is quite another; and, of course, overseas study automatically ranks high in the respectability stakes, whatever the level of instruction received.

I think of one preacher and theological teacher we know. Shortly after we arrived, we heard him preach. We did not understand much, of course, but were surprised by his quotations from Bertrand Russell in the course of his sermon. Some years later he asked for our help to arrange invitations for him on a visit to Scotland. He was involved in theological teaching, but all these years he had felt inferior because he did not have a PhD degree. Now he had the opportunity, and he was collecting data on Scottish church history. This bore little relation to his job, and his methods of research were highly questionable, but the carrot of the magic letters PhD was irresistible.

Many travel overseas for advanced study, often leaving family for several years. Some absorb the best and return greatly helped. Others never return. Still others, interested only in the doctoral certificate, return with a powerful credit to their pride and their power, but with little profit to their understanding of the gospel, or their ministry. A special service of public worship and thanksgiving for safe return (and advertisement of the achievements of the Reverend Doctor) is commonly a symbol of the latter type.

Distractions are manifold. No wonder the Lord was at pains to stress essentials to His hearers:

The Scriptures and the power of God.

You shall love the Lord your God with all your heart.
You shall love your neighbour as yourself.
What do you think of the Christ? Whose son is He?
It is the missionary's task to do the same. The voices are all too few and weak.

---

[1] The View that Scripture *contains* the Word of God rather than *is* the Word of God and that, while God speaks His living Word through the written word, that written Word itself is not necessarily free from error.

They bind heavy burdens, hard to bear, and lay them on men's shoulders; but they themselves will not move them with their finger.

They love the places of honour . . . and the best seats . . . and being called rabbi by men.

You shut the kingdom of heaven against men.

You tithe mint and dill and cummin, and have neglected the weightier matters of the law, justice, mercy, and faith.

O Jerusalem, Jerusalem . . . how often would I have gathered your children together as a hen gathers her brood under her wings, and you would not! (Matthew 23.4, 6-7, 13, 23, 37)

23

O Jerusalem, Jerusalem!

Matthew 23 is a terrifying chapter to deal with, especially when it is as penetratingly relevant as it so often is in Korea. A few words of explanation are in place.

Firstly, one only dares illustrate the chapter from observations in Korea, in the context of the whole. The whole of the Lord's contention with the Pharisees was set in the framework of the whole gospel story. We trust that taking the layout of a whole gospel and illustrating its themes and differing emphases preserves a measure of balance in the overall presentation. I personally believe that God's chosen method of revelation in Scripture, so much of which is history, is an important part of that revelation, and we are best preserved from imbalance and error by exposing our minds and our hearts to the whole sweep of Scripture as well as to its selected parts in detail. In so doing one is not at liberty to leave out the less palatable parts.

Secondly, the Lord's own cry at the end of the chapter gives a clue to the best standpoint from which to offer critique — one of compassion and personal involvement. *O Jerusalem, Jerusalem!* How often our hearts have cried, 'Oh Korea, Korea!' 'Would that even today you knew the things that make for peace!' (Luke 19.42)

Thirdly, the exhortations of Matthew 18.15-17 are relevant. 'If your brother sins against you, go and tell him his fault, between you and him alone' and so on. The context is of personal matters, but the principle remains that it is not right to talk behind people's backs of matters you are not prepared to say to their faces. People are sometimes surprised when we assure them that we have not said on furlough anything relating to Korea that we have not already said and taught both privately and publicly in

Korea and among those most concerned. Matthew 23.13-15 formed the text of a sermon in a Pusan church; Ezekiel 34.1-5 the substance of an address to theological students; I Peter 5.2-3 the basis of a word of encouragement at an ordination of elders at which nearly all the ministers in Masan were present. Examples could be multplied (chapter 12 contains another, of greetings at the General Assembly), but we have sought to speak with grace and clarity in the local situation first.

Fourthly, the Lord ends His words with sympathy, but begins them with a warning about sectarianism (23.2-3). The crowds, and His disciples whom He was addressing, were not to interpret His words as licence lightly to opt out of the framework and sling stones from outside. We have sought to live carefully and under authority within the framework of the Korean church. We have been privileged with formal acceptance and enjoyed a wide measure of personal and real acceptance. Only on this basis do we feel we have any right to speak clearly on the issues we see as important. Just as Luther and the early reformers had no desire to depart from the church of their day, but rather to reform from within, so our longing is to see reformation and revival within the framework of the existing structures. History would suggest that this is extremely difficult, but we are not absolved from trying. The great new surges of life in 'new wine bottles' are more spectacular and immediately spring to mind, but a careful perusal of church history will also reveal a host of less spectacular, but deep and effective reform movements within the existing framework. In the background from which we come ourselves, the history of Scripture Union and of Inter-Varsity Fellowship (now Universities and Colleges Christian Fellowship) over the last hundred years is one striking example. It is to this form of renewal that we are committed unless and until it proves unworkable.

Fifthly, words of our Lord such as those in Matthew chapter 23 are presumably recorded for our warning. If we are to preserve the balance of Scripture we cannot sidestep them where they are relevant. We need to heed the warnings if we are not to fall into the same errors.

Finally, as we saw in chapter 12, contemporary Pharisaism, all that it stood for, and those who were enmeshed in it, were roundly condemned by the Lord; but not all were like this. In spite of the prevailing climate there were godly men —

Nicodemus, of course, springs to mind. There were many others who secretly sympathized with the message of the gospel (John 12.42). Our equation of the Pharisees with the prevailing climate of attitudes and opinion in the ordained ministry of the Korean church is not to be applied to every individual Korean minister. Thank God, there are fine and godly men. But it remains true that the prevailing climate is such that it is very hard to remain faithful and humble. Men in such positions, especially those in leadership and engaged in training future ministers, need our prayers, not our condemnation. An example will illustrate how easy it is to lose balance.

A few years ago one of the largest Christian publishing houses in Korea began publishing Korean translations of Watchman Nee's books such as *The Normal Christian Life, Sit, Walk, Stand, The Spiritual Man*. Over a few years they produced almost the whole range of available titles, and these had a considerable impact on the church. Not a few ministers testified to an experience of the new birth, and informal ministers' Bible Study groups sprang up in a number of places — real foci of fellowship and spiritual growth. Not surprisingly, this provoked some official reaction, especially in view of Watchman Nee's rather strong stance against organized church structures. This in turn drove those who had experienced new life to condemn much of existing organized religion — 'The Central Church — Oh the minister's not born again there.' 'Hardly anyone born again in that church.' Such comments could readily be heard, and it can be imagined that they did nothing to promote harmony.

At the same time, the senior Korean pastor in charge of the radio station associated with the publishing house became more and more outspoken in his doctrine, gathered a following and, after much acrimony, broke away to form a 'Salvation Church' with a strong emphasis on the New Birth, and a reality of inner life and fellowship. However, within the course of a few years the ex-radio pastor was exerting his leadership so strongly that within the group it is commonly implied that there are very few real Christians outside their own fellowship. Church history repeats itself, and the would-be reformer must walk meekly and carefully.

Part of the normal cycle of church activities is the 'annual visitation'. Depending on the size of the church, for one or two weeks the minister, accompanied by three or four elders or lady deacons, will call on each church family in their homes and exchange prayer for refreshments before moving on. The group is unmistakable: the minister leads, carrying a small black satchel containing Bible and hymnbook. He is followed in dutiful order by his retinue. As he crosses the market place the deferential, 'Good afternoon, minister' will be acknowledged suitably. As he passes through the narrow lanes between houses, the teenage girls or young men home from the army who withdraw into doorways until the party is past, will be suitably ignored. As they enter the gateway into the house yard, a suitable discreet cough will summon the mother of the house from her kitchen where she is preparing refreshment suitable for the occasion. Mumbled apologies that father is at work, the children not yet home from school, and she is alone with granny and the toddler, will be greeted with an enigmatic grunt which is designed to produce a response of guilt by proxy — and is usually successful.

The party is ushered into the guest room, leaving their shoes at the door. 'Honourable minister, please come and sit over here where it is warm.' The not-unwilling reverend gentleman is ushered to the place of honour nearest to the underfloor heating.

When all are settled, the minister leads the little gathering in a hymn, short reading and homily, and long prayer. In the middle, granny withdraws hastily with the toddler. The damp patch remaining on the floor tells its own tale. The single glance cast on her retreating figure by the master of ceremonies is enough to achieve its aim of further humiliating toddler's mother. The content of the prayer will probably make this long-suffering lady feel she should double what she was planning to put in the harvest thank-offering next week — but that won't be easy to explain to husband: he wasn't here to hear the innuendoes. Perhaps a little deceit will carry the day? It seems the only way out.

Then come refreshments. A spread of cakes and fruit, coca cola, fizzy orange, hard-boiled eggs and, this year, ginger tea. Expensive, yes, but it had been too much hearing them talk about Mrs Han's ginger tea last year. 'Magnificent! Fit for a king!' was the assessment. Rising to go, the party don their shoes and, with suitable greetings and thanks, pass through the gate and make their way to the next house. Thus king and subject part mutually gratified, while granny begins to clear the dishes.

A caricature? Sadly, no. A composite picture, yes, but each element factually true. Universally true? Happily, no, but such is the trend that it is hard for a young man in the ministry not to conform to what is expected of him by his elders and his flock, as well as by his senior ministers.

- - - - - - - - - - - - - - - - - -

One friend describes how he travelled to his first presbytery meeting after his appointment as elder and how, as he sat near the back, tears filled his eyes as he scanned the rows of men, noting the plump and prosperous girth of the city pastors and, in contrast, the pinched outlines of the rural leaders. If the outlines of a man's soul could be visualized, perhaps the roles would be reversed.

It is little wonder that the Lord gave such clear instructions to His disciples in verses 8-12:

You are not to be called rabbi (teacher).

Call no man your father on earth, neither be called masters.

These titles are in turn appropriate to the Holy Spirit, our heavenly Father, and Christ Himself. When man usurps them it is expressive of that shift in basis of authority that we considered in chapter 21. No wonder the Lord cries out in disgust.

Woe to you . . . you shut the kingdom of heaven against men. (23.13)

In Korean it is common practice to address a man by his position or status — Mr Teacher, Mr Superintendent, Mr Manager, etc. — and this reflects the important role that status has in a Confucian society. This is reproduced in the church in a multiplicity of titles, many of which are unintelligible to the outsider — minister, elder, deacon, lady worker, moderator, keeper, etc. Excessive use of these terms all tends to reinforce the hierarchical system and, so far as it does, to undermine real fellowship in Christ (*you are all brethren* 23.8).

The bolstering of pride on the local scale is mirrored on a wider scale. When Korean church leaders speak, or are quoted internationally, it is common to note the emphasis on size, growth, numbers, influence, finances, buildings.

'Ours is the fastest growing church in Asia.'

'Our church is the biggest in Seoul (in the world).'

'Our people tithe faithfully.'
'We have dawn prayer meetings.'
'The spiritual hope of Asia lies with us.'
'There are so many Christians that God will protect our land.'
'Our city is the Jerusalem of Korea.'
When it becomes fashionable to talk this way, be sure that temptation abounds. *Whoever exalts himself will be humbled, and whoever humbles himself will be exalted.*

O Jerusalem, Jerusalem! 'Pray for the peace of Jerusalem.'

Nor is this all. The upshot is to build a religion of works to the neglect of grace. Thus multitudes of young men and women who earnestly want to know the truth about Jesus Christ are fed with a framework of religious subservience. Evangelism is vigorous (*you traverse land and sea to make a single proselyte* 23.15), but the end of it, in the Lord's words, *you make him twice as much a child of hell as yourselves.* How can this be? If a child of heaven is one who has tasted of grace and forgiveness, is not a child of hell one burdened with fear and guilt? Evangelism is good, but if the message is 'Come to church,' and when you get there the message is 'Keep on coming to church — and pay your tithes,' then men and women are being schooled in a religion of works that leads to death. The door of the kingdom of heaven has been shut and barred by those who *neither enter themselves nor allow those who would enter to go in.* (23.13) There are many within the church living in fear and burdened with unrelieved guilt. They desperately need to hear the liberating message of the gospel. And people say to us, 'Why do you need missionaries today in a developed situation like Korea?' The church desperately needs missionaries today while it is still day, and before the church plunges into a *rigor mortis* akin to the middle ages, or to oblivion like the early church in North Africa. *Therefore I send you prophets . . .* (23.34) It may be to a 'hopeless' ministry like that of Jeremiah and Ezekiel, but God still sends His prophets. Maybe He'll send you.

Two other strands come out of this chapter, both of which we have touched upon already.

Inside they are full of extortion and rapacity (23.25). Some manuscripts carry verse 14, *You devour widows' houses and for a pretence you make long prayers* . . . The parallel passage in Luke certainly has it. We saw how prayer may be used to manipulate people's giving. There are other instances of this. When the offering is received, offerings in envelopes are passed up to the minister who reads out the names of those who have given, distinguishing the tithes (one-tenth of income), and the special gifts (thank-offerings for a birthday, promotion, a church appointment as deacon or elder, recovery from sickness, birth of a child), from gifts to special church funds like the building fund, etc. In the prayer that follows, those whose names have been read out will commonly be specially prayed for. This is an extension and abuse of the earlier attractive practice of mentioning, and specially praying for, those who had some special personal joy or sorrow. Thus are men's susceptibilities played upon, and in the interests of church finances, giving all too easily becomes a means of merit or boasting, or a necessary precursor to obtaining the minister's priestly or shamanistic prayers (shades of medieval indulgences).

The other associated strand in this chapter is preoccupation with trivialities (23.16-22), the quibbling over what is a valid oath (23.23-24), endless discussions over details of tithing — straining out a gnat and swallowing a camel. The Koreans have a proverb for something that looks good on the outside, but inwardly is corrupt and sour (cf. 23.27). They say it is like the dog-apricot which grows on hedgerows, has a beautiful skin, but an intensely bitter taste. Just so, when endless time is consumed in discussions on church order, church buildings, presbytery business, policy on minor details of tithes and sabbaths in which freedom of conscience would be wiser, *the weightier matters of the law, justice and mercy and faith* are easily neglected.

- - - - - - - - - - - - - - - - -

When we have summer holidays in Korea, we go to one of a group of cabins high up in the mountains where it is cool and quiet. These are about four hours' walk up from the nearest village or habitation, so all stores have to be carried up. Men from the nearby village are glad to earn a day's wage in half a day by

227

carrying up loads of up to 100 lbs each — a moderate-sized tea-chest fully packed — while we climb unladen. It is as much as we can do to load these boxes into the car when we set off. The thought of carrying them up the mountain for four hours is totally beyond us, but the arrangement with the men who carry them is one of mutual profit, so we are content with it.

Often, though, when climbing that mountain trail, I have thought of the words of verse four: *They bind heavy burdens, hard to bear, and lay them on men's shoulders; but they themselves will not move them with their finger.* In a situation of personal contract to move loads up a mountain, it may be acceptable. As a picture of the church scene, it is horrific.

O Jerusalem! Jerusalem!

Pray for the peace of Jerusalem: and pray the Lord of the harvest that He will send out labourers into His harvest — men and women who will go with the liberating gospel of the Christ who said, *Come to Me all who labour and are heavy laden, and I will give you rest.*

His disciples came to point out to Him the buildings of the temple.

Take heed that no one leads you astray. Many will come in my name saying, 'I am the Christ,' and they will lead many astray.

Wars and rumours of wars.

They will deliver you up to tribulation, and put you to death.

Most men's love will grow cold.

False Christs and false prophets will arise and show great signs and wonders.

Who, then, is the faithful and wise servant, whom his master has set over his household, to give them their food at the proper time?

Blessed is that servant whom his master when he comes will find so doing. (Matthew 24.1, 4-5, 6, 9, 12, 24, 45-46)

24

False Christs

'We put an extra storey on the tower of our church when we were rebuilding, so that it would be taller than the Catholic Cultural Centre over there.' 'When we have finished, this church will have the tallest tower in our city, and everybody will be able to see it.' (That is a city where one of the existing large churches is modelled on Westminster Abbey.) 'Have you seen the Central Church? It's the largest church building in Asia.'

And when the largest Presbyterian church in Seoul (already seating two thousand at each of its three morning services) pulled down its buildings to build bigger, 'We will be the largest church in Seoul.' (I heard the same remark from another suburban church in Seoul engaged in rebuilding, so it seems there will be some disputed claims to the title.)

The provincial disciples, coming to the capital, were awed by the size and beauty of the temple. The Lord turned their attention away from buildings to the realities of the spiritual and political situation around. It was a time of immense change and insecurity, and it was perhaps natural that men's thoughts should focus on one of the most stable things they could see — a building. The situation is mirrored in Korea today. Immense economic progress and internal security do not hide the vulnerability of the Korean peninsula. The facts of geography make this inescapable. A small country shadowed by the giants of Russia, China, and Japan cannot hope for more than a somewhat precarious autonomy. The memories of recent history are still very strong. Anyone past middle life remembers the humiliation and hardship of Japanese domination which, beginning in 1910, only ended with the end of the second world war in 1945

(Roman domination of Israel in the days of our Lord is a helpful parallel). Still almost half of today's population was personally involved in the Korean war of 1950-53, with its enormous toll on life and property. Many now settled in the south were refugees from North Korea at that time, or are the children of such. Words such as those of 24.16-22, although spoken of different events, would evoke a host of bitter memories for many. 'This was our life 25 years ago.' Such memories leave deep scars.

These memories have been accurately and movingly documented in *The Triumph of Pastor Son* (IVP) and *Korean Pentecost* (Banner of Truth). Nor are memories the worst. The realities of a country divided by a line only thirty miles north of Seoul — much as you might draw a line across England north of Birmingham, or from San Francisco to New York across the States, and arbitrarily separate the two halves — are day to day, and close to all. (This line was established in 1945 when the Americans received Japanese surrender in the South, and the Russians 'liberated' the North. Apart from the vagaries of the Korean war, it has remained since.) The presence of a vast Communist army arraigned along the border, the necessary military and home guard service, the repeated incidents involving armed infiltrators from the North, the fact that many church and civic leaders can hear their names personally listed over North Korean radio as enemies of the state, the discovery of large tunnels constructed by the North Koreans under the border zone, tunnels capable of transmitting 7,000 men an hour — all these things, and many more besides, add up to a tense situation, threatened with long-term insecurity. It is not surprising that men look for 'salvation' in many directions: some in feverish activity to 'make money', some in emigration to America or elsewhere, some in the church, and some in the sects.

Within the church it is not surprising that there is a boom in church building. Some of this is healthy and necessary to accommodate growing numbers. Not a little of it becomes preoccupation with beautiful buildings for their own sake. One of the contributing factors to this trend is the deep-rooted sense of long-term insecurity. Paradoxically, of course, a building-centred church is least well equipped to stand in days of tribulation, but that doesn't prevent the trend. The attitude of the men of Babel sums up perennial human reaction to insecurity —
'Come, let us build ourselves a city and a tower with its top in

the heavens, and let us make a name for ourselves lest we be scattered abroad upon the face of the whole earth.' (Genesis 11.4)

Sadly, what they most feared was exactly what devolved upon them.

'Some in the church, and some in the sects . . .' Yes, the sects are active and powerful in Korea, and they constitute the main subject of this chapter.

- - - - - - - - - - - - - - - - -

'Can you spare 10p for missionary work?'

Walking down the main street of an English provincial town on market day, I was greeted by a courteous young man from the continent — perhaps Germany. On the opposite corner of the small side street the question was repeated by a smiling African girl. Returning from my shopping errand, I stopped to give a word of testimony to each, and later picked up a discarded leaflet, *One World*. Devotees of the Unification Church of Sun Myung Moon such as these can be found in many parts of Britian, and the western world.

It is beyond the scope of this chapter to examine in detail the doctrines and practices of the 'Moonies', as they have been called, but an examination of the contents of that leaflet will give some pointers.

Inside the front page are set out

PRINCIPLES OF THE ONE WORLD CRUSADE

1) We understand that the purpose of human life is to accomplish God's purpose. Individually we must become a temple of God in which His love and truth can dwell.
2) We understand the sacredness of the God-centred family. One blessing that God has given us is to share love in our families and in the great human family.
3) We understand that all mankind should love the creation as God's house and should be responsible for the environment and that there be no waste. Man's concern for creation must be spiritual as well as physical.
4) We understand that man never fulfilled his original purpose sons and daughters of God and Lord of creation at the beginning of History and fell from that purpose and position.

Since then, man has wandered in search of God and the truth. God has also been searching for His lost children. Due to Satanic spiritual influence, man has been unable to find God. All of his endeavours have been unable to be completed under the dominion and sovereignty of God's true love.

5) We understand that God sent Jesus Christ the true Son of God, to reunite mankind with God and to establish the Kingdom of Heaven on earth. He was rejected, as have been many of the great prophets and saints God has sent, and man is thus waiting for Christ's return.

6) We understand that today mankind is entering a new era in history because it is the time of the Second Coming of Christ when the Kingdom of God is actually to be established.

7) We understand that in this age, the materialistic ideologies and self-centredness that have characterised man's efforts for happiness will decline. In place of that will be the great world family centred on God. All mankind will be as brothers and sisters, and tyranny will be broken. Physical needs will be satisfied, and love, freedom, peace and all ideals will be realized in man's happiness.

The Christian will find superficial rapport with much of this. (This is deliberate, of course.)

However, each of these tenets could be shown from other literature to be understood in less than a full biblical sense. Central to it all is confusion over the person of Christ, and a side-stepping of the atonement. In chapter 16 we examined 'The Christ and The Cross.' These are crucial issues in understanding all the sects. Although, as here, promotional literature may use catch phrases such as 'Jesus Christ, the true Son of God,' investigation of the teachings reveals that He is accorded less than His true divinity. Similarly, the 'finished work of Christ' is qualified or undermined until, in one sense or another, human works contribute to or effect human salvation. Thus, later in the leaflet, under 'God and Man' it is said, 'Because man caused the fall, man must achieve this' (restoration to God-centred living).

Other headings from the leaflet reveal the subtle play on issues that interest Christians and thoughtful unbelievers in the West: Missionary News (a report of spiritual hunger in Japan); Searching for Freedom (a report of a dissident's suffering in Russia, with anti-Communist implications); Spas that heal ('healing' is a recurrent theme); Protection for the Child (a report of anti-tuberculosis vaccination of children in Nepal).

The Unification Church has been the most successful in the West, but it is only one of at least a dozen similar Korean sects — each with its attractive, persuasive leader, each with its distinctive doctrines centering on special revelations to the leader. The Unification Church is highly successful in Korea itself and is very 'Korean' in its emphases. The 'charismatic' leader, the tight authority structure, the big-business element, the intense religious fervour; all of these reflect Korean religion. Furthermore, 'unification' is a highly emotive word in Korea, because it is immediately linked to aspirations for reunification with North Korea. The strong anti-Communist stance of the Unification Church ('Communism is the expression of Satan' arising from 'Eve's illicit love affair with Satan'!) lends superficial credence to its interest in reunification of the country internally; hence its attractiveness. The Unification Church is the strongest religious group in the leading university in Seoul. All over the country the movement is putting up attractive modern buildings for worship and teaching, generally of modern design and materials, on an inverted 'V' form plan. They, too, have discovered the promotional value of church buildings!

Prominent among the other sects, about as large as the Unification Church and slightly older (30 years), is the 'Olive Branch Sect' of 'Elder' Park (like Moon, he began as a Presbyterian). This too has its worship halls widely spread throughout the country — distinctive buildings with a white tower, carrying a large red cross on their sides. Like Moon's group, its doctrines centre around distinctive revelations to its leader, and the group has widespread business interests. In both groups, youth membership is extensively used in the sects' factories. Work in the factories is regarded as part of their 'service for God.' No wages are paid; the workers are promised only their keep, clothes, housing, and other necessities. This, coupled with charitable 'non-profit' status (and thus tax-exemption), means that the profit margin is wide and available for the sects' promotion. Once again, Christ is less than fully divine, and works feature prominently in salvation.

Another emphasis prominent in the sects is that of spiritual healing. The attraction that the prospect of instant health has for men and women of every age and race is further enhanced by the expensiveness of conventional medical care. The sects are not slow to latch on to this — and to the potential financial benefit inherent in a healing ministry. One lady who came to us as a patient had spent three years on a prayer mountain run by yet another sect. With modern drugs, her tuberculous spine was well on the way to healing within six months of her coming to us, but I don't think we got nearly as far in healing the spiritual deformity of the doctrines she had imbibed over many years.

The healing emphasis, as we saw in chapter 8, is also prominent in the mainstream churches. The pastor of a large church in Seoul recently was prepared to lay hands on people in a healing service provided a suitable offering was made. Thus, once again the poor were effectively excluded.

The Mormons? Yes, there are currently over a hundred Mormon missionaries from America in Korea. As elsewhere, they are attractive well-dressed young men, diligently pursuing their business in pairs. Masan is one of their training centres, and there are usually about eight in the city. Until a number of business people came recently to the industrial zones, the Mormons and American Peace Corps volunteers were almost the only other westerners in Masan.

Normally they stay two years, and in that short time acquire remarkably good language. We are often surprised at the relative lack of success that they have in Korea. Perhaps the strong strands of American nationalism in their teaching makes the indigenous sects more attractive to the equally nationalistic Korean.

Jehovah's Witnesses? Yes, they too are easily seen. They are much more indigenous, and we not infrequently have Koreans at our door in twos selling the Korean edition of the Watchtower magazine. They are well established, but again cannot compete with the indigenous sects.

As we saw above, in all of these sects there is an inadequate view of the person of Christ (less than truly God incarnate), and an inadequate view of the work of Christ (in some sense it must be supplemented by my works for salvation).

It is no accident that within the framework of the mainstream churches, too, these are the key issues. While maintaining the orthodox framework of doctrine, popular religion tends to blur the sole authority of Christ with that of church and tradition; popular religion tends to dilute the sole sufficiency of Christ with an accretion of good works — church attendance, prayers, and tithes. The result is to make the distinction between the main-stream of Christianity and the sects less clear-cut than would appear on paper, and to leave many confused and dissatisfied.

Who, then, is the faithful and wise servant, whom his Master has set over his household?

In this confused and complex situation, where may the servant of Christ safely tread? Only in reasserting the sole authority of Scripture is there hope — and this not merely as a tenet of doctrine. In a world where many use 'Christ' words to mean a 'Christ' of their own construction, we proclaim the Christ of Scripture. We open the Scriptures with people to read the gospels that reveal the portrait of the only true Christ. We open the Scriptures with people to read Acts and the Epistles, where alone they may understand the full import of the cross and the relationship of faith and works, grace and law.

We are convinced that our task, alongside that of likeminded brethren, is to *give them their food at the proper time* — so to lead men to the Scriptures that through them they come to know Christ, to understand the wonder of His finished work, and to walk in His ways. It will readily be seen that our emphasis on Scripture Union ministries is a ready handmaid to this task.

Our first objective is for one missionary couple to develop this emphasis in each of the eleven provinces of Korea, besides single workers with students and young people. At the time of writing, we have missionaries in only three of these provinces. Two others where our missionaries have been, are now vacant. It will be no surprise that we are asking for fellow-labourers . . . in Hudson Taylor's words, 'willing, skilful workers'; in the words of this passage, *faithful and wise servants.*

'Pray ye therefore the Lord of the harvest . . .'

At midnight there was a cry, 'Behold, the bridegroom! Come out to meet him.'

Watch therefore, for you know neither the day nor the hour . . .

Well done, good and faithful servant; you have been faithful over a little, I will set you over much; enter into the joy of your master.

To everyone who has will more be given, and he will have abundance; but from him who has not, even what he has will be taken away.

Come, O blessed of my Father, inherit the kingdom prepared for you from the foundation of the world: for I was hungry and you gave me food, I was thirsty and you gave me drink, I was a stranger and you welcomed me, I was naked and you clothed me, I was sick and you visited me, I was in prison and you came to me. Lord, when . . .?

As you did it to one of the least of these my brethren, you did it to me. (Matthew 25.6, 13, 23, 29, 34-37, 40)

25

The sheep and the goats

'Give me oil in my lamp, keep me burning
Keep me burning till the break of day.'

Yes, Korean young people sing that too. Until recently
nothing was available in the way of Christian songs except the
standard hymn book. During the last four to five years Scripture
Union has produced two books of hymns, choruses, and songs,
with guitar chords (the guitar — and jeans — are as much a part of
today's youth culture in Korea as they are in the West). These
have been very popular, and other groups are now producing
similar books.

'Give me oil in my lamp.' It is one thing to sing with gusto. It
is quite another to be ready; ready for the Lord's return, ready
too for the tribulations that must precede that day.

It was July 1977. A conference centre in Seoul had been
booked, and all was ready for the opening of special five-year
celebrations for the birth of Korea Scripture Union. We were glad
to welcome two representatives from SU overseas to share in the
conference. One of these, with previous missionary experience in
Pakistan, commented sadly after listening, visiting, and looking
around, 'It seems a church totally unprepared for persecution.'
His experience of the church's suffering in an intensely Muslim
environment had taught him to look for those qualities that
would stand up under persecution, and they seemed largely
lacking. This is the more striking when the sufferings of the
comparatively recent past in Korea are remembered. It is a
common fault of old age to decry the state of modern youth, but
older saints in Korea not infrequently shake their heads in sorrow
at the building-centred, structure-centred emphasis of today's
world.

I think of old Pastor Oh, grey-haired and stooping. For years he ran a most effective Bible School in Taegu and then Pusan. His love of God's Word, and his love for people, shaped the lives of many. With the general upgrading of educational standards, his school was no longer recognized for pastoral training, and a few years ago he sadly consented to its absorption into the larger seminary. It is hard to find that same love today.

I think of Mr Ma, the carpenter, and remember seeing him one day in his lunch break from repair work on one of the mountain holiday cabins. He had found a quiet spot on the hillside under the shade of a small fir tree. His well-thumbed Bible was open, and he was poring over its pages. His whole demeanour carried the stamp of godliness so vividly portrayed in some of the old Dutch paintings.

I think of old Pastor Yune, father of the SU General Secretary, telling of a visit he had had that day. A young evangelist from the country had called on him, soliciting funds for his church building. Pastor Yune had spent a couple of hours seeking to show him that he would be better to concentrate his energies on his pastoral ministry locally, and to plan expansion within the capacity of the local congregation.

'Give me oil in my lamp . . .'

Watch, therefore, for you know neither the day nor the hour.

In the prevailing climate it is easy to become despondent, even cynical. Not a few missionaries have returned home disillusioned, even after years of service in Korea. This is particularly true of those whose position has been that of missionary-pastor within the church — often heavily committed in presbytery business, perhaps entrusted with the pastoral oversight of a group of distant and hard to reach rural churches. Most of the missionaries in this capacity have left within the last fifteen years, finding their position untenable. Looking for a spiritual ministry, they have too often found themselves sought after only for financial or political gain. A few men of outstanding calibre have remained and been able to maintain their ministry, but today the role of missionary-pastor is largely dead. The role of missionary-prophet is still desperately needed. Those who have remained have largely been able to shift their role in this direction, and those of us who have come more recently have found ourselves most commonly cast in this role. The pastor is an integral part of the system; the prophet stands outside the system, but is related to it, and speaks into it. In this capacity the scope is unlimited, and the welcome often warm.

It is easy to become pessimistic or cynical, but there is no need. In every age, and every church, God has His remnant. What is God's reply to Elijah? 'I have kept for Myself seven thousand men who have not bowed the knee to Baal.' So, too, at the present time, there is a remnant, chosen by grace. 'But if it is by grace, it is no longer on the basis of works; otherwise grace would no longer be grace.' (Romans 11.4-6).

We are not very optimistic for the Korean church on the scale that it is drawn organizationally, but God has His *good and faithful servants,* and we have every reason for optimism concerning the growth and impact of Korean Christians both within the church and nation, and beyond. It is the purpose of the remaining chapters to record some of the triumphs of grace against the generally sombre background we have already laid.

- - - - - - - - - - - - - - - - - -

It was a Saturday morning in June. The young girl at the door presented us with a vast bowl of 'mountain strawberries' (something more akin to a raspberry than a strawberry, growing on canes), with compliments from 'the superintendent.' We accepted gratefully, returning the bowl wrapped in a silk square for carrying.

In this case 'the superintendent' was the wife of an elderly Masan pastor, herself superintendent of one of the orphanages in Masan. For years we had seasonal gifts of fruit from this lady. At first we were embarrassed. Normally, gifts of this sort are a preliminary to requesting a favour. In the case of an orphanage, the most likely would be a request to solicit funds for the orphanage from the homeland. Over the years, we had come to discover that for this lady they were not gifts with an ulterior motive, but the genuine expression of a generous heart. She was grateful that we had come to serve the Lord in her country, and these were tokens of fellowship.

More than 25 years ago, in the turmoil of the Korean war, she and her husband were wakened one morning by cries outside their front gate. Going to investigate, they found a baby, crying lustily, abandoned on their doorstep. This was the first: others followed quickly, and as order returned in the aftermath of war they found that they had an orphanage — first a dozen children, then twenty, thirty, forty ... It was not long before they, and helpers whom the Lord sent, were caring for eighty children, with a high proportion of babies. Provision for these was uncertain in the extreme in the early stages. The kindness of neighbours ... armed forces relief ... prayer, and faith. Somehow they survived, and George Müller's experience of the wonderful faithfulness and provision of God was repeated many times over. Indeed, George Müller has been an inspiration to many Korean orphanages.

As the dust of war subsided, massive relief from America and the West poured in. Prominent in this was Christian welfare, and many agencies arranged sponsorships with orphanages. Our friends were among those linked to an American agency, and subsequently received help from friends in Britain too, through Kim Chin Kyung (our first Korean friend, who studied in Bristol).

Mrs Choi's experience was by no means isolated. Many orphanages sprang up in the wake of the war, the great majority of them Christian foundations. In Masan alone today there are at least a dozen such institutions. The initiative was almost entirely Christian compassion. Most orphanages have continued to the present time with strong Christian foundations. Government support is supplemented by sponsorships and grants from overseas relief agencies. Some institutions are better than others, but generally the ethos has been distinctively Christian.

Older teenagers leaving orphanages face tremendous problems. These are accentuated in a society where family connections are tremendously important for acceptance, job placements, marriage and so on. Various training and job placement schemes have been developed, and the problem is not one that has been left to moulder, either by government, or the orphanage leaders.

Over the last ten years government has, probably rightly, been trying to reduce the number of orphanages. Obviously the sort of need that was precipitated by the war no longer exists and orphanages are, to some extent, self-perpetuating institutions. When people know that orphanages exist and will care for abandoned babies, the temptation to desert in times of stress — family strife, financial crisis, unmarried motherhood — is stronger. The existence of too large a number of such institutions can thus be a catalyst to undesirable social trends.

Although we have generally a high esteem for the work that

has been and still is being done by many orphanages, in our opinion their support does not rank as a very high priority for the generosity of overseas relief agencies, or individual sponsors.

Not only is the need declining, but the perpetuation of overseas aid cuts the initiative of local responsibility. Government does a lot. It would be encouraging to see more sponsorship and support from the wealthy churches on the spot.

For the same reasons we are not greatly enthusiastic about the sponsorships of children in their own homes (albeit very poor homes) organized by some agencies for Korea. Such giving is healthy and helpful to the giver, but is perhaps better directed to economically more needy disaster areas where there is little prospect of local initiative.

- - - - - - - - - - - - - - - - -

He was a young man, and not very sick. He had been referred to us by a friend in the office of a Pusan hospital, because he had tuberculosis of the spine in the early stages. His home was poor and difficult, so we admitted him to our wards for a period of three months. In other circumstances we would have treated him as an out-patient. While with us, he was hardworking and helpful. Often he would be busy with a broom, and when it came to the Christmas show and nativity play he was the natural choice for compere.

But all was not well. There were tales of his borrowing money from other patients and not returning it. Clearly he had an eye for the girls. More than once he disappeared for a night or two without notice. Finally, he vanished without trace. Extensive searching by the out-patient staff finally revealed that he had been picked up by the police on charges of fraud and rape. He received a three-year sentence, and was committed to Pusan gaol.

We were introduced to a wholesale watch salesman, elder of a Pusan church, who for many years had made visitation of the Pusan gaol his particular Christian service. Through his good offices, and the co-operation of the prison authorities, we were able to continue supervision of this man's treatment. Later he was transferred to Masan gaol.

Prison visitation, prison services, distribution of Christian literature to prisoners and personal evangelism among them, has been the chosen ministry of a number of Korean Christians like this elder. It is hard and tiring work and demands a high level of commitment to persist in it, but many is the ex-prisoner who testifies to faith in Christ first found through such men.

Our patient wrote to us from prison, expressing genuine repentance for his sins, telling of his reading of God's Word and asking for our prayers. Recently discharged from prison, he came with a word of thanks and a testimony of faith. We trust that he will continue in that path.

- - - - - - - - - - - - - - - - - -

Mr Kim, our hospital business manager, asked me if I would interrupt my out-patients for a minute to meet a man in his office. Following him, I was introduced to a smartly-dressed man in his thirties, a minister I had not met before from a church in Ulsan, a new industrial city about three hours from us.

He explained his purpose in calling. A poor neighbour of his, not one of his church members, had an eighteen-year-old daughter who had returned home from factory work in Seoul with very bad tuberculosis in the chest; it was also affecting one ankle. With the girl's father the minister had sought help locally, but the reaction had either been 'hopeless,' or desperately expensive treatment. Could we help? We were glad to be able to, and arranged for her admission the following week. I asked the minister to send a note with the girl so that we would know who it was, but he insisted that he would bring her personally. True to his word, the following Monday he arrived with this very sick girl. To save fares, the father had not come. We began treatment, and slowly she improved.

Some six weeks after her admission was the annual autumn festival of *chusok* when everybody heads for home and there are great family celebrations. In a society where only a minority have private cars, public transport is in great demand on such occasions. It is a public holiday, but we had arranged some special food for the patients on our wards who could not go home (the atmosphere is somewhat akin to that of Christmas in the West — in its secular connotations). Coming up in the middle of the day to spend a little time with the patients, we were surprised and delighted to meet this young minister again. With him was the girl's father — a simple, labouring man. The minister had taken the trouble to brave the crowded buses on this holiday

day, facing a three-hour journey either way, and he was prepared to spend a good part of the day at the hospital so that this man and his daughter could be together on this family festival. Mother was dead and the father would not have braved the journey on his own. It was touching to see him in his simple rough clothes, beside the young man in his clerical suit.

Later that morning, we saw the jacket of that clerical suit doffed, sleeves rolled up, and the minister, with a large basket of apples, going round the wards, handing them out, spiced, with a word of cheer to each patient. *I was sick and you visited me.* We took heart. This is the stuff of which the pastoral ministry is made up. *Well done, good and faithful servant.*

The Son of man will be delivered up to be crucified.

They took counsel together in order to arrest Jesus by stealth and kill him.

Truly I say to you, one of you will betray me.

Before the cock crows you will deny me three times.

Are you still sleeping and taking your rest?

The one I shall kiss is the man; seize him.

Then all the disciples forsook him and fled.

He has uttered blasphemy ... what is your judgement ... he deserves death.

Then they spat in his face, and struck him; and some slapped him.

I do not know the man.

Peter went out and wept bitterly. (Matthew 26.2, 4, 15, 21, 45, 48, 56, 65-7, 74-5)

An alabaster flask of very expensive ointment.

She has done a beautiful thing to me.

Wherever this gospel is preached in the whole world, what she has done will be told in memory of her.

The Son of Man goes as it is written of him.

Drink of it, all of you; for this is my blood of the covenant which is poured out for many for the forgiveness of sins.

That day when I drink it new with you in my Father's kingdom.

After I am raised up, I will go before you to Galilee.

Do you think that I cannot appeal to my Father, and He will at once send me twelve legions of angels? But how then should the scriptures be fulfilled that it must be so?

All this has taken place, that the scriptures of the prophets might be fulfilled.

Hereafter you shall see the Son of man seated at the right hand of power and coming on the clouds of heaven. (Matthew 26.7, 10, 13, 18, 24, 27-9, 32, 53-4, 56, 64)

26

Thy kingdom come

The verses at the head of this chapter from Matthew chapter 26 are deliberately set out to contrast the ugly and foreboding backcloth with the amazing poise and confidence of the Lord.

The scene is horrific. His enemies are consumed in plots, bribes, violence, false justice, hatred and abuse. His friends are stumbled with love of money, betrayal, sleep, fear, denial.

And through it all the Lord stands firm, touched by a beautiful act, confident of the fulfilment of Scripture and the ultimate triumph of His kingdom, choosing the pathway of faith and eschewing force in spite of the immense cost.

So it is with the work of the gospel everywhere and at all times. The discovery of human sin (not least one's own sinfulness) is frightening, and it is no help to the cause of the kingdom to minimize this. Sometimes the forces working for destruction both within and outside the church appear overwhelming. In the preceding chapters we have touched on many of these as they relate to Korea. But if this leaves us with a sense of despair and defeat, then we are totally foreign to the spirit of the gospel.

'I will build my church, and the gates of hell shall not prevail against it,' said the Lord. His demeanour and actions in the current chapter amply endorse this confidence. In the darkest hour He stands confident; deeply moved by the depths of human sin and the suffering entailed in atonement, yes; but disappointed in His Father's ordering of affairs? — emphatically no!

We have very often been tempted to disillusionment and despair by the things we have seen said and done by the 'friends' of Christ (one expects it from His enemies), but again and again it has been the loving act of an ordinary person (inconspicuous to human eyes, but not insignificant to divine eyes) that has given hope. We have often feared for the future and still do, but the Scripture cannot be broken and warns us to expect no different. The amazing thing is that in spite of the failings of His people, the future of Christ's kingdom is assured. Faced with over-whelming opposition we have often been tempted towards the use of 'force' — not twelve legions of angels, but money or ecclesiastical politics are powerful weapons. It is hard to take a stand of faith, allowing God to vindicate His Name; it involves many hidden Gethsemanes — *My Father, if it be possible, let this cup pass from me; nevertheless, not as I will, but as Thou wilt* — and each new missionary has to tread the same path, fight the same personal battles, and come through with faith deepened. I don't think there is a member of our missionary team in Korea, man or woman, but that has had periods of strong crying and tears. One by one, each has come to discover that faith is not so much our holding on to God, as the knowledge that God still has hold of us, when we can't hold on any longer. The Lord's word that 'the servant is not greater than his master' still stands. The missionary task is still an intensely demanding one in the context of developing and already highly-developed churches, just as it has been and still is for those pioneering in unchurched regions. After each fresh conflict, one is brought back to basics with deeper understanding. Among those basics are these three: The kindness of a loving heart is beautiful in God's sight. The Word of God is true and immensely powerful. Faith is always vindicated by God — and much of the work of faith is to refrain from human force.

For our encouragement let us look at some incidents from modern Korea that illustrate these.

- - - - - - - - - - - - - - - - - -

Granny was 62 years old, and had suffered from tuberculosis of the spine for 35 years without treatemnt. For the last fourteen of those years she had had a discharge of pus from her hip, and she was severely deformed. She was with us for three months, during which time we discovered that she had had some Christian teaching in her youth, but had never applied it. Her son was a Buddhist priest, now quite high up in the hierarchy in Seoul. She lived in a country village two hours from Masan. Quite early in her stay her heart warmed to the gospel, and with great joy she announced her faith in Christ. Day after day in the wards she would greet us with a smiling face. She could barely read, but when the regular Sunday and Tuesday services came round, she would join in the singing lustily and listen to the message eagerly.

While she was in the wards the patients began, on their own initiative, fellowship meetings in the evenings — informal times of hymn singing, prayer and Bible reading. Rarely was there any Christian among them of more than a few weeks standing, and when there was, the tendency was to let him dominate — with consequent loss of spontaneity. For the most part, these meetings had a warmth and refreshing vitality about them that was a delight to see. We only rarely attended, and that more as passing spectator than as integral partaker. Granny was always to be seen at the heart of these gatherings, drinking in the words of truth, and rejoicing in the singing.

One day she passed me an envelope, saying it was a little gift for the hospital. Inside I found 10,000 won — enough to cover her food expenses for three weeks. Only rarely did we receive money gifts from patients, and then generally from patients somewhat better off than the majority of ours, who felt some responsibility towards the institution where they had received treatment for minimal expense. More commonly, we received gifts in kind — a chicken, some apples or eggs, a bag of potatoes or nuts. Granny most certainly did not come within the bracket of the better-off, but we felt constrained to accept her gift as the token of a loving heart.

Two other facts underlined to us the beauty of her generosity. The first is always with us, namely the acrid atmosphere relating to financial dealings in medicine all around us. It is common assumption that the patient is out to pay as little as possible. In this prevailing climate, it is hard to maintain, from the institution's point of view, the attitude of *giving* to the patients the best service at the least expense, and it is harder still from the patient's point of view to break through to *giving* from a generous heart for the welfare of others, and to *trusting* that the institution will not abuse that generosity. This mutual trust is, we believe, precious in God's sight.

Then, secondly, a few weeks after that morning, granny announced that she was going home. We would have preferred her to stay one more month, but it was not a matter vital to her recovery and future welfare. We acceded, and on the morning of granny's departure, almost the whole hospital — staff and patients — gathered at the front door. Granny mopped her tears and climbed into the hospital Land Rover, stifling her sobs, while her friends of the evening fellowship sang 'God be with you till we meet again.' This, too, was punctuated with sobs until the car drew away, and all returned to the day's routine.

Later that day I learned that the principal reason for granny's early departure was that she didn't have enough money for her food to stay longer, and she didn't want to be dependent on others. Such, sometimes, is the cost of giving, and such giving is not forgotten before God.

- - - - - - - - - - - - - - - - - -

The central lesson of our years in Korea has undoubtedly been that the Word of God is true and powerful, and that it is the principal tool in the hands of Christ's servants for the work of His kingdom. Once bring the words of this book to bear upon the lives of even the most hopeless, and amazing things happen.

Kim Sun Kyung was a girl of 14 from the outskirts of Pusan. She had had a septic condition of the bones for many years and kept developing abscesses all over her body. What was worse, shortly before admission to the hospital the infection had attacked both ears and she was almost totally deaf. Treatment was a long slow process and she was in hospital on and off for almost two years. Towards the end of that time she wrote a letter to the Lord. Her septic condition was gradually clearing up but she could only just walk because both her hips were very stiff. She still could not hear. This is what she wrote:

' † Immanuel †

Loving and merciful Lord! Lord, I did not know You. I used to try believing any religion that claimed it would make me better. However, there was no result, no benefit at all. My heart just got worse and worse.

Since I was admitted to this hospital, I have come to know You, Father God. When I first read the hymn book and the Bible I just went through the motions, but little by little as I read, my interest was awakened and now I see it all.

Now, by Your grace, Lord, I am able to look around this beautiful world. Lord, I give You my thanks again. I see now what a wonderful and courageous Person You are, O Son of God. From now on I mean to do good and to learn carefully as I follow You. As I learn many things I mean to pass them on to my family that all of them may believe too.

Dear Lord, I have one matter that troubles me. Because I cannot hear, I cannot join in when the other patients meet for worship. Because I cannot learn the hymns and hear the Bible message my heart is sore. Nevertheless when I read hymns and the Bible on my own my heart is comforted, so I have endured it until now. I pray, Lord, that sometime You will remember me and cause me to hear again.

Dear Lord, I want to promise before You that I will follow You to the end. I pray all these things through the Name of our Lord Jesus Christ, Amen.

Ward No. 3   Kim Sun Kyung'

In spite of what she says, she used faithfully to attend worship services and, with the help of others, she would find the hymns and the Bible passage and follow them carefully. When we had a hospital party she sang a solo to the assembled company and was awarded a prize 'for effort'.

She is still deaf and a hearing-aid did not help her. Medically her prospects of hearing again are dim, but the Lord has her in His hand. As she continues to read His Word He will lead her on.

The Word of truth backed up by kindness does indeed have a tremendous impact, and Jesus is still able to save to the uttermost.

The aspect of faith that, casting itself upon God, refuses to call upon *twelve legions of angels* is one that is easily neglected in today's security-conscious world. Yet, perhaps it is one of the strands of thought, possible the main one, that is included in the Lord's word to His disciples, 'If any man would come after me, let him deny himself and take up his cross and follow me.' Simple trust in God may lead through deep waters of suffering, but without it, *how should the scriptures be fulfilled, that it must be so?*

The following story is one in which I found myself seeking to be an angel (if not a legion of angels), unbidden, and deserving of the rebuke 'Get behind me, Satan! You are a hindrance to me; for you are not on the side of God, but of men.' Let me hasten to add the rebuke was from the Lord, not from the person concerned.

Soon Beki was nineteen, though from his height alone you would have thought him half that age. He first came to us at a particularly difficult stage in the hospital. We were still only allowed to admit children, and the papers required were complicated and difficult to obtain. A young Korean doctor who had little sympathy for our work or its aims was temporarily working with us, and responsible for admissions. The whole future of the work was in doubt, and I had little power to influence things one way or another, except by recourse to prayer. I remember looking on in helpless horror at the tears welling up in Soon Beki's eyes as he was refused admission and sent away for yet more papers that he had little prospect of obtaining.

We enrolled him for treatment in out-patients which was the only section over which I had jurisdiction at that time. Later, we learned more of the cause of his tears. Not only was there the frustration of years of chronic disease — tuberculosis eroding his lower spine and both his hips — but also the frustration of his living conditions. He lived in the country an hour and a half away, with his elder brother's family. His parents were dead, and his brother's wife hated this deformed little brother-in-law. She took every opportunity of making her displeasure known and, for Soon Beki, the thought of returning to this, when he had hoped for the peace of a hospital bed, had proved too much. Happily, the story did not end there. Within a few months the situation in the hospital had changed, and we were able to admit him to the wards. Over the next six months he made good progress, and was able to leave at the end of that time walking quite well, with only one crutch. During his time in hospital he came to trust the Lord, and he went out determined to live as a Christian.

Having been free of him for six months, his sister-in-law was even less willing to contemplate having him back. He did go back to that home, but it quickly became evident that it was an untenable situation.

It was some time before we saw him again, and we knew nothing of this. When he did return to us, we found that he was living in a lodging house in the city of Taegu, and making his living by selling chewing gum on the trains. Day after day he would set out to earn that day's keep. Hitching a ride on a train, he would peddle gum among the passengers. Sometimes the guard would turn him off; sometimes he would turn a blind eye. Occasionally someone would give him 100 won; more often the standard 20 or 30 won. Night after night he would return to the lodging house to count his gains and rest in preparation for the next day. When Sunday came around, he would go to church in the morning, to one of the large city churches with smartly-dressed gentlemen and ladies. This, of itself, required a lot of courage for him, clad only in the best of his shabby clothes. Then Sunday afternoon he would be out peddling again, for he couldn't afford to miss a day. 'I think the Lord will understand,' he said apologetically, conscious of prevalent strict Sabbatarian attitudes. Several of us listened with tears in our eyes as he recounted his adventures with a mixture of humour and pathos. Such a man, not infrequently, has a penetrating understanding of human nature, and his descriptions of disdainful passengers and superior church members, defy translation.

Moved by his courage and indomitable spirit, we offered him the train fare for his visit to us, and said he was welcome to come and stay any time he needed to.

'Thank you,' he said, but no, he wouldn't accept our offer. He must learn to make his way in the world just like anyone else. He was saving up money to go into a technical training course. Later on, if we could introduce him to one, he would be grateful, but he would pay his way. Meanwhile, the Lord would take care of him.

And so, declining 'angels' help', and trusting himself to the heavenly Father he had learned to love, he shuffled off, a little figure with a crutch, but holding within that undistinguished frame a great big heart of faith. 'Has not God chosen those who are poor in this world to be rich in faith and heirs of the kingdom which He has promised to those who love Him?' (James 2.5)

Not long afterwards he returned once more, having saved 80,000 won from his chewing gum sales. We were able to get him a place in a training school run by Christians in Pusan, where he learned watch repairs for six months. After his 'graduation' from there, (and baptism), he rented premises in Masan and ran an effective little watch repair shop. 'Please send me some of your ex-patients,' he said, 'I will take them in and help them get started too.'

There is a fine line between charity that is true kindness, and charity that saps the nerve of faith, and makes people spiritual paupers as well as economic ones. Pray for missionaries involved in medical or other social works, the courage of faith that leads people towards stepping out in faith on their own, rather than towards dependency.

They took counsel against Jesus to put him to death.
Judas . . . 'I have sinned in betraying innocent blood' . . . he went and hanged himself.
His blood be on us and on our children.
Pilate . . . delivered him to be crucified.
Jesus cried again with a loud voice and yielded up his spirit.
The tombs . . . were opened, and many bodies of the saints who had fallen asleep were raised.
Joseph took the body, and wrapped it in a clean linen shroud, and laid it in his own new tomb. (Matthew 27.2, 3-5, 25, 26, 50, 52, 59-60)

27

Thy will be done

One of the strongest evidences for the truth of the gospel is the attitude of Christians in the face of death. The gospel has a death at its centre — the death of the Son of God — and creates in its adherents an attitude to death in total contrast to that of the pagan world. Furthermore, faced with death, very many of the distractions of life fall away, leaving the core of faith in God. Love of money, pride of achievement, strife over supremacy, the quest for human praise: only the most hardened hypocrite can cling to these face to face with the ultimate journey. In our present day death-denying western culture, we are in danger of losing the full impact of the gospel in this respect. Not so in Korea — nor, for that matter, in most of the rest of the world. Most of mankind, for most of history, has had very clearly-expressed attitudes towards death. Our modern western preoccupation with the temporal world, and refusal to look beyond. is a short-lived and geographically limited quirk of history.

Funerals, and the dead, play an important part in Korean social structures. Funerals are most commonly conducted by Buddhist priests, but the overall attitude towards the dead is far more influenced by Confucian thought than Buddhist. Thus, as we have seen, keeping of a deceased relative's memorial day is far more important than thoughts of reincarnation. It has been said that Confucianism teaches a man to respect his father after he is dead, while Christianity teaches him to honour his parents while they are alive. There is some truth in this.

The word that has been traditionally translated 'filial piety' is one of great emotive content in Korean. Not only does it include careful tending of the family graves and offerings there twice a year, and keeping the annual memorial days with ceremonies and offerings in the house, but it expresses also a deep sense of respect for the ancestors, an attempt to live along the lines of which they would have approved, and a training of one's children to do likewise. In the values system of Korean society, it ranks very high. It will be seen that the onus of responsibility is all on the younger generation, and that this can be abused by the older ones, demanding excessive loyalty. Indeed, it is the reverse of Paul's adage, 'Children ought not to lay up for their parents, but parents for their children,' (2 Cor. 12.14).

Traditionally, a dutiful son should renounce all other activity and camp at his father's graveside for three years' mourning following his father's death. This is probably never practised nowadays, but it is still faintly shocking for a son or daughter to marry within a year of a parent's death.

Traditional funerals are elaborate and expensive. With the social pressure to express grief and devotion, the family are ready prey to the professional undertaker. Common village practice is more communal, and has many attractive features. When the church elder who had founded both our village church and the one in the government sanatorium died, we, as part of the community, were inevitably involved. The body was laid in state in the principal room of the house, with one of his sons in constant attendance, and his photograph and personal possessions on a table beside. Most of the village community gathered in the house and yard, or in adjacent houses, making paper flowers for the funeral bier, talking, eating, passing the whole night together. In a relatively small community like the village where we live on the outskirts of Masan, this group included the Christians and non-Christians indiscriminately.

Others of the men were constructing the bier of stout poles. The simple wooden coffin would be laid on this, and then enclosed in an elaborate tiered case. Looking something like a wedding cake, this was of white paper on a frame of thin wooden lathes, and decorated with a vast number of white paper flowers. In contrast with the subdued hush, drawn shutters and general shunning of a house in the West where there has been a death, this corporate effort lent support to the family, and had many attractive elements.

Korean graves are most commonly on the mountains, preferably near the person's original home. Elder Kim's home was in

North Korea, so land was granted on the hillside above the hospital and village which he had served for more than twenty years. So, the coffin was borne on the shoulders of village men a short walk up the hillside for a simple service, which we were not able to attend.

An increasing number of city dwellers are cremated, but a common sight, too, is the undertaker's bus, white with a black stripe, taking the coffin and chief mourners, after initial ceremonies in the house, to the graveside for the burial. Some of these grave-sites are easily accessible, but others are far up in the mountains, involving the funeral procession in several hours' walking. One brand of diviner makes a living by selecting auspicious grave sites for enquiring families. These should generally be on a south or east-facing slope. At the site, a grave is prepared in advance, and after the burial, earth is heaped up in a smooth mound over the spot, and laid with tufts of grass. Most grave mounds are about the size of a mini car with the wheels off, though some are much bigger. Everywhere, the hillsides are studded with these mounds. Especially in the autumn they may easily be spotted where the long grass has been cleared around them in preparation for the autumn festival offerings.

One of my earliest experiences in Korea, a few weeks after arriving, was to attend the funeral of the father of a young doctor friend, a Christian. Besides the long drive out to the Seoul common burial ground, and the vast hillside of grave-sites that lay there, my chief memory of that occasion is of the young doctor's concern over what he should wear. Traditional mourning dress for close relatives is hemp clothing (sackcloth), with a sackcloth hat and a straw rope girdle. Women mourners would wear a white turban tied up with straw rope. This friend associated these with Confucian attitudes to mourning, and wished to make a specifically Christian stand, while not needlessly offending family sensitivities. In the end, he compromised by wearing a Western suit with a hemp hat and sackcloth flashes, in the same way that a Western mourner might wear black. Perhaps more important was his sister's willingness to postpone her marriage for a year from the father's death. In the event, I think she married a few months later.

Most people have a deep longing to die in their own home. Probably two strands of thought motivate this in the minds of most. The peace and security of one's own home, with one's own family around, is comforting when treading the last lonely road. Also, it is commonly held that the peace of the dead one's spirit in the after-life is assured if he dies in his own home. This, not unnaturally, presents problems in hospital work. One does not want to offend susceptibilities, and certainly the first of these motives is a healthy and attractive one. On the other hand, one does not want to send a man home to die when further stay in hospital might have saved him. In our situation, we have very few patients who die while in our hands. Tuberculosis of the bones and joints that we are treating is chronic and, for the most part, eminently treatable. Over a period of two years with adult patients in the wards, we had only two men that we sent home in this way. In each case the patient himself and his relatives wanted it, and both died within a few hours of reaching home. Theoretically, one is faced with tantalizing issues of conscience. In practice, nearly always the issues are very clear, and the decisions largely made for one.

A brief account of two very different funerals will illustrate the immense change of outlook that the gospel engenders.

A few years ago Mr Jee's father died. It will be remembered that Mr Jee, our hospital driver, came from a very traditional family, steeped in the Buddhist and Confucian thought-patterns of Korea. Mr Jee's elder brother, as oldest son, was the chief mourner. Mr Jee himself was also, of course, intimately involved.

We visited the home in Masan on the eve of the funeral to pay our respects to the family. The atmosphere of gloom, mingled with the strong smell of drink, pervaded the house. Mourning is traditionally loud and tearful (cf Matthew 9.23) and, although the house was quiet when we called, the faces of all the family bore the marks of this strenuous effort. Next day we accompanied the funeral party by car to the mountains behind Masan, and joined the crowd around the grave-site. Again, the atmosphere of loud wailing and tears, laced with large quantities of alcohol, dominated the scene. The family, clothed in sackcloth, staggered behind the bier, apparently bowed down with grief — grief that could be instantly controlled by women as well as men when instructions needed to be given to the bearers, or a visitor welcomed: an overt display of grief, too, that could be solaced in the abundance of alcohol so readily available. Grief expressed according to accepted patterns . . . grief a token of filial piety . . . a healthy expression of genuine feeling . . . a cover for fear on the part of those who 'all their lifetime are subject to bondage through fear of death.' Yes, all of these elements are there, but perhaps behind them all, the deep awareness of the transitoriness of human life, and the despairing ignorance concerning the here-after. It is not surprising that Buddhism finds its greatest appeal and most common popular expression at funerals.

What a contrast is the atmosphere of a truly Christian funeral. Kim Chin Kyung, our first Korean friend, had spent a good part of his life in Masan. His elderly widowed mother still lived in Masan and we saw her from time to time. She died one April in very tragic circumstances. She had been attending the funeral of a friend in the country. As is the custom, the hostess had stoked the under-floor heating system hotter than usual as an expression of hospitality; but the floor of the old country house could not bear it, and during the night carbon monoxide from the briquette coal beneath seeped through the cracked floor, poisoning the old lady. She was found in a coma the next morning, and died in hospital 48 hours later.

She had been a staunch Christian all her life; a real warrior for the faith, and one of an inner group of brave men and women who had stood by their convictions during the Japanese occupa-tion, refusing to bow to Japanese Shinto shrines, and being an inspiration to many others. Several of her contemporaries and companions had died in prison in the Second World War, and others, still surviving, had suffered much at that time. Sadly, as we saw in chapters 3 and 4, peace and freedom had led to strife and factionalism among some of these in the intervening years.

Now, however, they were all gathered for a triumphant funeral service. Crowded into the narrow courtyard of her cramped Masan home were a strange mixture of leading pastors, friends, and family. With curious neighbours peeking over the walls, the assembly sang hymns, prayed, and listened to Scripture. The minister emphasized that she had gone to her reward, and exhorted all to like faith. Strife among those present was not forgotten, and for discerning eyes, the allocation of parts in the service to different people was a reflection of this. Yet even this could not detract from the fact that eternity was in view, and in the light of eternity such pettiness was seen for what it is.

As the procession formed up in the roadway outside the house for the walk to the hillside a mile away, more hymns were sung. The family wore sackcloth mourning, and tears were far from absent, but the atmosphere of darkness and despair was nowhere to be found. The funeral bier was decorated in white, but prominent among the designs were white crosses. As the column of mourners proceeded down the main street out of town towards the hills, it made a striking visible testimony to the worth of the gospel.

At the grave-site high on the hills a simple service of committal was enacted. Many of her contemporaries had not managed the climb, but in that group of family and friends was a warmth of fellowship in Christ that gave a glimpse of heaven.

In the work of the kingdom there is much to discourage and much that causes concern but when, faced with the ultimate test, it is found that we do 'not grieve as others that have no hope' (1 Thess. 4.13), there is a bright future and confidence that 'He shall see the fruit of the travail of his soul and be satisfied' (Isaiah 53.11).

For fear of him the guards trembled . . . but the angel said to the women, 'Do not be afraid'.

Jesus met them and said . . . 'Do not be afraid'.

Jesus came and said to them, 'All authority in heaven and on earth has been given to me. Go, therefore, and make disciples of all nations, baptizing them in the name of the Father and of the Son and of the Holy Spirit, teaching them to observe all that I have commanded you; and lo, I am with you always, to the close of the age.' (Matthew 28. 4-5, 9-10, 18-20)

28

Do not be afraid

Seven am on a Thursday. We made a strange group, the six of us gathered round the white-clothed table of a side room in the Station Grill at Seoul Railway station. We had met over breakfast to work towards the forming of a Korea Home Council of Overseas Missionary Fellowship. The purpose of this would be to channel Korean missionaries through OMF for service in other countries of East Asia. In Japan, Philippines, Hong Kong and, more recently, Malaysia, Taiwan and Indonesia, such home councils have also been prepared to take responsibility for channelling missionaries to the Indian sub-continent and West Asia through the Bible and Medical Missionary Fellowship. This too was in our thinking. In each case the purpose was to provide a link between the sending churches at home and the field of operation overseas. This was the second in a series of two-monthly meetings that would probably extend over a period of two years before definite steps could be taken. Who were we, and why was the projected time-scale so drawn out?

Dr Chun Chaeok was probably the most experienced among us. A refined and very able lady, she had spent fourteen years as a missionary in Pakistan, working closely with BMMF missionaries in student and lay-training work. She had also spent two years at London Bible College and, more recently, a year in America to complete her doctorate. Originally she had been sent to Pakistan by a committee of staff of her university, Ehwa Women's University, a Methodist foundation in Seoul. Now she was back on the staff of that University, teaching courses on a Christian view of culture — a lone biblical voice in a predominantly modernist academic atmosphere. With extensive first-hand experience as a missionary and further academic study of the subject of missions, she was well equipped to make a major contribution.

Mr Yang was elder of a Presbyterian church in Seoul. Managing his own private firm for the production of glass ampoules for injection fluids, he had travelled overseas to Europe, America and East Asia on a number of occasions. He was also chairman of the missionary committee of his church, and personally deeply committed to the spread of the gospel at home and overseas. In his earlier days he had given much time to tract distribution in the streets of Seoul (no easy thing for a budding business tycoon), and he had personally supervised, and not infrequently personally supplemented, the disciplined giving of the church's missionary committee to the support of an OMF missionary family. More recently, the church had commissioned a young pastor and his family for service among Koreans in West Germany (predominantly nurses, nurse-aides, and mine workers). The church undertook their full support in a disciplined and orderly way.

Mr Lee had been a leader in student work in Seoul for more than ten years. He had been overseas on two occasions to leaders' conferences organized by the International Fellowship of Evangelical Students and was anxious for fresh and wider fellowship with the churches locally and student work internationally. The group with which he worked had increasingly concentrated on training gifted graduates who were emigrating to America (and to a lesser extent Canada, West Germany and elsewhere). These were given intensive Bible training and commissioned as lay-missionaries, supporting themselves in their professional capacities, and seeking to establish cells in the circles in which they found themselves. Many of these graduates were doctors and nurses, and much of their overseas activity was concentrated in hospitals in America and West Germany. The idea of harnessing the natural trends of emigration to the purposes of the gospel was a good one, but the organization of separate groups without reference to existing Christian work and answerable to headquarters in Seoul was less healthy. It smacked too much of the worst propagation of sectarian loyalties overseas by nineteenth century (and some twentieth century) Western missions. Mr Lee was well aware of this and, while equally committed to the world-wide task of mission, was looking for healthier channels. Both he and Mr Yang had a working knowledge of English.

Mr Yune, as general secretary of Korea Scripture Union, was

the member whom we knew best. He had long been involved in prayer for missionaries, notably some OMF missionaries in Thailand. He had known well the ordained missionary and his family who had been sent some fifteen years earlier by his denomination's general assembly for work in Taiwan. He well knew the problems that had been associated with this, and had visited the missionary in Taiwan in 1973. It was no easy thing to be a lone missionary answerable to a board in the homeland, the membership of which was changing annually and very few of whom had first-hand experience of Christian work overseas. Yet he laboured faithfully for many years. Yes, Mr Yune was aware of some of the pitfalls in the missionary enterprise. He had travelled not only in East Asia, but also to Australia. He knew OMF intimately and was well aware of, and attracted by, the principles that led Hudson Taylor to his distinctive policies.

These bear repeating, for they stand in stark contrast to the dominant trends in Korean thinking about overseas missionary work, and are as important today as they were a hundred years ago — and largely for the same reasons.

Hudson Taylor adopted his distinctive financial policy for two reasons. Firstly, he did not want to divert funds from existing agencies. He wished to avoid the competitive image. Secondly, he wanted God's financial provision to be a testimony to the reality of the work of God in an age preoccupied with human works in the spiritual sphere.

Hudson Taylor sited his headquarters 'on the spot' in China, rather than in the homelands, to minimize the snares of policies dictated from far away that were not suited to the real life situation on the field.

Hudson Taylor emphasized not only the adoption of Chinese dress, but that his missionaries should accommodate themselves to local patterns of life in all respects commensurate with reasonable health and safety, and befitting the gospel. This particularly related, and relates, to what we now call 'standard of living'. For the sake of the gospel, it was important to minimize the gulf.

Hudson Taylor worked on an interdenominational basis, emphasizing the things held in common rather than the peripheral differences of denominational emphasis. Further, he used women as well as men, unordained as well as ordained missionaries and, latterly, missionaries from an increasing variety of countries. The decision at the Centenary of the CIM in 1965 to open the doors of the mission to Asians for service in lands other than their own was the natural extension of this existing policy.

All this, Mr Yune knew, endorsed, and longed to see reproduced in Korea, with the Korean churches channelling missionaries through OMF to the other lands of Asia. He further knew, from his intimate knowledge of Korean church life and his work with Scripture Union, that only a close attention to Scripture on the part of all involved in such a venture would ensure that valuable biblical emphases would be preserved against the overwhelming prevalent preoccupation with organization, finance and statistics.

These four members provided an interesting (and deliberate) blend of the different approaches to missionary involvement abroad in Korea today: independent agency − local church − denominational − lay − ordained − overseas Korean − 'cross-cultural' − Asian lands and Western lands. None was a forceful, widely-recognized leader. None had large resources behind him or her. They came as individuals rather than representatives of their groups or other agencies.

The other two members of that little breakfast group were myself and one other OMF missionary. He was appointed scribe of the group. He was already producing (three times a year) a broadsheet of missionary prayer topics around Asia. He was commissioned by the group to produce an introductory leaflet about OMF, and Korean sound-tracks to several of the OMF audio-visual productions widely used in the Western home countries. The group further agreed to organize a public meeting presenting our approach to overseas missions. The group was later strengthened by cooption of additional members and continued to meet as a planning committee over the next two years. It was formally constituted as the Korean Home Council of OMF in May 1980, and the first candidates for membership of OMF from the Korean church were interviewed at that time.

From the start of OMF's work in Korea in 1969, the stimulation of interest in overseas missions among the Korean churches and help to Korean Christians whom God had called as missionaries, was seen as one of the principal aims of the mission in Korea. Nearly ten years later, why so little, and so slow? Of the little group gathered to work and pray for progress towards this goal, none was beyond his early 40's, none a recognized Christian leader on a national scale, none even ordained. Why so insignificant? To understand some of the problems associated with launching a home council in Korea it is necessary to go back a bit.

Like many other aspects of Christian life, the early history of the Korean Church with regard to missionary endeavour is thrilling. When the first presbytery of the Korean Church was formed in the early years of the present century, they decided that one of their first tasks should be to despatch a missionary overseas. When volunteers were called for, every man in the presbytery rose to offer. One pastor was selected, and, together with his family, despatched to Shanghai, China, for missionary service — the first overseas missionary of the Korean Church. Others were later sent north to Manchuria, but through the period of Japanese domination and the vicissitudes of war, the sending of missionaries overseas was rarely a feasible proposition. Nonetheless, churches sprang up among the considerable numbers of Koreans resident in Japan and North America. Sometimes it was possible to send pastors to these congregations from the churches in Korea. More recently, in the 25 years since the Korean war, large numbers of Korean pastors have either opted to remain in America after an initial study period, or have emigrated to pastor existing congregations or found new ones among the Korean community there.

More recently still, and especially over the last ten years, interest in overseas missionary work has sprung up in many quarters. The varied involvement of the different members of our little breakfast group is illustrative of this. Dr Chun produced figures for us from all the major denominations and all the different missionary groups that could be identified, showing a total of 247 Korean missionaries at the end of 1976. However, when this total was broken down into different groups — those subsequently returned home, those ministering to Korean congregations, those who were primarily emigrants in secular jobs, etc. — she showed us that those currently involved in cross-cultural missionary work (that is, primarily involved in spreading the gospel among people of a different race) numbered less than twenty. When motives are mixed — competitive spirit, personal kingdom building, the desire to be seen to be doing the 'right thing', the desire to have something of which to boast — statistics and figures can easily become artificially inflated.

The experience of one Korean missionary is illustrative of the problems faced by those who do seek a ministry in a difficult cross-cultural situation and by those who seek to send and support them. An invitation was received by leaders of his church at an international gathering from the leaders of a church in another Asian country to send a co-operating, ordained missionary. The man in question was a junior minister in a large church of several thousand members with five ordained ministers. His church (independent of the presbytery or other groups) selected him and his family. It was proposed that he enter that country on a tourist visa and seek to change this afterwards – a move doomed to failure according to the country's immigration regulations. He received almost no other specific training – his theological course and ordination were deemed enough. Funds for his support were quite adequate, but arrangements for their transfer were flimsy in view of the complex regulations relating to foreign exchange control.

Eventually, having resolved the visa problems, he arrived in his place of work. Almost no preparations had been made for language study, and it was not long before his wife found the contrast between that rural and mountainous area and sophisticated Seoul too great to endure, and moved to the capital. He followed later, and now they are ministering largely to Koreans in the capital. Willingness and sacrifice, yes, but sadly thwarted through lack of preparation, support and knowhow. Inevitably there are many problems in an infant missionary movement, but it is encouraging that there are those with a sense of call to this work and those who are prepared to translate their enthusiasm into action.

Another problem that some have run up against is that of persistent rivalry among church leadership. Spiritual leadership is co-operative. Natural leadership tends towards competitiveness. In a general atmosphere where this sort of competitiveness dominates the scene, even spiritual leadership that seeks to be co-operative cannot afford to become too prominent. Hence our contentment with a younger and relatively unknown group of co-workers. For the time being at least, we want to keep our channels open to as wide a consensus of the Christian public as possible. The time may come when this proves unworkable, but for the moment we are content to work slowly and quietly. 'Content' is perhaps the wrong word if it implies that we will be satisfied with only a marginal influence on the whole. Rather, our priorities as a missionary movement leave us no option for the present, the prevailing climate being what it is.

We have spoken largely of method in the missionary enterprise. Still more important is the message that missionaries take with them. The eleven disciples were commissioned by the Lord of heaven and earth to go to all peoples (it took them a while to realize this meant others besides Jews), to make disciples of Jesus, baptized in the Name of the Trinity (it still takes missionaries time to realize that this is more important than sectarian loyalty to the sending denomination), teaching them to observe all that Jesus commanded. It is still an oft-repeated failing that missionaries, taken up with the mechanics of operating 'the mission' or the mission's institutions or 'the church', are failing so to open Scripture before their hearers that these see and understand the teachings of Jesus and obey them. Another danger also exists.

Through the pages of Acts and the Epistles may be traced two contemporaneous missionary movements. The first, and more familiar one, is that of Peter and Paul. Yet at every turn alongside this is the missionary movement of the Judaisers dogging Paul's footsteps. These were cultural missionaries — imposing Jewish traditions upon their recipients. Worse, they were the missionaries of a system of law and a ministry of death. No wonder Paul used strong words (Gal 5. 11-12, Phil. 3. 2-3). These were the emissaries of the religious system so roundly condemned by the Lord (Matthew 23. 15). Plausible and zealous, orthodox in their view of written Scripture, yet they were the messengers of bondage and strife. It is inevitable that where the sending church is enmeshed in this web of religious tenets, some of its emissaries will propagate the same views. Too often has this been the case in the history of Western missions, and history has a knack of repeating itself.

All that we have said and shown of the practical weakness on Scripture in Korean church life will help us to understand that a rapidly-expanding missionary programme from the Korean church is fraught with danger. The essential place of an effective biblical movement within the church as the precursor to effective biblical missionary outreach will also be seen. Once again we come back to the key contribution that can be made through Scripture Union — a contribution fundamental to all other aspects of healthy growth. 'Reformation and Revival through a return to the Scriptures" Yes, and out of that reformation and revival will spring a life-giving missionary movement.

The nation of Israel that cried out, 'Crucify Him, crucify Him', yet became the cradle of the gospel, the source of the little band that turned the world upside down and which has gone on through all the vicissitudes of history to become today's worldwide church. In the same way we believe there will be a growing band of Korea's sons and daughters, chosen by God, who will go to the ends of the earth at His command to make disciples of all nations, baptizing them in the Name of the Father and of the Son and of the Holy Spirit and teaching them to observe all that Jesus has commanded. As they add their service to the annals of church history, He will be true to His promise, 'Lo, I am with you always, to the close of the age.'

****